T0210885

Game Development 2042

This book is a fast-paced look at the next two decades of the games industry with a focus on game design, the evolution of gaming markets around the world, the future of technology, Artificial Intelligence, Big Data, crypto-currency, and the art and business of creating and publishing hit games.

The book contains interviews with a dozen veteran games industry luminaries, who have collectively created many of the greatest hits of the last twenty years and grossed tens of billions of dollars in revenue for companies like Electronic Arts, Facebook, Apple, Activision, Microsoft, Amazon, Supercell, Netflix, Warner Brothers, and others.

Game Development 2042 is meant for game developers, anyone with a financial interest in the games business, and for gamers who want to know what the future holds. Mobile, console, PC, web, free-to-play, play-to-earn, and other businesses are discussed in depth with specific examples.

Tim Fields has been making and operating games and leading game publishing companies for more than 25 years. Along the way he has been a part of bringing games to life in franchises like *Call of Duty, Halo,* Marvel, Disney, *Need for Speed, Fast and Furious, Transformers, Dungeons & Dragons*, and many more, winning multiple Editor's Choice and other awards, and generated billions of dollars in earnings. This is his fifth book on the games industry. He recently served as the CEO of mobile game publisher Kabam and currently works at Wizards of the Coast, bringing beloved franchises to life as digital games. Tim also runs an AI focused research company called MainBrain.AI.

Game Development 2042
The Future of Game Design, Development, and Publishing

Tim Fields

CRC Press
Taylor & Francis Group
Boca Raton London New York

CRC Press is an imprint of the
Taylor & Francis Group, an **informa** business

Cover Image credit: NASA and the NSSDCA

First Edition published 2023
by CRC Press
6000 Broken Sound Parkway NW, Suite 300, Boca Raton, FL 33487-2742

and by CRC Press
4 Park Square, Milton Park, Abingdon, Oxon, OX14 4RN

CRC Press is an imprint of Taylor & Francis Group, LLC

Library of Congress Cataloging-in-Publication Data
Names: Fields, Tim, author.
Title: Game development 2042 : the future of game design, development, and publishing / Tim Fields.
Description: Boca Raton, FL : CRC Press, 2023. | Includes bibliographical references and index. | Summary: "This book explores the future of game design, development, and publishing, extrapolating the next two decades through the lens of the industry's evolution over the last ten years and the technical advances in recent adjacent markets"– Provided by publisher.
Identifiers: LCCN 2022015809 (print) | LCCN 2022015810 (ebook) | ISBN 9781032272092 (hardback) | ISBN 9781032272054 (paperback) | ISBN 9781003291800 (ebook)
Subjects: LCSH: Video games–Forecasting.
Classification: LCC GV1469.3 .F54 2023 (print) | LCC GV1469.3 (ebook) | DDC 794.801/12–dc23/eng/20220623
LC record available at https://lccn.loc.gov/2022015809
LC ebook record available at https://lccn.loc.gov/2022015810

ISBN: 978-1-032-27209-2 (hbk)
ISBN: 978-1-032-27205-4 (pbk)
ISBN: 978-1-003-29180-0 (ebk)

DOI: 10.1201/9781003291800

Typeset in Minion
by codeMantra

This book is dedicated to William Gibson, who taught us how to see the future by looking at the world around us. And to Dr. Stout, always.

Contents

Game Development 2042

THIS BOOK IS AN exploration of the future of Game Development and Publishing through the lens of the industry's evolution over the last decade. We will focus our attention on several significant trends that I believe speak to the future shape of the games business. Along the way, we will visit with a dozen or so games industry luminaries from different countries, different walks of life and hear their thoughts on the future.

INTRODUCTION

> Today's leaders shouldn't be reading management books, they should be reading science fiction.
>
> – *Melany Hamill, Executive Producer,*
> Marvel Contest of Champions

The global video games business is quickly approaching a $200 billion dollar per year business. From the basements of inventors and university mainframe computer labs, gaming has taken up residence on every television and in billions of people's pockets around the globe. And we are just getting started.

The industry and market tastes evolve so very quickly that advice or publications on techniques, software tools, or specific design approaches often become obsolete before they can even be posted on a blog, much less printed and distributed to bookstores.

So what if – rather than trying to catalog the way things are done today and capture the shape of the industry – what if we instead look into a crystal ball to determine where the business is likely to go?

DOI: 10.1201/9781003291800-1

1

Prognostication is a notoriously difficult trick to pull off effectively. Humans are poor at guessing what the future holds; we have a tendency to anchor on imagining small changes based on current trajectories rather than envision the kinds of sea-change shifts that technological revolution can bring about.

At the turn of the nineteenth century, horses and the carriages they drew were the only significant means of transportation in most cities. In 1890, urban planners in New York City despaired of coming up with a solution to the 45,000 tons of manure horses deposited in the city each month. In 1898, they convened to discuss solutions to this problem. Within 15 years, motorized vehicles outnumbered horses in the city. The manure crisis was no longer a concern, no thanks to the efforts of the dedicated urban planners.[1]

More recently in the gaming space, few would have predicted in 2000 that the rise of smartphones would increase the number of gamers 30-fold in over just two decades. The ubiquity of cellular or high-speed wireless networks was imaginable, but not to most people at the time. Even poor-quality 2018-era deep-fake videos would have been persuasive evidence in a criminal court in 2000. And the rise of decentralized currency structures not backed by any government fiat which would drive game economies would have been inexplicable to even the digiterati of that time.

The point here is that the future is hard to predict, but also that there is incredible advantage to trying; even when our predictions are inaccurate, the way they can stoke the imaginations of creators and entrepreneurs can lead to life-changing results for billions, and huge profits for those brave enough to be pioneers.

And one of the wonderful tandem dances that writing, technology, and business can perform together is when each informs and inspires the other. In the mid nineteen eighties, science fiction author William Gibson wrote compellingly of a future of digital spaces that transcended the boundaries of nations. A generation of technologists and game makers were so inspired by his visions that we set about creating echoes of the world he envisioned. Our creations, in turn, inspired later generations of science fiction writers like Earnest Cline to keep riffing on these themes, which in turn inspired the next generation of game makers and inventors. And beyond just gaming, science fiction films like *Blade Runner* inspired modern AI artists like Refik Anadol to create new types of programs in which machine learning systems use data to create more art. And so the snake keeps eating its own tail and growing stronger. Art influences life which prompts the creation of more art, in a virtuous cycle of imagineering, invention, and creation.

This book will seek to extrapolate from the shape of today's game industry at the beginning 2022. We will try to imagine the types of major changes – both evolutionary and revolutionary – which will come to pass by the year 2042.

Inspired by the works of visionaries like Ray Bradbury, William Gibson, Ray Kurtzweil, Ted Chaing, Kai-Fu Lee, and informed by 26 years of working tirelessly alongside some of the brightest and most dedicated technologists and game makers across North America, Europe, and Asia, I hope that this book will galvanize the next generations of game makers to dream of all that can be, then set out to bring their visions to life.

If I have any fear in setting down these thoughts it is only that would-be futurists – especially those who are too steeped in the constraints and business realities of their field – are more likely to err on the side of imagining too little change, rather than dreaming big enough. However, as a business leader, game designer, and software developer first, and a futurist second, I will seek to constrain the majority of these speculations to extrapolating on technologies and trends which exist in the market today, rather than relying upon truly speculative "breakthrough" technologies like quantum computing, 100-fold increases in power production, teleportation, singularity level Brain-Computer-Interfaces, or similar. In any case, while some of these may come to pass – as radical a shift as the car was to the horse and buggy – they will likely remain very unevenly distributed. Social gaming is inherently the most powerful, profitable, and observable when it is mass-market and mainstream across the globe. So at the risk of under-speculating, most of the game technology developments conjured here will remain grounded in technologies we have proven today, which could feasibly be made available to billions over the next two decades. And, as we are reminded by the observations of Roy Amara, famous Stanford researcher, "We tend to overestimate the impact of a new technology in the short term and underestimate its impact in the long term." Even many technologies which have been with us for years or decades now are still not being applied to anything close to their potential. Photolithography, parallel processing, distributed computation, lithium-ion electrochemistry, deep learning, and many other technologies from last century will continue to transform our world for the next century.

If we are not going to rely upon teleportation, time travel, or other speculative fictional technologies to try to predict the future, what broad innovations or trends will we try to apply in these pages?

I believe there are six major forces in play which we can use as guides for our exploration:

- Hardware advance in CPU power, battery power, and input accessibility

- Pervasive machine learning and autonomy fueled by vast increase in data

- Ubiquity of high-speed, high-capacity data networks

- Network effect of social networks and human connectivity

- Increases in the amount of leisure time available for humanity

Let's talk about each of these vectors of advancement in turn.

Hardware Advances in CPU Power, Input Accessibility, and Battery Power

We've all been living with Moore's Law long enough that it now seems a given to most of us that computing power will continue to increase significantly every few years. For those who may have forgotten, Gordon Moore, founder of Intel made the observation in 1965 that the number of transistors on a chip doubles every two years while the cost halves. This has been broadly shorthanded into the phrase that "computing power doubles every two years." And this golden rule and all the exponential growth that regular doubling entails has, indeed, led to profound transformation in our ability to process staggering amounts of information. As a result, the phone in your pocket currently in 2022 has literally millions of times more processing power than the computers NASA used to put men on the moon in 1969. While there are some practical physical limitations we are starting to run into having to do with heat at an atomic level which threaten to slow these advances, there are similar advances in parallelism, chip specialization in dedicated graphics and AI processing which look likely to continue this inexorable march. And the fact of exponential growth here is not to be overlooked: By 2042, we can expect nearly free computing power with billions of times more calculations per second than was possible in 2020. Literally. This means far more sophisticated simulations and games which can do a lot more easily. How to properly use all of this power is one of the chief challenges of game design in the coming decades.

One of the opportunities unlocked by all of this processing power is the ability for us to significantly improve the number of inputs available to software. Broadly speaking, as designers we should learn to think about inputs in the broadest possible sense. Traditionally, these have been keyboard entries, joystick or controller button presses, mouse movements, and the like. More recently basic haptics (screen touches, taps, swipes) have unlocked a new era of computing and gaming by unlocking the power of smartphones and touch screen displays of all types. Some game devices, like the Wii or Xbox Kinect have added basic camera inputs which allowed player movements to be interpreted so users could dance around. We should expect the sophistication of inputs to increase dramatically in coming years. Voice control, yes, but also real world inputs from dozens of device families: from camera-enabled microdrones the size of fruit flies to wearable devices to biometric inputs potentially even at a nanotech in-vivo level. (What do current neurotransmitter and serotonin levels suggest about a player's stress level? Are they having fun?) And then, we can anticipate the connection of game simulations to a large number of external data-streams that can provide information which could change the game experience. (Which other people in the subway did the player's gaze linger on? How are they socially connected to our player, if at all?) What will all of these new types of information input allow us to do as game makers? This is a question well worthy of exploration.

Fifty years ago, the idea of being able to do almost any computing without a hardwired connection to grid power would have seemed science fiction. Now thanks to lithium-ion batteries, we can game for most of the day without charging up. And while battery power is not increasing at nearly the rate of bandwidth or processing power, it is continuing to improve such that we are able to do much more on a variety of smaller devices than most of us even dreamed of 30 years ago. What will this technology enable on smart devices? Local-field communications? Wearable technology? Internet of Things? And how do we translate all of this into more accessible, more compelling entertainment available anywhere and everywhere?

Pervasive Machine Learning and Autonomy Fueled by Vast Increase in Data

In May 1997, IBM's computer Deep Blue beat Gary Kasparov, the world's top chess player at the time. Chess was long considered a standard for measuring machine intelligence; this was the first baby step of domain specific Artificial Intelligence (AI) measuring itself against humans. In March of

2016 Google's DeepMind AI AlphaGo beat Lee Sedol, the world's top Go player at the time, wielding a computing power of around 30,000 times that of Deep Blue. Because the complexity of Go is considered so much higher than chess, we could think of this as AI's first toddling steps across a room. Five years later, AI is starting to walk around, exploring different rooms of the house. Within the next ten years it will learn to sprint, maybe running metaphorical marathons. By 2042, we should expect that Artificial Intelligence may well have started inventing its own new means of locomotion, allowing it to do things we have not yet contemplated.

Recognized AI expert Kai-Fu Lee estimates that "AI has penetrated less than 10% of our industries" as of 2021.[2] When we talk about AI, there are two main types of technological implementation that we are referring to. The first of these is "machine learning," which describes the way that large volumes of data can be synthesized, and then mined for patterns. Based on these patterns, and studying the probability of a thing occurring based on the frequency of that outcome having occurred within the datasets studied, one can make predictions about what is likely to happen next. As a simple example to illustrate the way this works, consider the likelihood of a particular train being on time tomorrow. How many times has that train run between those two locations? Of those, how many times did something alter the on-time arrival? This level of predictive analysis is quite basic, and has been the basis for actuarial science, insurance policies, and many other businesses for a long time. But what if you took it a step farther and looked for correlations between day of the week, amount of precipitation, or other factors. Then what if you further refined your estimate of the likelihood of the train being late tomorrow, forecast to be a rainy Monday? This kind of data analysis and correlation detection has been possible for a long time, but the introduction of computers made it possible to quickly process far larger amounts of data. In the last few decades, the advent of advanced and generalized machine learning software and hardware has made it possible for us to digest extremely large datasets and cross-reference many of them very quickly. At the same time, the amount of data available has expanded at truly staggering rates. Lee reckons that the "size" of the internet in 2020 is more than one trillion times the size of the internet in 1995. The result has been a huge boom in our ability to predict many things with high degrees of accuracy. This is Machine Learning. Consider the corresponding increase in predictive power that another 20 years of these increases – processing power doubling every year and volume of data expanding dramatically faster still – will have on deep learning by 2042.

The second major technological force that people refer to as "Artificial Intelligence" usually refers to some level of machine driven autonomous behavior. A self-driving car is one high rent example of this which has long been a holy grail to the automotive industry, insurance companies, and stressed chauffeur-parents the world over. But there are many simpler tasks which can be undertaken with high degrees of autonomy: Roomba brand vacuuming robots which clean carpets without much human intervention is one example, drones that can track a video subject as they jog through the park while avoiding nearby trees and other obstacles is another example. While there are a host of subset technologies ("machine vision" and many others) which allow for these kinds of behaviors, we can generally think of them as creating a level of autonomy for computer run agents. And due to the rapid improvements in computing power and data volume described above these autonomous behaviors can optimize themselves very effectively over time. The capacity of these systems to learn and improve themselves is without precedent in human history until now.

Both of these broad categories of technology are in use in many video games today, but I suggest that their current incarnations and influence on the gamers' (and developers'!) experience is quite shallow. Over the next two decades, we should expect massive evolution in this area.

Ubiquity of High-Speed High-Capacity Data Networks

In 2000, the idea that many cities would have high-capacity Wi-Fi everywhere would have been a hard concept to even explain to most people in the world. Few of them had ever been on Wi-Fi at all. High-speed cellular data networks that would allow us to stream High Definition video from YouTube were still almost a decade in the future, as were devices that would make this easy. By now, there are few populated places in the world where this is not both possible, but experienced daily by millions of people.

Low earth orbit satellite swarms can now connect anyone anywhere to the sum of human knowledge with low latency and very high upload and download speeds. And in populated places the world over both the cellular and fiber-optic infrastructure to transmit massive amounts of data are increasing rapidly, pushed forward by massive investments from governments and private companies like Google. These infrastructure improvements are even making their way to corners of the globe not usually known for advanced technology.

And our capacity to store and access staggering volumes of data is increasing at the same time. Always available high-speed connection from anywhere to vast stores of information is truly a new thing for humanity. When coupled with computing power and advanced AI techniques, this trio of forces makes the next 20 years quite a bit different than the last 20, and will make our technical capabilities largely unrecognizable to even the digital elites of the 1990s.

Network Effect of Social Networks and Human Connectivity

The network effect is a phenomenon in which the usefulness of a network increases based on the scale of the network. At the risk of oversimplifying, as more people and more devices get connected to the internet the internet becomes more useful.

For games, this translates to more gamers online in any given region, time zone, language, game, or game mode. This makes matchmaking faster and higher quality. It makes finding friends with shared interests easier to do, which means that games can be built which celebrate those interests. More users and players means more people to sell your virtual goods to, more people to trade with, more users playing games and adding to the stores of data that Machine Learning AI can use to improve the games. All of these trends result in still more people enjoying games and playing them more, in a virtuous cycle. More gamers online make online gaming better for gamers. More gamers generating content make AI get smarter faster. More users watching streaming content online make content streamers and the platforms that host them more powerful. Network effects accelerate many elements of the gaming business.

Increases in the Amount of Leisure Time Available for Humanity

In 2020, as a result of the pandemic, millions of workers the world over stepped back from their jobs, at least for a while. While many pundits and eager social reformers declared this to be the beginning of a fundamental shift in the balance of power between labor and capital, or an inevitable withdrawal in disgust at the inequalities found in so-called late-stage capitalism, I suspect it reflects something simpler and less politically charged: Across much of the world, standards of living have risen massively over the last 100 years as a result of productivity, the application of technology, reduction in food scarcity, and advancements in social safety nets. The annual number of working hours per worker has steadily declined, from around 3,000 hours per year in 1870 to 2,000 hours per year by 1970, and down to 1,500 hours per year in 2017.[3] Consider that: The average worker's time spent doing work has cut in half in the last two centuries.

While available free time differs significantly by country, by age group, by education levels, and even by gender, over the last 200 years humans have steadily found themselves with more free time for leisure.

And this has all been true before much robotic automation and Artificial Intelligence have started to shift the nature of work much. Over the next 100 years, we should expect billions of people to have measurably more leisure time. Some will devote this to learning more, sleeping more, exercise, or other activities. But many will spend it gaming. In the future, more people will have more time to devote to games.

A ROADMAP

How shall we spend the next hundred thousand words or so?

- **Chapter 1: A Global Community of Players** will look at the way demographics are changing the addressable market population of gamers across the world.

- **Chapter 2: How to Reach the World** will provide a high level look at some of the forces we must consider when thinking about games as a global business.

- **Chapter 3: The Evolution of Game Design** will look at some of the significant factors in the way games are designed that can influence their effectiveness in driving adoption, engagement, and retention.

- **Chapter 4: Web 3 Gaming: Crypto, Play to Earn, NFT** will look at the implications of new technologies enabled by blockchain technology on game development.

- **Chapter 5: Devices and Platforms** will look at the kind of hardware and software platforms people game on, and explore their evolution.

- **Chapter 6: Inputs and Feedback Mechanisms** will investigate ways we can get information from and communicate the game to players.

- **Chapter 7: Business Models** will look at the ways games can generate revenue for creators, publishers, and players.

- **Chapter 8: Data and Analytics** studies the way the vast increase in data changes the way we make and operate games.

- **Chapter 9: Artificially Intelligent Characters** explores the impact of sophisticated conversational AI and photorealistic characters on gaming.

- **Chapter 10: The Future of Game Development** looks at the way the tools and organizational structures we use to create and operate games are likely to change over the next 20 years.

Along the way, we will periodically pause to converse with industry experts, covering aspects of each of these topics in their own words.

Who Is This Book For?

This book is written by a lifelong gaming industry insider; I grew up in this world and have devoted most every waking minute to it for more than 25 years. And many of the experts interviewed in this book are also deep industry experts. As a result, this book is written for those who are professionals in the gaming business.

But this book is focused on the future, which means that those who are just starting in this fascinating space are likely to benefit more from this kind of a discussion than folks who are later in their careers. To all of the new game makers, or those who hope to become game makers, welcome! The future we are talking about here is the one you will create.

And this book is for gamers. If you love games, gamer culture, and talking with your gamer friends about the games you love, this book is for you too. Hopefully this journey into what might become will get you even more excited about your wonderful pastime.

I believe the greatest thing this book could do for you is not to provide you with answers for what the future must be like, but to arm you with dozens of razor-sharp questions which you can use to sculpt the future you want to be a part of. If our journey together here goes well it will allow you to make better games, positively influence the lives of millions of people you will never meet, create great businesses which generate huge amounts of value for your players, your employees, your investors, your country, and you.

We all have an incredible opportunity and responsibility to entertain the world. First, we must imagine what is possible, then create that future.

This book will help us all try to do just that.

NOTES

1 https://hbr.org/2017/07/why-business-leaders-need-to-read-more-science-fiction.

2 https://www.penguinrandomhouse.com/books/653310/ai-2041-by-kai-fu-lee-and-chen-qiufan/

3 https://ourworldindata.org/time-use.

CHAPTER 1

A Global Community of Players

GAMING LIGHTS THE WORLD

For us to gaze into the crystal ball of the future of gaming, we need to first think about the most important group: the gamers! Who are they? Where are they? And perhaps, more importantly, where will they be? What will they want in 2042?

Who are the gamers of the future?

For years, the world assigned gamers a stereotype: we can imagine the cliché of a lonely acne-scarred, socially maladroit boy in some backroom of his parent's house, living out violent fantasies with a controller in hand. But by 2020, the world had come to realize this was a media projection that did little to reflect the diversity of those who loved games around the world. Gamers come from most walks of life, represented by all genders, age groups, and ethnic backgrounds, from all countries. And as games got more diverse, more affordable, more accessible, this population expanded and widened even further.

There are three billion gamers in the world in 2022. This is more humans than populated the entire globe in 1950. The whole world games (Figure 1.1).

And while video-gaming started in universities in the United States and England before moving into arcades and homes in North America, Japan, and Western Europe, by 2022 the major markets for gaming had expanded. In 2020, the People's Republic of China was the world's largest

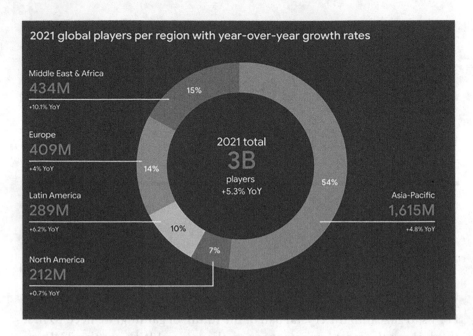

FIGURE 1.1 As of the end of 2021, there are over three billion gamers in the world.[1] (*Image Credit*: Google for Games report.)

gaming market both by players and by revenue. The United States, the UK, France, Germany, Italy, Australia, South Korea, Japan, and Russia all represent large and mature markets for PC and console gaming, and the entire world now plays games on mobile devices.

We can expect this trend of broadening geographic markets and increasingly diverse population of gamers to continue.

In 2022, there are 7.9 billion people on the Earth. 38% of them – three billion in total – identify as gamers, and many of these are still of a generation who grew up before gaming had entered the mainstream in their cultures or before any accessible devices or networks existed upon which to play social games. By 2042, the global population will reach 9.3 billion. It seems reasonable to expect that a full half of these will play social games online. Then, by 2040, we should expect this number to approach 4.5 billion gamers, as device penetration increases, populations age, and the world's total population increases.

Let's take a look at some of the bigger markets today and their projected demographic shifts to try to quantify and imagine what this worldwide population of gamers will look like by 2042. An in-depth look at every gaming community in the world today would be vastly outside the scope of this book. To that end, we will focus on the largest markets or those in

FIGURE 1.2 Anywhere you see lights here, people can play online games. (*Image Credit*: NASA/NOAA.)

which we can expect to see significant changes over the coming decade. To any countries whose gamers get short shrift in these pages, I can only ask forgiveness in advance.

For each country, we will look first at a satellite view at night. Consider: Anywhere there is sufficient electricity to illuminate the land, and certainly anywhere with a dense enough population to glow at midnight, there is a population of gamers. Today and for the next 20 years, all of them will have access to high-quality, free online multiplayer games. As we will discuss, even the network infrastructure to allow high-speed gaming is rapidly becoming untethered from the Earth. Where there is light there can be social gaming, and there will be. (Figure 1.2).

There is a worldwide community of players coming, which will soon exceed the total population of the Earth on the day I was born. And every one of them could conceivably play the games you will make.

POPULATION GROWTH

Let's look at the world population and demographics by region today and in 2042. From there, we can start to think about where these gamers will live and begin to contemplate how they might choose to interact with games.

A note on the reliability of demographic projections from the UN:

> Projections can only illustrate potential trajectories of population change. The projections in this report will hold true only if all assumptions about future fertility, mortality, and international

migration hold true as well. Because these assumptions of demographic change are based on historical trends in births, deaths, and international migration, the projections do not predict any potential impact of future policy decisions or exceptional historic events, such as natural disasters.

First, let's look briefly at the global population growth; most of us have a vague sense of human populations over time, but the profound impact of the logarithmic scale of growth is easy to underestimate. We didn't just add a lot of people in the last hundred years; we quadrupled the total number of humans alive at the start of the Great Depression. While education, birth control, and rising standards of living have curbed population growth in many regions, we are still adding humans to the planet at an incredible clip.[2] And every one of them could be a gamer (Figure 1.3).

While birth rates are changing, so are other critical demographic factors that will influence the coming generations of gamers. In the developed world, particularly the United States, China, Canada, and Europe,

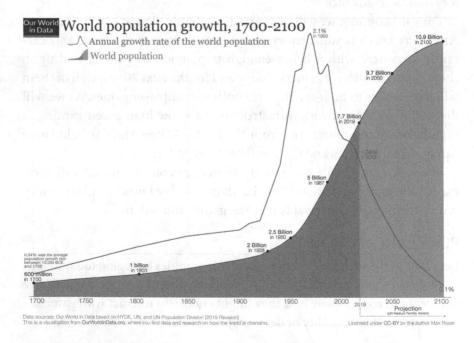

FIGURE 1.3 The rate of human population growth has slowed in the last 20 years, but we are still adding gamers to the world at an astounding rate. (*Image Credit*: UN Population Division.)

Annual number of births by world region

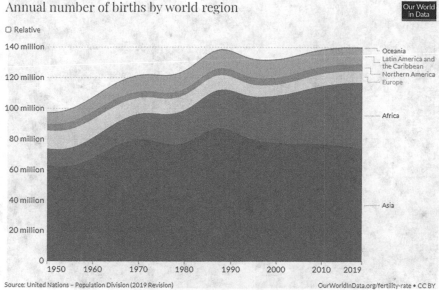

Source: United Nations – Population Division (2019 Revision)   OurWorldInData.org/fertility-rate • CC BY

FIGURE 1.4   Across the developed world, declining birth rates are leading to significant demographic shifts over the coming decades, moving from population growth to contraction in many of 2021's top gaming markets. (*Image Credit*: The World Factbook, US Central Intelligence Agency.)

the populations are aging. Birth rates are in decline. The wealthy are living longer and having more time for leisure with more disposable income. As age reduces mobility, these citizens will increasingly spend more time on stationary recreation like gaming (Figure 1.4).

United States and Canada

Right now, the United States and its northern neighbor, Canada, comprise over 175M gamers[3] with high levels of disposable income. They play on high-end consoles, PCs, and mobile phones. They also consume significant amounts of gaming content on Twitch, YouTube, and other online services. Revenue from the region is fairly evenly distributed between different platforms (Figure 1.5).

Because the propensity to spend on games is high here, disproportionate amounts of marketing budgets are devoted to this region. These high-value users can generate significant Return On Investment (ROI) from paid User Acquisition (UA) efforts in a short period. Since many automated ad-purchasing processes measure the effectiveness of UA efforts based on payback period for UA costs, the region remains one of the most desirable

FIGURE 1.5 The United States and Canada. (*Image Credit*: NASA/NOAA.)

and expensive to advertise in. In other words, higher value users are more expensive to acquire.

Based on Google's and NewZoo's reports from the beginning of 2022, North America should be described as a mature market, in which shared gameplay, platform-agnostic gaming, community participation, streamers, and spectators can all be collectively described as "gaming" in the region.[4]

How are the gaming populations of the US and Canada changing?

Today, 17% of the US population and 18.5% of the Canadian population is over the age of 65. By 2042, this will be 22%. The US and Canada are aging. This impacts the number of new gamers that will join the party from these regions (Figure 1.6).

At the same time, both the US and Canada are increasing in ethnic diversity. We can expect a lower percentage of the population of the United States who are Caucasian each year for the next 20. At the same time, we see a significant increase in the percentage of foreign-born residents in the US.

This means that the cultural backgrounds, reference points, and languages will become less homogenous and the need for a more varied cultural and ethnic representation in games will continue to increase. Games are no longer for or by white-males, and this will increasingly be true. This

Population by Age Group: Projections 2020 to 2060
The population is projected to reach 404 million by 2060.
(In millions)

Characteristic	Population						Change from 2016 to 2060	
	2016	2020	2030	2040	2050	2060	Number	Percent
Total population	323.1	332.6	355.1	373.5	388.9	404.5	81.4	25.2
Under 18 years.	73.6	74.0	75.7	77.1	78.2	80.1	6.5	8.8
18 to 44 years.	116.0	119.2	125.0	126.4	129.6	132.7	16.7	14.4
45 to 64 years.	84.3	83.4	81.3	89.1	95.4	97.0	12.7	15.1
65 years and over	49.2	56.1	73.1	80.8	85.7	94.7	45.4	92.3
85 years and over	6.4	6.7	9.1	14.4	18.6	19.0	12.6	198.1
100 years and over	0.1	0.1	0.1	0.2	0.4	0.6	0.5	618.3

Note: The official population estimates for the United States are shown for 2016; the projections use the Vintage 2016 population estimate for July 1, 2016, as the base population for projecting from 2017 to 2060.
Source: U.S. Census Bureau, 2017 National Population Projections.

FIGURE 1.6   By 2035, older adults will outnumber children for the first time in US history.[5] (*Image Credit*: U.S. Census Bureau, 2017.)

will result in a need for a broader spectrum of heroes, and greater avoidance of racially archetypical villains. This has been further advanced by social movements in North America over the last few years. These factors will further increase the demand for high-quality language localization.

North America also plays host to many of the great game development and publishing companies of the last 20 years. Electronic Arts, Activision, Microsoft, Apple, Google, Facebook, and incredible game makers too numerous to name are headquartered in North America. Many of the historically iconic institutions of the gaming business – from venerable pen and paper games to the original Game Developers Conference – began in the United States before spreading across the globe.

Europe

Collectively, Europe comes in just behind Asia as the world's biggest single market for gamers. In 2021, between 200 and 500 million gamers called Europe home.[6] (Differences in which elements of the Middle East get lumped into Europe account for different populations attributed in different studies.) The UK, Germany, France, and Italy led the region, but PC and mobile gaming are huge in every country in the area. Sony, Nintendo, and Microsoft all also sell lots of consoles in the region. While mobile gamers in this region game for less time on average, they have a higher propensity to spend on games.[7] Every country in Europe can proudly boast of truly great game development companies and publishers. Strong school systems and universities drive innovative research and development (R&D) projects in basic and applied sciences throughout the region. These same places also generate solid programmers, designers, and artists every year to fuel the creation of impressive games. Scandinavian countries, long-time leaders

FIGURE 1.7   Europe. (*Image Credit*: European Space Agency.)

in mobile technology and publishing, continue to punch far above their weight class in mobile, PC, and console development. (Figure 1.7).

Overall, the population of Europe will undergo significant changes over the coming decades. The average lifespan is increasing. Birth rates and the population are in decline. The EU population as a percentage of the world population is in decline as well.[8] Since the end of the Colonial era, when the great powers of Europe dominated the globe, Europe has slowly watched its cultural, military, and economic influence wane. According to a Price Waterhouse Cooper report from 2020, "The EU27 share of world GDP could be down to less than 10% by 2050, smaller than India."[9]

Europe will remain an important gaming market, with hundreds of millions of gamers who spend. But we can expect the importance of the European market relative to emerging markets to decline in the next two decades, as a function of meta-layer demographic shifts in population (Figures 1.8 and 1.9).

Russia

Russia had over 65 million gamers in 2018, mostly playing on PCs and mobile devices. Personal computers like the venerable Commodore 64 were smuggled into the Soviet Union in the early 1980s, and since then,

Map 2 – Crude rate of total population change in NUTS 3 regions, 2018

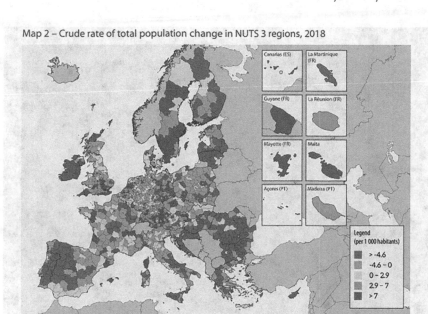

Source: Eurostat.

FIGURE 1.8   European populations are projected to be in decline over the next two decades. (*Image Credit*: Eurostat.)

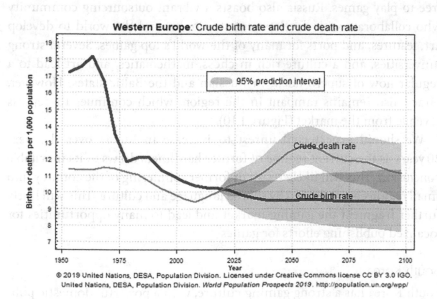

FIGURE 1.9   There will be fewer European gamers in 2040 than there are today. (*Image Credit*: United Nations.)

FIGURE 1.10   Moscow by night from ISS. (*Image Credit*: NASA/NOAA.)

there has been a strong game development and hacker culture in Russia. In 2020, Russian publisher Playrix dominated global charts in mobile free-to-play games. Russia also boasts a vibrant outsourcing community who collaborate with development studios around the world to develop art, features, and ports for many of the world's top games. Several strong universities, and a culture rich in chess, mathematics, and art lead to a regular flow of superb talent in Russian and the Baltic states. However, piracy also remains rampant in the region, which continues to depress revenue from the market (Figure 1.10).

We should expect civil unrest to increase in Russia over the next 20 years as the current regime of former hardliners draws to its inevitable conclusion. This will likely result in former splintering of the country into small regions more unified by shared language and culture. This will likely further fragment the gaming market and lead to many opportunities for localized publishing efforts for games.

South Korea

South Korea has a strong gaming culture, with a powerful domestic publishing business that has expanded across the world over the last decade. More than 56% of the South Korean population identified as gamers in

FIGURE 1.11   Seoul, South Korea by night. (*Image Credit*: NASA/NOAA.)

2018,[10] totaling almost 30 million. South Korean MMORPGs, which followed in the footsteps of early online fantasy MMORPGs like *Ultima Online*, have dominated the market in the region for decades. In recent years, Korean entertainment from KPop music like BTS (who have their own line of video games) to Korean cinema (like the hyper-violent *Oldboy* or *Squid Games* to Academy award-winning social black comedy like *Parasite*) has experienced an incredible worldwide explosion. Korean creators and entertainers are now enjoyed globally, representing a massive entertainment export industry. Companies like Big Hit Entertainment, NCSoft, Nexxon, and Netmarble as well as hundreds of smaller developers and publishers employ thousands of young, well-educated Koreans (Figure 1.11).

However, the population is in decline. The population of South Korea is expected to peak around 2022, and enter a period of significant decline over the next few decades, barring significant changes in immigration policy or birth rates. The Korean economy and per capita GDP increase has been stellar over the last decade; however, this is unlikely to continue due to these demographic changes.

We should expect Korean giants, particularly the big three domestic publishers, to continue to enjoy banner sales and some high level of export business from the West, Europe, Taiwan, and Japan. Because of the strong relationships between the government and the Korean games industry, the regulatory climate in the country will likely remain favorable for game

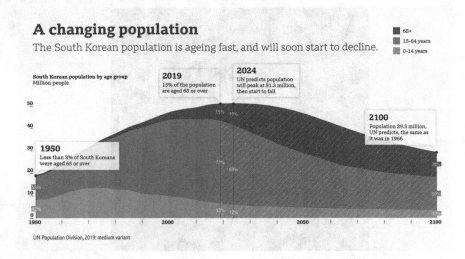

A changing population

The South Korean population is ageing fast, and will soon start to decline.

FIGURE 1.12 South Korea, a gaming giant, enjoys strong domestic and foreign market sales. The impressive population and per-capita GDP growth here are likely to slow in coming decades, forcing South Korean publishers to focus their efforts on exporting to other markets. (*Image Credit*: UN Population Division.)

makers. South Korea will also remain a trendsetter for cultural tastes, legal decision-making precedents, healthcare technology, and game economy design for the next ten years (Figure 1.12).

These changes are described starkly in a UN Report:

> The pace of population ageing in the Republic of Korea is projected to be one of the fastest in the world. With zero immigration in the future, the proportion aged 65 or older in the total population would increase from 5.6 per cent to 24.7 per cent between 1995 and 2050. The proportion of elderly would be 24.0 per cent in 2050.[11]

2020 UN Report on Demographics

South Korea is a gaming giant right now, combining a strong gaming culture, several large publishers who build games of terrific quality, global ambitions. Coupled with a film and music entertainment industry that is enjoying a current boom in worldwide appeal, South Korea looks strong for the next decade. But demographic shifts are likely to slow this growth over the next decade and beyond.

Japan

Japan is a country full of gamers.

FIGURE 1.13   Tokyo Bay at night. (*Image Credit*: NASA/NOAA.)

Japan loves games. Millions of daily gamers and some of the most accomplished game development studios in the world call Tokyo and Osaka home. Nintendo may well be the best-known brand in the world for gaming. Legendary creators like Kojima, Yoshi Ono, Shigeru Miyamoto, and From Software call Japan home. The domestic market for arcades, pachinko, Nintendo consoles and games, and home-grown mobile games is dedicated and powerful. Japan had 125M citizens in 2020, and 76M of them were gamers (Figure 1.13).

It's hard to find a game maker in the world who was not strongly influenced by games from Japan. Everyone has a story of playing Street Fighter 2 Turbo on an old Nintendo in an Akihabara street tournament, the first time they got a sword in Zelda, dodging barrels thrown by that damn dirty ape, *Donkey Kong*, or the moment they finally beat the first boss in a *Dark Souls* game. *Pokémon, Monster Hunter, Resident Evil*, and dozens of other iconic gaming franchises were born here.

Yet, Japan's domestic games market remains overwhelmingly dense and hard for foreign companies to penetrate. It tends to be very difficult for companies outside of Japan to greatly excite Japanese players. Mostly, the games that sell well and monetize in Japan on all platforms for most of the last 20 years are Japanese games. Role-playing games (JRPGs!), puzzle games, and simulation games reign supreme.[12] Consoles are ubiquitous, but they are overwhelmingly Sony or Nintendo consoles. Mobile phone gamers still pay homage to genre-defining games like *Puzzles & Dragons* every week in a market that reached almost $14 billion annually in 2020.[13]

Japan was early to the demographic downturn that is beginning to characterize the developed world. Birth rates in Japan have been low for 20 years, and the country's near-zero immigration policies are starting to change. Japanese citizens have the longest life expectancy in the world, but there will be 15 million fewer of them by 2030 than there are today.[14]

It will remain difficult for foreign-made products to do hugely well in Japan. But, even a small slice of the country's gaming attention can be huge. And exports from beloved gaming brands will remain strong for the next decade. By 2040, however, I would expect even perineal behemoths like Sony and Nintendo to have been absorbed by rival corporations whose home markets simply offer scale Japan cannot match. Nintendo may have laughed at Microsoft's effort to purchase them at the beginning of the century.[15] I predict that eventually the economic might of tech giants in the US, China, and India will end up absorbing even the legends of this proud island country just as we have all been absorbing lessons from their grand-master game makers for the last 40 years.

China

There's no country harder to predict than China right now, in early 2022. Who would have thought that the world's largest gaming market a year ago would have suddenly slammed down a draconian series of edicts to cripple the world's largest publishers? A recent report in the gaming news-site Kotaku informs us that more than 14,000 game development companies have gone under in the last year as a result of the Party's newfound zeal targeting the games business.[16] Who would have expected a billion gamers to suddenly have to change their schedules and login information and ultimately, play a lot less?

What happened next? VPN, already incredibly common, became a necessity and a bit of diplomatic fiction accepted by seemingly everyone. And the advent of satellite dishes that could be fit into a briefcase and plugged into a car battery via USB gave all of the citizens access to a Low Earth Orbit level of high-speed connectivity without (as much) censorship. The biggest gaming market in the world got bigger than ever by 2030… Or did it?

It's hard to say today.

Games made in China and run by massive teams of incredibly skilled and dedicated game makers are top of the world charts on mobile and PC

FIGURE 1.14   Cities of Northern China. (*Image Credit*: NASA/NOAA.)

in terms of users and revenue. The vast teams arrayed by major publishers like Tencent and NetEase continue to deliver games with deep technical skill and superb design innovation. As it has been true for the last decade, still will it remain for the next ten years: to see the future of gaming, look to China. There certainly is no country with a more impressive and formidable group of professional game makers in the world. Easily more than a hundred thousand Chinese citizens make a living from the gaming industry (Figure 1.14).

And some of these games are very, very good. In fact, there are hundreds of games killed in China each year by developers who want to do better and publishers who understand the business well and push technology and design to make great games. And hundreds of even better games published every month. Until recently.

Game licenses are now a hard-to-get rarity, very limited in their number and carefully allocated by party policies and favoritism. And so now grand publishers may be limited to a few games a month they can release. So the Chinese publishers – many, powerful, skilled, with deep pockets and great tech – have turned more of their gaze outward. Tencent, NetEase,

Huawei, and a hundred other powerful players in the games industry will continue to scour the globe for markets and talent to continue the techniques they honed to razor's edge in Beijing, Shanghai, and Shenzhen over the last decade.

If video games are the spiritual opium[17] of the masses, as the Party described them in 2021, then they are likely to remain as much a flashpoint for East–West relations as the original crop of opium did in the nineteenth century. The sums involved are so great and the access to user identities and data is such a complicated topic that the Chinese gaming market, and Chinese game publishers, will both remain the single most powerful group in the gaming market for the next 20 years.

China likely overtook the US in the field of AI research in 2019.[18] In the next two decades, China will drive incredible innovations in computer gaming, mobile phone technology, game design, economy design, live operations techniques, deployment, and many more fields. But this advance in the craft will be slowed if game makers in the country are not allowed to deliver their games to the world's biggest gaming market: their friends and families.

China's demographics are also suddenly in flux and hard to predict. Just a few months ago, China was also projected to begin slowing in population growth within the next decade.[19] Yet the government recently loosened the reins on controversial two-child policy from 2016 and is now, as of 2022 encouraging couples to have more children. In any case, the Chinese population will remain well over one billion for the next 80 years at least. And that's a lot of gamers.

ON EMERGING MARKETS

Purchasing Power of Markets by 2050

The world economy will continue to grow much faster than the population.

This is even truer in Emerging Markets than in advanced economies. Price Waterhouse Coopers, a consulting agency, projects that *"emerging markets will grow about twice as fast as advanced economies on average"* between 2020 and 2050 (Figure 1.15).

As the consulting firm PWC tells us:

> We expect this growth [in global GDP] to be driven largely by emerging market and developing countries, with the E7 economies of Brazil, China, India, Indonesia, Mexico, Russia and Turkey growing at an annual average rate of almost 3.5% over the

FIGURE 1.15 The ranking of economic power by country will change significantly over the next 30 years as demographic shift alters GDP for many countries.[20] (*Image Credit*: Visual Capitalist.)

next 34 years, compared to just 1.6% for the advanced G7 nations of Canada, France, Germany, Italy, Japan, the UK and the US. We will continue to see the shift in global economic power away from established advanced economies, especially those in Europe, towards emerging economies in Asia and elsewhere.[21]

Let's look at where these world economies spend their gaming cash.

In 2021, Mobile gaming took home $93.2B in gross revenue. Console gaming followed, with $50.1B, and then PC gaming at $36.7B.

Let's take a look at some of the most exciting emerging markets which are rising to prominence in the gaming industry over the coming years (Figure 1.16).

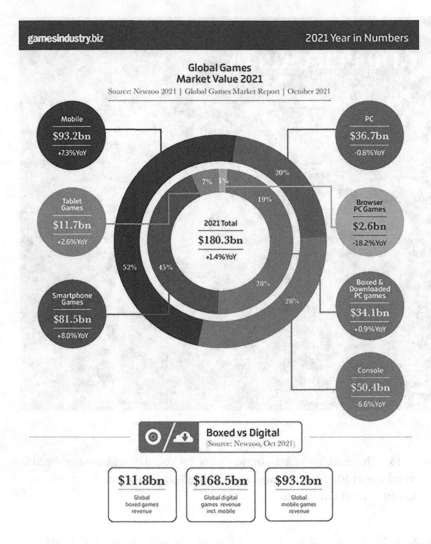

FIGURE 1.16 By the end of 2021 the global market for games had shifted to mobile first. We should expect this trend to continue. (*Image Credit*: GamesIndustry.biz/ Gamer Network Limited.)

Southeast Asia

If there is anywhere that online gaming has clearly exploded over the last few years, it is Southeast Asia. From the northern mountains of Vietnam to the southern tip of the Indonesian archipelago, millions of gamers have joined the party since 2015. And this region is continuing to emerge as a powerhouse for gamer populations, publishing, revenue, and game development. Indeed, it is estimated that more than $4.4 billion on revenue originated from the region in 2019.[22] Further, 82% of those living in urban areas identify themselves as gamers. High-speed cellular networks, widespread adoption of mobile phones (and PCs), and the growth of mainstream free-to-play competitive games have unlocked gaming as a pastime for a youthful population. Widespread use of English (it is the official language of the Philippines, Malaysia, and wealthy Singapore) makes it easy for many gamers to play Western games as well (Figure 1.17).

However, the market is far from uniform. Thailand, Singapore, and the Philippines have quite different cultures and gaming tastes. Strategy games, particularly mobile MOBAs like Mobile Legends or *Honor of Kings*, do well in the region, but so do sports games like *FIFA* and shooters like Garena's massive hit *Free Fire*. Millions in the region tune in to watch eSports events, particularly *PlayerUnknown's Battlegrounds* and *League of Legends* tournaments. Play-to-earn games built around the emerging blockchain and NFT technologies have attracted a lot of attention to the region in 2021 as well, as Vietnamese developer's Sky Mavis' *Axie Infinity* drew in huge numbers of users with the promise of being able to earn Ethereum by collecting and battling.

Indonesia is the most populous country in the region: over a quarter billion people today and growing rapidly. The Philippines comes in next, with just over a hundred million citizens. Vietnam and Thailand follow.

FIGURE 1.17 Bangkok at night. (*Image Credit*: NASA/NOAA.)

About half the population live in sprawling urban centers like Jakarta or the region's undisputed melting pot, Singapore, a city-state where you can discuss video games over bespoke cocktails served by Malay men in drag while listening to a nearby call to prayer from one of the cities many mosques. In recent years, Singapore has become something of a regional hub for media companies and game publishers alike. Disney, Electronic Arts, Microsoft, and Garena all have big offices there, as do hundreds of smaller developers.

Over the next two decades, Southeast Asia collectively is poised to be one of the most exciting regions in the world for the emergence of large new population of connected gamers and the new business models and technologies it will take to engage them.

Let's take a closer look at a few of the countries that comprise this region.

Indonesia

In recent years, Indonesia, a disparate collection of thousands of islands in a South Pacific archipelago, has grown in stature as a gaming center (Figure 1.18).

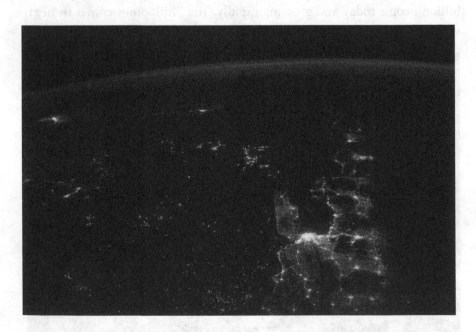

FIGURE 1.18 The cities of Java, Indonesia. (*Image Credit*: NASA/NOAA.)

- Indonesia's population will continue to grow to approximately 250 million people by 2050.[23]

- Indonesia is expected to be the fourth largest economy in the world by 2025, just behind China, the USA, and India.

- Purchasing power is growing, but the population is still relatively poor. This forces game developers to focus on alternative business models like advertising, sachet-pricing IAP, or emerging pay-to-earn models.

- Almost exclusively mobile gamers, with some limited PC access.[24]

- Indonesia's population is very young, on average.[25]

This combination of a large population of highly connected mobile gamers whose tastes for sophisticated Western and North Asian products demands advanced publishing efforts represents a huge opportunity for game makers from across the world.

Vietnam

Vietnam has not been a major gaming market until fairly recently. Consoles are almost nonexistent, and the PC Café culture that led to widespread online gaming in other countries never took hold in Vietnam. But mobile gaming has changed all of that. Vietnam is expected to generate $280 million in revenue for game makers in 2021.[26] This gross dollar value is expected to roughly double over the next 5 years. Vietnam is a near-perfect example of an emerging market, with some local developers and specific taste in games.

Vietnam is expected to reach 109M people by 2050, with fairly constrained growth. The population is also aging.

- Median age in 2015 was 30.5 years, expected to increase to 41 by 2050.[27]

- Rapid growth in per capita GDP, from $6300 in 2016 to $28,200 by 2050.[28]

In 2020, approximately 75% of Vietnamese, between 16 and 24, reported that they played online games daily.[29]

Combining these data points suggests a robust addressable market of gamers with disposable income for gaming.

As a satellite of the Chinese economy, but one that has not yet started running into the caps on growth that are beginning to plague the Middle Kingdom, Vietnam appears poised for further market growth: this means more gamers with more income.

India

India is among the most rapidly growing gaming markets in the world in 2020 (Figure 1.19). "By 2050 the population of India is expected to surpass that of China with an estimated population of 1.67 billion people."[30]

2050 is also expected to be roughly the peak of India's population growth.[31]

India's population averages 26.8 years old, in a prime gaming age bracket. While this is expected to increase to 35 by the year 2040, this would still mean a population of well over a billion people in peak gaming age. Indeed, the consulting firm KPMG expects the gaming market in India to grow from $1.8 billion to almost $4 billion per year by 2025.[32]

For this reason alone, I expect India to become the world's top gaming population by 2040. However, when coupled with the incredible growth in mobile data usage from 2018 to 2022 and the widespread availability of

FIGURE 1.19   Cities of India (*Image Credit*: NASA/NOAA.)

affordable, high-quality gaming devices, India is very likely to be home to the largest active number of gamers in the world within the next few years. Indeed, in the Summer of 2021, India was reported to be home to over 400 million gamers. We should expect that to approach 700 million by 2025, likely over a billion by 2035 (Figure 1.20).

Mobile data use and bandwidth have increased massively in just a few years in India.[33]

Combine the availability of high bandwidth mobile devices with the increase in per capita and disposable income, a lack of repressive governmental approach to the gaming market and we could reasonably expect India to be the top gaming market in the world by 2030. Smartphones drive the vast majority of this gaming action. While the same kinds of games which are popular the world over are popular in India, there is a strong focus on regional brands and tastes as well. (For example, Cricket, the sport, is very popular there, as is a card game called *Teen Patti*.) Virtually no one in India plays games on the PC (9%), and even fewer on consoles. With a rainbow of local languages and dialects, games which localize into

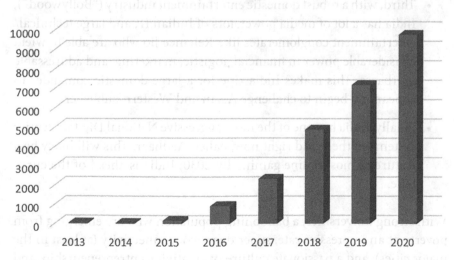

FIGURE 1.20 India's usage of mobile bandwidth has grown at an incredible rate over the last decade. (*Image Credit*: Data from Statista, Image credit Tim Fields.)

Hindi, Bengali, and even Tamil or Urdu can attract a large population. However, the propensity to spend on games is still low in India, such that monetizing Indian gamers remains a challenge today.

There are a few other interesting high-level trends to be aware of when thinking about gaming in India.

- First, while Indian cities like Bangalore and Hyderabad have long been hubs for technical outsourcing and customer support centers, there is a rapidly developing local game development and publishing market now as well. In fact, a number of Indian studios and publishers are pushing to bring products from the Indian market to the West.

- Second, while government regulation of gaming is much less protectionist and restrictive in India than it is in China, there have recently been some overtures made at bringing the trade war between the two countries into the gaming space. Specifically, Tencent products like WeChat and games like PUBG have recently been banned in India.[34] Given the ongoing border and trade issues between the two countries, we should expect this trend to continue.

- Third, with a robust domestic entertainment industry ("Bollywood"), India has a lot of media power, lots of Indian IP, and large technical/entertainment conglomerates like Reliance Jio who are able to wield considerable power in financial, logistic, marketing, and addressable userbases. This makes India ripe for a large domestic contender to appear and begin to challenge Asian and Western publishers.

- Finally, India has one of the most aggressive National Digital Identity systems in the world right now, called Aadhaar. This will likely be a feature of most online gaming by 2030; India is ahead of the curve here.

With strong universities, a ballooning population who are emerging from poverty at an impressive rate, super degree of connectivity (at least in the major cities), and a passionate culture of creativity, entrepreneurship, and technology-focused development, India has rapidly emerged as a powerhouse of game makers and publishers with designs on their own mighty domestic market as well as international ambitions.

INTERVIEW WITH ZAID AZMI: INTERACTIVE FICTION FOR THE WORLD

Zaid Azmi is the CEO and founder of KahaniBox, an interactive fiction development studio in New Delhi, India.

TF: First, can you tell us who you are and tell us about your role in the games business?

Zaid: I'm Zaid, and I'm the founder of *KahaniBox*, which is India's first Choose Your Own Adventure-styled story game in local languages. I've been in the gaming industry only for the last three years. Overall I've been working for the last 12 years in different domains, mostly in tech startups in India.

Building a game was kind of a new thing, but it was something of my interest. I've been playing a lot of interactive fiction-based games for over two decades, and in India, storytelling is one of the primary forms of entertainment. It bothered me a bit that there were no other platforms that provided interactive fiction in Indian languages and contexts. Hence, I started building *KahaniBox* in 2019.

TF: How big of an audience do you believe there is for the types of interactive stories that you're building?

Zaid: Bollywood movies and TV shows currently entertain the 1.3 billion people that we have in India. We build similar stories that people love watching, but we take a step further and provide them a much more interactive experience. So we envision ourselves to be the Netflix for interactive fiction, and we want to be able to entertain anyone who has a smartphone in India.

TF: What are some of the advances in technology that you think will make interactive storytelling even better over the next ten years?

Zaid: That's a good question. I think it has to be the evolution of platforms. By platforms, I mean, the tools which are available for creating interactive stories. Right now, there are only a very few skilled people who can create good interactive fiction. Because working with branched narratives and making sure the audience is continuously engaged is not easy.

Just like Unity made it possible for a single developer to create award-winning games, similar evolution will happen for interactive story game engines, which are currently not very resourceful and easy to use.

TF: Do you imagine interactive fiction platforms, like the one you're creating, to be something that you allow thousands of users to create content for? Like *Roblox* has done with gaming.

Zaid: Definitely! When I started building *KahaniBox*, my belief was that creating high-quality interactive fiction is a very skilled thing to do and it will always be a few game studios that would continue to create good interactive story games. Because you need a solid understanding of storytelling and game mechanics, both, to build a great interactive fiction story, and not a lot of people have that.

But if you look at what YouTube and iPhones have done – They have made people learn cinematography and storytelling, and now there are thousands of creators on YouTube who have millions in following and they create very professional content that keeps their followers very entertained. So I think similarly in gaming overall, and not just interactive fiction, once we have platforms that are even simpler than *Roblox*, lot of individual creators who have no prior background in game development, will eventually learn the game mechanics and create brilliant games.

TF: We have seen Artificial Intelligence write some stories. Do you believe that AI will be able to create interactive fiction for your players, at some point?

Zaid: Yeah, definitely. So, GPT-3 is very fascinating, and there are already games like *AI Dungeon*, where you type something in the story, and the AI tells you what happens next. In the future, it might be that you only need to write a few sentences, and then AI can build a very interesting story that is hours long. I think AI will make a very important impact in game development and in the media/entertainment industry in general.

TF: One of the things that impressed me about you and your company when we first met was the way you were looking at games as a way of reaching a huge audience who have not traditionally been gamers. How do you see the world of gamers evolving over the next 20 years?

Zaid: In India, I think interactive storytelling has huge potential and it will at some point be more popular than Bollywood. Because currently, we produce the second-highest number of movies in the world and Bollywood is the most popular form of entertainment for Indians, or we can say that storytelling is the primary form of entertainment in India. And when we watch any movie or TV show, we all have these thoughts like "Why did this character die?", "Why did the story end this way?", "What if this/that would have happened in the story?". That's what exactly interactive storytelling allows you to do. So for a lot of users gaming could primarily mean interactive storytelling in India.

I also think people would start valuing digital game characters much more than Hollywood or Bollywood stars. There are some very iconic characters already from games like *GTA*, *Final Fantasy*, *Splinter Cell*, and hundreds of others. People get these characters tattooed on their bodies. Over the next 10–20 years, I think the majority of celebrities that people admire won't be actually real.

TF: Of all of the game maker conferences I've been to in the last few years, the Game Developers Conference in India, there in Hyderabad, had the most energy, and it felt like the game development community in India was really excited about the future. Can you tell me how you see game development in India evolving over the next few years?

Zaid: Gaming has very recently started to become mainstream in India. It happened with the growth of great quality but affordable smartphones and almost free mobile data. Previously people didn't have a platform to access good games because we are not a country where people buy consoles and PCs for gaming. More than 90% of the gaming users are on mobile and India still has almost 500 million users with no smartphones yet. So mobile game development has great potential in India. There are some state governments who are promoting local game development and people are now seriously considering game development as a career choice, which was not very common few years ago. We still don't have a lot of good places where people can learn game development but hopefully, that will change soon.

TF: What do you think will be the first game to reach one billion DAU?

Zaid: In India?

TF: Or anywhere.

Zaid: I think it has to be a social multiplayer kind of game but not sure which one would it be.

TF: What advice do you have for young people who want to get into the game's business the way you have?

Zaid: Yeah, I think, specifically, for people from India, I'm really tired of seeing these gaming companies producing the same kind of games again and again. Every game studio in India will have a Rummy game because it makes you money. Every game studio will have a Caram, a Ludo game. We do not take enough risks, which is really a shame because we as a country are a content powerhouse. We have Bollywood, 50+ OTT streaming apps, thousands of individual popular creators on YouTube and other platforms. I don't know why nobody picks up this task of creating the next AAA game out of India, which should have already happened. So my advice is to try to do something which has not been done yet and try to build something amazing inspired by our history and culture. There's way too much money being pumped into the Indian startup ecosystem so money isn't the problem.

There are so many games from the West like *The Last of Us, God of War*. Recently, I played *Ghost of Tsushima* who's story has really stuck with me. I literally cried two or three times while playing that game. It's an amazing story, beautiful visuals, great music – I think that's the best game I've ever played and that game should have gotten the Oscars.

In India, we have such a diverse history and culture that I think there can be a game like *Ghost of Tsushima* or *God of War or The Last of Us* from India, for sure. It's just that nobody has done it yet. Maybe we will build it at *KahaniBox*, but who knows?

Latin America

Diverse and populous, Latin America is host to several hundred million gamers today. (290 million in 2021 according to Google.) In 2021, Latin America generated more than $3.5 billion in mobile revenue.[35] But this is just the tip of the iceberg, as PC and console gaming generated another $4 billion in the same year, for a total of more than $7 billion. And we should expect this to grow to more than $5 billion in mobile revenue alone over the next few years. Most of this growth will continue to be on Google Play Store and through the PC (Figures 1.21 and 1.22).

Brazil, Mexico, Argentina, and Colombia are the top gaming populations in the region. As 5G networking continues to expand through dense urban populations, we can expect a huge boom in online gamers. Strategy,

FIGURE 1.21   Brazil at night. (*Image Credit*: NASA/NOAA.)

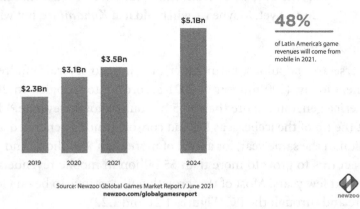

FIGURE 1.22 Latin America gaming culture and revenues are growing rapidly. (*Image Credit*: NewZoo.)

shooters, and racing games tend to be the most popular, and Latin America shows a strong trend toward more core games, with fewer casual or puzzle games than in many regions.

Correspondingly, eSports based on competitive games like *Free Fire* and *Arena of Valor* are popular.

Latin America is the youngest and most rapidly growing market for games in the world today. But, due to low disposable income per capita, monetizing users here remains a challenge. To succeed in the region, games need to custom tailor their monetization approach with localized content and payment options.

Let's dive deeper into a few particular countries in the region.

Brazil

Featuring the largest population in Latin America, Brazil features millions of gamers and a number of very high-quality game development studios.

- Population of Brazil was 208 million in 2018.

- Expected to peak in 2047 at 233 million.

- Aging, from 33.5 in 2020 to an average 45.1 in 2050.[36]

- Disposable income increasing from $2265 in 2011 to a projected $9771 by 2050.

- 62M active gamers in 2020.

- Mobile first (70%), with console and PC too expensive for most players.

With over 60 million Portuguese speaking gamers, as a market, Brazil alone justifies localizing game content into Portuguese. In 2020, Brazilian players generated gross revenues of $1.6 billion dollars, and we should definitely expect this to increase significantly over the coming decade. More than a third of Brazilian gamers identify themselves as core gamers, making competitive games like shooters, racing games, and strategy games popular.[37] "Competition" is regularly ranked highly by Brazilian players as a reason they play.

No major game release or "Go to Market" strategy is complete without having determined an approach to engaging the players from Brazil. And as their disposable income triples over the next three decades, Brazil's importance to the market will continue to grow.

Mexico

- 121 million in 2015, expected to exceed 145 million by 2050.

- Rapidly aging, from 27.9 in 2015 to 42 years old by 2050.

- In 2019, there were 72.6 million gamers in Mexico.

- Per capita GDP $19,100 in 2020, projected to continue to increase rapidly until 2050.[38]

Mexico represents the second largest market in Latin America by population, but the highest grossing country in the region. In 2019, Mexico generated $1.8 billion in revenue from the gaming business.[39] Console and PC retail sales are strong still in Mexico, representing about 40% of the total market. Racing games, sports games, and shooters are popular, with *Call of Duty, Free Fire,* and *Fortnite* topping the charts in 2021.[40]

Mexico also boasts a number of high-quality art outsource houses as well as several game development studios in Monterrey and Mexico City.

Over the next decade, we should expect significant decline in the retail market here and a migration toward digital distribution mechanisms that offer benefits to consumers and publishers alike.

The Middle East and Africa

Finally, let's look at four countries in the Middle East – Turkey, Saudi Arabia, Egypt, and Israel – which show signs of rapidly emerging into large gaming populations. There are currently around 100M gamers in this broad and diverse region. A number of local game streamers have recently emerged, and are being picked up by regional television broadcasters. Many regional governments like Saudi Arabia, UAE, and Dubai are putting resources into building out eSports facilities hoping to capitalize on a youthful population motivated to participate in competitive gaming tournaments. Many of them are currently underserved by games or devices fit for the region. This represents a good opportunity for international and domestic publishers alike.

Within a few years, some experts suggest that the Middle East will reach a market size of around $6 billion per year.[41] Indeed, Saudi Arabia, UAE, and Egypt alone grossed more than $1.7 billion in 2021 according to a recent study from Niko Partners[42] though the bulk of that came from Saudi Arabia. The region is marked by extreme differences in wealth, connectivity, and device availability. Generally speaking, mobile gaming dominates the region. (Though some reports suggest a significant growth in PC gaming as well in coming years.[43]) Clearly some countries (Iraq, Yemen, and Syria at the time of this writing) are sufficiently war-torn that they lack a sufficient infrastructure to support gaming. However, there are many bright spots, and the presence of a common written language (Arabic) makes tailoring games to be played across the region possible.

Saudi Arabia

The Kingdom of Saudi Arabia is pushing hard to emerge from almost a century of medieval theocratic darkness and government repression into a modern economy who can participate in enjoying and creating entertainment on the world stage. Saudi Arabian players spent more than $1 billion on gaming in 2021.[44] But beyond just playing games, the Kingdom has other ambitions as well.

Recognizing the need to diversify their income from being purely petroleum based, the Saudi Royal family have embarked on an ambitious mission to transform the Kingdom over the next decade. This "Vision 2030" initiative includes targeting film, animation, and gaming as opportunities to put the Kingdom's youthful, digitally savvy population to work in new ways.

As *The Economist* puts it in December 2021[45]:

> The conservative kingdom has become suddenly serious about the business of fun. It plans to invest $64bn in entertainment over the ten years to 2030, and hopes consumers will double their entertainment outlay from 2.9% to 6% of household spending.

From special effects creation studios, to full blown film production, to the creation of a robust domestic video game production industry, the Kingdom of Saudi Arabia (KSA) has big plans. Along with this effort, they are constructing new cities in the desert, including the futuristic NEOM, along the Western edge of the country bordering Egypt and Jordan. The Kingdom is pouring billions into creating a new city which is expected to be a hub for digital content creation, partnering with Bollywood for film production,[46] but also hoping to attract game development and publishing.

- 34 million citizens in 2020, expected to increase to 44 million by 2050.

- Despite earlier predictions from around 2011, Per capita GDP growth is expected to slow to almost zero over the next ten years as a result of instability in the petroleum market.[47]

- Estimated 21 million mobile-first gamers in 2020.[48]

In addition to a sizeable youthful population of gamers, we should expect to see Saudi productions begin to enter the market over the coming years.

While KSA's entry into the modern age has not always been smooth, a multitude of dedicated gamers, and what appears to be a sincere effort from the royal family to make gaming a big part of the country in the coming decades is very encouraging.

INTERVIEW WITH HIS ROYAL HIGHNESS PRINCE FASIL BIN BANDAR: THE BRIGHT FUTURE OF GAMES

Faisal bin Bandar bin Sultan is a Saudi Royal and the president of the Saudi Esports Federation (SEF) and the Arab eSports Federation since 2017. He is also vice president of the Global Esports Federation.

HRH: I look forward to speaking to you today. I have to admit I'm honored and humbled that you would consider talking to me for research, for a book. I consider myself just a humble gamer. Thank you.

TF: I believe that there are a lot of cool things going on in the Kingdom and in the region that I don't think most gamers and most game makers in the world know about. So, I think it's a great chance to tell us some stories that are important, cool, and inspiring, and I hope people would enjoy reading about them.

HRH: We're really excited about everything that's happening and growing over here. We are a culture of gamers—very young, very intense gamers, which I enjoy very much. One of the things that I find here that I get along a lot with the gamers here, I am a very gracious loser. I will always take a good game, I will congratulate you, follow you, talk you up, but I am a terrible winner. And when I win, I will not let you forget it. It's been a lot of fun being a gamer, being a part of the Federation, to get to interact with the community. Being intent to interact with them gives you a real sense of who the community is. And it's something I get very excited and very passionate about talking about, so I'm very excited to talk to you today.

TF: Okay. Why don't we start? Can you tell us a bit about your role in the gaming business?

HRH: As I said, I'm an avid gamer. I have been through much of my life. I am disappointed that the growth of eSports came after my peak. In my day, I was quite a good *FIFA* and Madden player. I took part in a few tournaments when I was younger. Before there was any money in it, it was all for bragging rights. The official pursuit of this as an industry and as a business came when I was appointed as president of the Saudi Esports Federation.

So I have to do an in-depth deep dive into PC gaming, some of the more popular games at the time, really start to gain some experience on the industry side of things. It was a huge learning curve. Something that I enjoyed, and I still enjoy immensely. And it's one of the fun things about this as an industry. It changes so regularly, that there's always a learning curve. You're never in front of the eight ball unless you're creating the game. And even then, there's always something to catch up to. Seeing the growth that's happened in the last five years, not just locally but regionally with the creation of the Arab ESports Federation, with our entry into the Global ESports Federation, as well as the International ESports Federation. I was just appointed recently, Vice President for the MENA region, I guess would be West Asia for the GEF, the Global ESports Federation.

It's an honor to be among all these individuals and to be able to do more for this community, both locally, regionally, and internationally, and with the goal toward the Olympic movement. I think one of the things that I always tried to bring to all of these, whether it's the federations, whether it's the ministry here, the government work that's happening, and the initiatives that are being taken. Growing up as a gamer, the one thing I was trying to bring things back to is, let's remember that this is gaming, let's remember that this is about having fun. Let's not forget that at the base of everything we're doing, it's that fun factor. And if you're not having fun, or if you're not creating something that people will have fun doing, you're really in the wrong business.

TF: Well said. eSports has grown from something that was just played as a hobby for a fairly small number of people to a global phenomenon that delights millions of spectators around the world. How do you imagine the evolution of eSports over the next 20 years?

HRH: One of the interesting evolutions that we've seen is that originally eSports was essentially a marketing tool for developers. I can think back to the days of the first eSports on MTV in the 90s with Nintendo. It was really an opportunity for developers to get involved and put some money behind it, a little bit of money at the time. Although at the time, it seemed like a lot. It really started to grow already into its own beast. I started seeing, even now, games being created as an eSport rather than an eSport being created to further the excitement of a game, which is a big change for me. That, to me, puts it in the same sphere as more traditional sports.

And then you bring into that the unique ability to interact with your community over eSports. This really has the potential to become the biggest spectator sport, you're already not far off. I mean, I think there are only three or four events that are bigger than big eSports events at this current time. It would be the Super Bowl, maybe the Olympics, and I think the NBA championships, had more spectators than eSports events. And I'm not sure much else did. But you're getting to a point where populations get younger, you have already reached a generation that doesn't know sports without eSports being a part of it. And they're only getting younger. So this is their sport, this is their opportunity for growth.

The lines between electronic and traditional sports are continuing to blur. And as they blur eSports is already growing at phenomenal rates. That growth can't be surpassed by traditional sports that have been around for 100 years.

TF: You mentioned young people. I know that up until recently, the Middle East in general and the Kingdom of Saudi Arabia in particular, has had a very modest domestic games development industry. But I know there are many young people in the country who would love to make their own games, tell their own stories. How do you envision the Kingdom of Saudi Arabia's game development landscape changing over the next decade?

HRH: Culturally, as a region, we have a long history of storytelling, of that oral tradition. Going back to the days of the ancient Egyptians, the ancient Babylonians, to the pre-Islamic days, to the Islamic days, to the current day, it's a rich history of storytelling. Giving our community, our next generation, the opportunity is important. Storytelling is a gift, and we can give young people the opportunity to have a new avenue to tell those stories.

We have a rich history in poetry, rich history in storytelling, rich history in film and TV that's starting to be showcased now. We're giving them another avenue which is gaming, which really allows you to tell a story in a unique way. It's something that I get very excited about. It's something I dreamed about doing when I was younger. My son and I started playing Zelda together. He's already decided how he wants to change Zelda and create a new game and bring in the Dragon Riders from *How to Train Your Dragon* and how to do these different things with this game. He says, "We'll just get them to send us a chip and we'll put it in our story!" It's a little bit more complicated than that, but I like how he is thinking.

Giving them the tools to be able to take those ideas and really showcase the talent that they have. Of course, we would love to have AAA games being created in Saudi. But what's more important is to get the story started, because once people get started telling their stories in this medium, we will get to AAA games in time.

One of the things that I think is very interesting, with the evolution of technology and where everything is now, where more people are able to create things at great quality. In the past, you had two real avenues of game creation: You had the Indie gamers who were really pushing the boundaries creatively, but doing things with smaller budgets and therefore lower graphics. And then you had the AAA companies creating those great graphics, the great scenes. The Indie gamers would create something, push the boundaries, create something that's popular, the AAA companies would buy that and then move that into that AAA sphere.

We have an interesting crossroads now, and what gets me excited for our region. You have the ability now to take those

Indie style games, but they can create output that's AAA level of quality. The tools are there. It's fun to see what can come out of it. Especially where we are geographically.

I'd say a good half the population is influenced by Japanese gaming and anime and all of that, and the other half is impacted by Western gaming and animation and that sort of thing. They're taking those influences, but really bringing those cultural aspects into their ideas and putting their own their upbringing to it. It's really interesting.

There's a young man I had the pleasure of talking to a few days ago, studying at NYU. He's studying game development. He created a game based on *Dragon Ball Z,* like a fan game that he and some of his classmates created, which I very much enjoy.

We started talking about what's going on and we could help, and about what we need as an industry here. What I like to do is, rather than tell people my ideas, I like to get people to tell me what they need to succeed. My father used to always tell us, "God gave you two ears and one mouth for a reason." I like to listen and then have the opportunity to adjust and pivot what we're doing here is based on the needs of the people here who are creating.

Talking to people in the community, there is a lot of opportunity with academies like the Misk Academy and other academies that are coming in here. DigiPen. We're talking with Full Sail about doing something here. All of these groups work with government entities on hackathons and other ways to give people a chance to showcase their skills. We are providing the tools for this community and this next generation to do what they need to do, and then get out of their way, and let them mold the future and where we're going. We want to let them innovate and take the risks that they want to take, and give them the tools really showcase what they're doing.

TF: I read exciting things about Neom as a new city of the future, where special effects, film, game development, and even an eSports academy will thrive. What can you tell us about plans for gaming and game development in this new city?

HRH: I get really excited about a lot of these giga-projects here. Neom is one of them. Qiddiya is another great one. The opportunity to build out an infrastructure that's built for the future, built with gaming in mind, game production, with future technologies, with green technologies and all these things is very exciting to me. For me, what this shows is not how ambitious Neom is or how ambitious Qiddiya is. Qiddiya is a sports-focused city.

What that tells me is how ambitious we are as a nation. We are getting the full and complete support and government backing that we need to help the community get to that next level. A lot of these plans have been announced. Neom is going to be one of the cities of the future. Qiddiya, being closer to Riyadh, is one of the cultural centers and the sports center, and we're working very closely with those, among others.

A lot of things will be announced with those very soon that I'm not allowed to talk about yet. But, what I can say is within the next ten years, the backing that we're getting from the government, the excitement we have from the community, and the ability to not recreate the wheel, but to take what's existing out there and put those tools on show here, we are well on the way to our 2030 plan as a federation to be a global hub for gaming and for eSports. We did a survey throughout our events for over a year, covering about 30,000 members of our community. One of the things we found is the vast majority are not just excited about watching eSports, but actually want to follow an educational path and a career path within eSports and gaming.

It's our job to make sure they have the opportunity to follow their dreams. Whatever you want to do, whatever you are interested in, whether that's art, production, acting, writing, poetry, music, anything you're interested in, there is a career path within gaming and within eSports. We've had a lot of good feedback and a lot of support from even the older generations.

TF: Do you have any other predictions of what the world of gaming will look like by the year 2042?

HRH: One of the things that I think is pretty interesting is the normalization of the Metaverse. The Metaverse is something that's new to people outside of gaming, it was really what gamers really lived for a long time. Look at *Ready Player One*, that kind of juxtaposition of the virtual world and the real world and how people's lives interact between those.

How do we get to a healthy place with that virtual world? Whether it's for commerce, whether it's for the community, whether it's communication, or the future of social media. How do we anchor that in a way that we don't lose our real-world communication? Nothing can replace sitting with someone face to face, having a coffee, laughing, that human interaction. How do we keep that, but not hold back that virtual growth? It is going to be so interesting to see how that evolves.

CONTINUING IN THE LEVANT

Turkey

In recent years, Turkey has emerged as a center of excellence for hypercasual development and publishing and is home to a number of development studios like Rolic and Peak Games who are rapidly becoming household names, at least within the business driven by a hot M&A in which Western publishers sought out value from Turkish developers. Straddling the cultural boundaries between Europe and the Middle East, with more than a little influence from Russia and the United States, Turkey continues to embrace its historical role as a meeting ground for international trade. Despite mild political and economic instability, Turkish developers and games both cast a large shadow on the global stage in 2021 (Figure 1.23).

The population of Turkey is growing, from 85 million in 2020 to just under 100 million by 2050. It's a youthful population, averaging 31.5 today,

FIGURE 1.23 Istanbul at night. (*Image Credit*: NASA/NOAA.)

but moving into middle age over the next 20 years. 36 million of those identified as gamers in 2020, generating gross revenues of $880 million dollars, mostly though mobile games and PC gaming.[49] In fact, more than 80% of Turkish gamers play on mobile devices as their primary platform.[50]

Shooters like PubG, eSports (MOBAs), and a host of more casual (even hypercasual!) games dominated the charts in Turkey over the last few years, speaking to a diverse culture of gamers in the country.

While Turkey's population is not so vast as to make it a top territory for most publishers, it's outsized contributions to game development make the next two decades a very exciting time to watch Turkey.

Egypt

Egypt is a rapidly growing country with a youthful population who have modest levels of disposable income compared to other places in the region. Mobile gaming dominates in the region, with more 92% of 16- to 34-year olds in Egypt reporting as having played a mobile game on their phone[51] (Figure 1.24).

- The population is 102 million in 2020 almost doubling to 190 million by 2050.

- Average age of 24.6 increasing to 29.7 by 2050.

FIGURE 1.24 Cairo and the Nile at night. (*Image Credit*: NASA/NOAA.)

Twitch and YouTube drive a lot of local awareness of eSports, making games like *Counterstrike, Fortnight,* and MOBAs like *League of Legends* and *Defense of the Ancients 2* (DOTA2) popular.

Egypt is generally regarded as the largest gaming market in the Arabic-speaking world today, and the sheer increase in population will fuel an increase here.

Games that pay attention to the needs of this market can achieve huge popularity in the coming decades.

Israel

Israel is home to a number of the world's top technology companies, including a few game publishers and small firms that drive the tools that are making mobile gaming popular across the world (Figure 1.25).

With a relatively small population of fewer than ten million people in 2020, expecting only modest growth over the next few decades, Israel is more important to watch as a source of technical talent and capital than as a large consumer market.

FIGURE 1.25   Night lights of the Levant. (*Image Credit*: NASA/NOAA.)

Playtika, Plarium, and modding company Overwolf have all grabbed headlines in the last year as they put out games and gaming software that is played by hundreds of millions. Israel will continue to fill an oversize role in the game-making world, particularly as adjacent regions in Africa and the Middle East develop larger consumer populations that Israeli companies can service at healthy margins.

The Rest of Africa

There are a lot of people in Africa, and 186 million of them are gamers. Generally speaking Africa can be thought of as existing in two parts: North Africa is culturally most similar to the Middle East. The rest of Africa, outside of South Africa, is a different matter altogether. Currently, this represents roughly a quarter billion dollar per year market for the gaming industry. In 2021, South Africa generated $290 million in revenue, Nigeria $185 million, Ghana, Ghana, Kenya, and Ethiopia next.[52] And the population of the region is expected to explode in the next two decades: Today, there are approximately 1.3 billion humans in Africa. By 2040, the total population of the continent is projected to exceed two billion.[53]

There are a few obstacles we need to overcome before we can start seeing large numbers of gamers in Africa. The first of these is bandwidth infrastructure. Consider that games like *Fortnite* consume around 50 MB of data per user per hour; this is well outside of the capacity for the telcos in most cities in the region. However, this is rapidly increasing. Among other infrastructure projects, many spearheaded by the Chinese Belt and Road Initiative, Google is running new subsea cables from Portugal to South Africa, stopping in Lagos, Nigeria along the way; this effort is called the Equiano[54] after Olaudah Equiano, a Nigerian writer. The cable is expected to increase the available network capacity by more than 20 times its current capability. At the same time, there has been an absolute explosion of mobile devices in the region. Approximately 300 million Africans used a smartphone in 2019.[55] Of these, 177 million of them played a game on the phone. Payment methods and low levels of disposable income are serious barriers, but a number of startups are pushing to resolve this,[56] and we should expect consolidation in regional mobile carriers to help reduce some of the complexities with payment methods (Figure 1.26).

But there is huge opportunity here: two-thirds of the population of Africa are under 25 years old today.[57] When Africans play games, they play on mobile phones. (According to a 2021 study, 95% of gaming activity in Africa is on a mobile device.) There is a strong collection of initiatives to

FIGURE 1.26 Africa by night reveals a few major population centers and a lot of darkness. (*Image Credit*: NASA.)

educate and improve the possibilities for a home-grown game development business in the region. Indeed, VC firm Andreessen Horowitz has recently invested $20 million in an Africa mobile-first publisher called Carry1st,[58] who focuses on Web3 games and facilitating payments using locally accepted payment systems. We should expect gaming adjacent venture capital to continue to move into the region.

Publishers are starting to pay attention as well,[59] and this will increase as efforts over the next few years yield public results. Nigeria, South Africa, and Kenya are all poised to become significant markets, in ways that will benefit gamers, the region, and those developers and publishers who are courageous enough to dedicate resources here.

ZOOMING OUT

Conclusions Based on this Research and Demographic Data

We can project with high accuracy how many people the Earth will have by 2042. And we know the propensity of people in different regions to play games. Based on this light analysis we can make a few conclusions which seem clear to me:

- Total addressable market will continue to grow rapidly, adding one to two billion new gamers by 2030.

- Almost all of these new gamers will come from emerging markets.

- Most will be mobile first, PC second, and few will ever own dedicated gaming consoles.

- The revenue derived from the gaming industry will increasingly be made on mobile-first game devices, which are ubiquitous and affordable across the world, particularly in emerging markets.

- Increased purchasing power, plus alternative means of monetizing (advertising, play to earn, gamers for hire), use of non-fiat currencies to drive gaming economies will make it possible to monetize players we could not reach before.

- South Asia, the Middle East, and Central and South America will drive gaming tastes.

There is a planet full of gamers coming, and very few of them look like a Western media cliché.

How to Tailor for a Region

To build games for the whole world we need to focus first on those commonalities which unite gamers. We will talk more about the reasons people play games in a coming chapter, and about some of the most common motivators which different major game genres appeal to. But simply releasing a single game for the entire world is no longer considered the best route to success. To win in emerging markets we have to tailor many aspects of the software to each different market, or at least the ones that provide the most strategic or economic value to your particular game. Let's look at some techniques for helping increase the odds of success in different markets:

To start, let's accept that most gamers in emerging markets play on mobile phones first, PC a distant second, and other platforms barely at all. And of these gamers, the majority of them play on the Android operating system.[60] And the rate that new gamers are joining the fold in many of these markets is particularly impressive in a world where the growth of gamers in the US, Europe, Japan, Korea, and Taiwan is expected to be largely flat after 2025. And while gamers in India, Brazil, Russia, the Philippines, and other emerging markets do not currently spend nearly at the per user levels of their fellows in North America, South Korea, or the UK, they do spend. And the amount that they are willing (and able!) to spend is growing rapidly. We have every indication that lower Average Revenue Per Paying User (ARPPU) is more a function of disposable income than of desire. So there are definitely customers out there. How to best attract them?

First, the game needs to function well on in the gaming ecosystem. What are the minimum specifications of the phone or PC that you expect to be able to play the game? How does that compare with expected market penetration of devices at that caliber in the year you expect to release the game? How does the game deal with finite resources like RAM, disk footprint, or bandwidth. (Many places still have metered cellular bandwidth and Wi-Fi access is still limited.) While these factors will continue to improve over the coming years, they will always be finite, and understanding the target market will help increase your odds of success. Where to run hosting may be a factor as well, particularly if the game has core gameplay dependent on low latency (like shooters or fighting games). Of course, if people cannot easily read or understand the User Interface in a game they are less likely to enjoy it; so localization into regional languages is critical. This tends to extend beyond just the software as well though. Marketing materials, customer service, billing support, and so on will be much more effective at attracting and retaining users if they are served up in a gamer's native language. Unsurprisingly, marketing and other aspects of publishing in a particular region are almost always much more successful if conducted by an entity familiar with the region. To that end, many developers find that recruiting local publishers to cover a particular region yields far better results than just releasing a game into the market cold. The price of a game or In App Purchases (IAP) needs to be tailored to that region. Correspondingly, offers and events are far more effective when they correspond with local holidays.

By combining a number of these techniques for each market in which a game wants to succeed, I expect that many games could engage players from around the globe. Of course, this is a lot of work, but no one ever said making the whole world love your game would be easy!

Ultimately, why do we care how many gamers there are in the world? Why should we care about getting more people in hitherto underserved areas to play games?

There are two reasons studies like those in this chapter are encouraging to me:

> First, the games industry provides fulfilling employment and occupation for many people. Expanding the market for these kinds of

leisure goods can generate huge profits for anyone invested in the business. And since gaming is largely environmentally neutral to create and enjoy, (some concerns about the power cost of block-chain efforts notwithstanding) and is not clearly harmful to its consumers as some products are, this is a good business to expand.

The second reason it is so encouraging to imagine billions more gamers entering the world over the next two decades is that I genuinely believe that the games we create do good for the world. Games bring people and populations together, to adventure together, solve puzzles collaboratively, or to engage in friendly competition. The world is filled with stories of lovers who first met in online games and ended up having long and happy lives together. Games can allow the weak to feel powerful, the lonely to make friends, and those trapped by disability or circumstance to explore and experience a simulacra of experience which might otherwise be denied to them. The games we create bring color to lives which are sometimes gray. And because they can carry the games we make with them in their pockets, to school, and sometimes into the rooms where their days will end, we are able to deliver on a level of intimacy that truly can positively impact the lives of millions.

Entertaining the world is a noble calling, and I sincerely believe that Earth is a more fun, better place with more gamers in it.

NOTES

1 https://games.withgoogle.com/reports/.
2 https://www.worldometers.info/world-population/world-population-projections/.
3 https://www.insiderintelligence.com/insights/us-gaming-industry-ecosystem/.
4 https://games.withgoogle.com/reports/.
5 https://www.census.gov/content/dam/Census/library/publications/2020/demo/p25-1144.pdf.
6 https://www.statista.com/statistics/293304/number-video-gamers/.
7 https://games.withgoogle.com/reports/.
8 https://www.europarl.europa.eu/RegData/etudes/STUD/2020/646181/EPRS_STU(2020)646181_EN.pdf.
9 https://www.pwc.com/gx/en/world-2050/assets/pwc-the-world-in-2050-full-report-feb-2017.pdf.
10 https://productcoalition.com/the-korean-game-market-a-comprehensive-overview-77d461832ff7.
11 https://www.un.org/en/development/desa/population/publications/pdf/ageing/replacement-chap4-ko.pdf.

12 https://newzoo.com/insights/articles/the-gamers-powering-japans-22-1-billion-games-market-consumer-motivations-behavior-data/.
13 https://www.serkantoto.com/2021/08/12/japan-mobile-gaming-market-size/.
14 https://demographic-challenge.com/demographic-change-in-japan.html.
15 https://www.independent.co.uk/life-style/gadgets-and-tech/nintendo-microsoft-laughed-purchase-b1784509.html.
16 https://www.polygon.com/22869159/china-video-games-crackdown-restrictions-super-buckyball-tournament.
17 https://www.reuters.com/technology/tencent-falls-after-china-media-calls-online-gaming-spiritual-opium-2021-08-03/.
18 https://www.forbes.com/sites/richkarlgaard/2020/11/12/china-has-caught-up-to-us-in-ai-says-ai-expert-kai-fu-lee/.
19 https://www.nytimes.com/interactive/2019/01/17/world/asia/china-population-crisis.html.
20 https://www.pwc.com/gx/en/world-2050/assets/pwc-the-world-in-2050-full-report-feb-2017.pdf.
21 https://www.pwc.com/gx/en/research-insights/economy/the-world-in-2050.html.
22 https://newzoo.com/insights/articles/southeast-asia-games-market-esports-game-streaming-spending-playing-engagement/.
23 https://www.theworldcounts.com/populations/world/continents/asia/countries/indonesia/people.
24 https://www.statista.com/statistics/1116224/indonesia-share-of-online-gamers/.
25 http://proximityone.com/future_of_indonesia.htm.
26 https://www.statista.com/outlook/dmo/digital-media/video-games/vietnam.
27 https://www.statista.com/statistics/444584/average-age-of-the-population-in-vietnam/.
28 https://unchartedterritories.tomaspueyo.com/p/us-gdp-per-capita.
29 https://www.statista.com/statistics/1117962/vietnam-share-of-online-gamers-by-age/.
30 https://sdg.iisd.org/news/indias-population-expected-to-surpass-chinas-by-2050-world-population-data-sheet/.
31 https://theprint.in/opinion/slowing-population-growth-means-time-is-running-out-for-india-to-get-rich/468793/.
32 https://www.gamesindustry.biz/articles/2021-06-23-indias-gaming-market-to-grow-113-percent-by-2025-kpmg-in-india.
33 https://www.statista.com/statistics/918855/india-total-mobile-data-usage/.
34 https://economictimes.indiatimes.com/tech/funding/krafton-may-invest-more-to-build-digital-ecosystem-in-india/articleshow/84342350.cms.
35 https://newzoo.com/insights/articles/insights-into-latin-americas-3-5-billion-mobile-games-market-players-payers-revenues-esports-market-dynamics/.
36 https://www.populationpyramid.net/brazil/2050/.

37 https://newzoo.com/insights/articles/brazilian-games-market-consumer-insights-brazils-mobile-players-are-likelier-to-play-competitive-midcore-games/.
38 https://carnegieendowment.org/files/World_Order_in_2050.pdf.
39 https://www.mexicanist.com/l/mexico-videogames-industry/.
40 https://today.in-24.com/News/311158.html.
41 https://www.capacitymedia.com/articles/3828610/e-gaming-and-the-6bn-middle-east-opportunity.
42 https://www.gamesindustry.biz/articles/2022-01-10-saudi-arabia-united-arab-emirates-and-egypt-markets-worth-usd1-76bn-in-2021.
43 http://www.tradearabia.com/news/IT_384014.html.
44 https://venturebeat.com/2022/01/07/niko-partners-big-middle-east-countries-will-hit-85-8m-players-3-1b-in-revenues-by-2025/.
45 https://www.economist.com/books-and-arts/2021/12/18/after-banning-cinema-for-decades-saudi-arabia-is-making-movies.
46 https://economictimes.indiatimes.com/news/international/saudi-arabia/-how-saudi-arabias-neom-aims-to-be-bollywoods-next-powerhouse-production-partner/articleshow/85293554.cms.
47 https://www.thehindubusinessline.com/economy/Saudi-Arabia-to-have-6th-highest-per-capita-GDP-by-2050-Report/article20107285.ece.
48 https://newzoo.com/insights/articles/saudi-arabia-gamers-and-games-market-mobile-player-spending-consumer-research.
49 https://restofworld.org/2021/turkey-gaming-peak/.
50 https://games.withgoogle.com/reports/.
51 https://english.ahram.org.eg/NewsContent/40/163/422913/Advertising/Advertisement/Egypt-Online-Gaming-Industry-on-the-Rise.aspx.
52 https://www.pocketgamer.biz/news/77614/95-per-cent-of-gamers-in-africa-choose-mobile-says-newzoo/.
53 https://www.statista.com/statistics/1224205/forecast-of-the-total-population-of-africa/.
54 https://cloud.google.com/blog/products/infrastructure/introducing-equiano-a-subsea-cable-from-portugal-to-south-africa.
55 https://medium.com/kampaytoken/mobile-gaming-in-africa-cc8bb6d7c49b.
56 https://techcrunch.com/2021/07/13/nigeria-leads-mobile-app-market-growth-in-africa-as-use-of-gaming-apps-surge-44-from-q1-2020/.
57 https://www.gamesindustry.biz/articles/2021-01-12-what-does-2021-hold-for-the-african-games-industry.
58 https://www.forbes.com/sites/tobyshapshak/2022/01/19/african-mobile-games-publisher-carry1st-is-andreessen-horowitzs-african-investment-with-20m-series-a.
59 https://venturebeat.com/2021/05/04/carry1st-raises-6-million-for-mobile-games-in-africa/.
60 https://medium.com/googleplaydev/winning-in-emerging-markets-3007c1b780a.

CHAPTER 2

How to Reach the World

HOW TO REACH THE WORLD?

Most of us started making games or working in the games business because we loved games and the kinds of expressions and experiences the medium allowed. Most people who make games started by making the kind of games they wanted to play, mimicking the greats in the business. And while there are a lot of commonalities in the kinds of games players and game makers in different parts of the world grew up loving, there's a lot that is regional. At some point, either to grow a business or for reasons of ego, most of us start to become interested in how to bring our games to a larger audience.

The games business is now truly global, and, as we saw in the last chapter, game makers of the future have the very real opportunity to delight any player anywhere there is electricity. From my perspective, the massive growth in total addressable market over the last decade and the next two continue to make game development one of the most exciting businesses in the world. We can now entertain the whole world. In fact, we already are in some ways. How does this truly global dynamic change the way we need to think about making, distributing, and operating games over the next 20 years?

There are a number of lenses we can evaluate this question through. Indeed, much of this book will concern itself with deep dives into the future of technology filtered through this question. Let's look at an overview of a few key themes here.

DOI: 10.1201/9781003291800-3

THE IMPACT OF GLOBALISM ON GAME DESIGN

I believe that the types of core fantasy-fulfillment games satisfy for users tend to be universal to the human condition. Even the "core toys" themselves: matching three, lining up the cross hairs, mastering a double-jump, combining characters in a unique and clever way, etc., tend to be broadly satisfying across cultures and languages. But different people in different places have vastly different amounts of disposable income to spend on leisure activities like games. For some, shelling out $70 USD on the newest *Call of Duty* or *Need for Speed* game from a big publisher is just the price of a weekend's diversion. For others, a game isn't worth playing unless it can earn them a few dollars a day to supplement their income. It takes very different approaches to excite and capture both types of players, let alone players who are anywhere in between these spectrums.

Beyond the amount of money players have to spend (and the mechanics by which they are able to spend it), which device they have access to, the place and ways in which they want to play may differ greatly. Someone who plays mobile MOBA games during their two-hour bus ride home to a Manila suburb each night likely engages very differently than a PC gamer with a haptic chair and a VR headset in Santa Rosa, California. What is a target session length? What languages is a game translated into? Which devices can it support? How much memory and bandwidth does it consume? How does the technology that powers games dictate how popular it can be?

And the creative wrapper or themes of different games will appeal to different players in different places. While there are some types of characters, stories, and worlds that may have near-universal appeal, many do not. And even when character or gameplay archetypes ("defeat the villain") or objectives ("score the goal") can be understood by almost anyone, the ways they need to be packaged differ. Imagine how the victory sequence over a Bollywood gangster boss might be celebrated as opposed to defeating a Korean demon-monster in a game. Consider the difference between a winning play in Cricket as opposed to scoring that crucial conversion in the last seconds of a game of *Madden Football*, or a brilliant checkmate move in a chess game. Regional tastes differ. Different creative wrappers appeal to different people.

Yet at the same time, for the last decade, and likely for the next few, we have entered a world of winner-take-most zeitgeists, in which the biggest hits of any year – Marvel movies, *Genshin Impact, League of Legends,* and so on – end up capturing imaginations and wallets around the globe. Which intellectual property (IP) has truly global reach and which ones don't? Why? Why do some games manage to capture massive audiences while others don't make it out of a small niche audience?

DISTRIBUTION MECHANISMS

Right now, there are three major ways to get a player to play your game.

- Offer it for download on a mobile phone storefront (Apple and Android, most notably, but also via console manufacturers' or carriers' store apps)

- Offer it for download through a web storefront (like Steam or Epic Store)

- Sell it in a retail store

Each of these three mechanisms for distribution has advantages and disadvantages, and different storefronts vary widely in their effectiveness in different countries. Of course, offering a game on as many devices and distributing it through as many different channels as possible is the best way to reach a massive audience. Some games, like *Minecraft*, have led the charge here, attempting to be available anywhere users can look at games. Then, big games like *Fortnite* also regularly allow cross-platform play, which means that you can download it anywhere and play it on almost anything. This should be the holy grail for game makers from now on; but of course, this takes a huge amount of staff, years, a lot of hard work, business and legal agreements with a huge number of partners, and is generally outside of the capabilities of any but largest and most successful global publishers.

The more channels you can distribute your game on and the more devices it can run on, the more players you can reach. Still, this doesn't guarantee the number of players you can attract and retain.

USER ACQUISITION

The top games in the world today, in 2022, attract hundreds of millions of players. But most games ever made will reach fewer than a thousand players. Why? What techniques do game publishers use to attract big audiences?

User Acquisition (UA) is a broad collection of techniques that capture marketing, brand marketing, paid digital advertisements, the use of influencers, and even some techniques within a piece of software designed to help players find the game like App Store Optimization (ASO). As the sheer number of games in the world increases (currently estimated at well over 2,000,000 total distinct games![1]), one of the biggest challenges is attracting users to a particular game. Of course, the techniques used vary significantly between big tentpole AAA releases like Activision's *Call of Duty*, or even bigger mobile free-to-play games like Tencent's *Honor of Kings*. The complexity of this UA discipline and the marketing efforts required to launch global hits will continue to increase.

Broadly speaking, there are a few ways that publishers can get the word out about their games. They can advertise them on social media like Facebook, WeChat, Kakao, TikTok, or on the web. They can advertise them in public spaces, like billboards or Times Square. They can advertise them on the target devices themselves, on the PlayStation Store, or on the Apple iTunes Store. They can pay influencers on Twitch or YouTube to generate content about the games that are then viewed by potential players. Tens of billions of dollars are spent each year on these activities. (Electronic Arts alone disclosed a total marketing budget of more than $680M in their fiscal year 2021.[2])

And advertising is also regularly served up within games themselves via a complex network of ad providers. Since a big percentage of all advertisements shown to players in games are for other games, (for obvious reasons) digital advertising is a somewhat incestuous ecosystem. Moreover, because of the way ad providers bill advertisers for impressions, this is an area that has historically been ripe with fraud. (Imagine fake impressions generated by bots, false installs, bad data, and the like.)

There's an additional host of complexity that we will discuss in this book dealing with how advertisers can best target players who are likely to become paying customers. This is an area of technology that is changing rapidly, from the rise of Machine Learning (ML) algorithms that learn how to surface certain ads to certain types of users, to seemingly small changes in the type of data provided by networks that end up having massive seismic shifts in the economics of this business.

BUILDING COMMUNITIES

It is telling that in 2021, many games launch their efforts at community building before they've even built a playable version of the game. As has always been the case, the best way to get new players excited about a game is when their friends tell them about it. As online communities from YouTube to Twitch to Discord to WeChat to Kakao to TikTok all continue to overtake real-life communities as places where people gather to discuss things that excite them, they take on an ever more important role in informing players about new games. The role of "Community Manager", who once mostly spent their time answering questions or dealing with trolls on forums, has been elevated to whole teams within a publisher. When run well, these teams can set up, curate, cultivate, and grow thriving online spaces in which players can congregate and invite their friends to speculate about new games, team up, swap strategies, and even deliver their own fan fictions about the games.

A well thought out and well executed plan for building communities in every major market you want a game to succeed in is now as (or more) essential than a strategy for deploying marketing assets. Communities recruit players, help them make friends, and keep them engaged for years when done well.

HOW TO REACH THE WORLD, THEN KEEP THEM PLAYING

Throughout this book, as we explore the topics above, we will be focused on two primary goals. The first of these will be how we can get more people to play a game. The second is how we can drive higher engagement from players.

The observant may raise an eyebrow at techniques for monetizing players and increasing revenues not being mentioned as a primary goal. This is because, as a game maker, I truly believe that driving awareness and engagement are the hardest and most important things to do with the games we create in order to reach the world. When players love a game, they will pay for it, they will buy merchandise associated with it, they will tell their friends about it, they will attend eSports events to watch it. In all these ways (and more!) players will fuel the financial growth of games that they love. Raising awareness in an increasingly crowded landscape, then building and operating games that drive deep and long-term engagement from players is the surest route to real financial success in the gaming business.

This is true today, and will be increasingly true over the coming decades.

INTERVIEW WITH AARON LOEB: THE FUTURE OF COMMUNITIES

Aaron Loeb is an award-winning playwright and the Chief Business Officer at Scopely, a top mobile game publisher. He lives in London.

TF: Hello! Tell us about your history in the games business and what you do in your current role.

Aaron Loeb: My name is Aaron Loeb and I started in the games business making paper and pencil role-playing games in the previous century. In the early 90s, I was a designer for games like Underground. And then in the mid-90s, in the early days of the commercial internet, I got into writing about video games. I became a journalist and was an editor for one of the first commercial websites covering video games.

   As a critic for many years, I always really wanted to make video games instead of just writing about them. And so, I got an out-of-the-blue opportunity to go be a producer making games in 2000 at a little shop called Planet Moon Studios. Their biggest game at that time was a game called *Giants: Citizen Kabuto*. I worked there for about ten years, starting as a producer. And by the time I was done, I was the CEO. Around 2011, we sold that company to BigPoint. It was right at the time that the free-to-play revolution was sweeping the West. And I got very excited about changing to that, because I was pretty disillusioned with the premium console business: You could spend years working on something, release it, and if nobody bought it, it felt like years wasted. But free-to-play could get you in front of players fast and felt like you could reach millions of players much more easily, which is what I was excited about: reaching a big audience.

So I went to EA and joined their Playfish division and that became EA Mobile. I was lucky enough to be the GM of a game called *Simpsons: Tapped Out*, when it was relaunching. It was a giant hit. I think it reached about 250 million people. I learned a ton about free-to-play during that period. But then I started to come to the conclusion that I wasn't learning fast enough. I got an opportunity to go join a company called Kabam as the head of their North American Studios and learned a whole next level amount of stuff about free-to-play. When I joined Kabam, we had launched this even bigger hit called *Marvel Contest of Champions*, which was awesome. We went through this series of selling the company over and over again. And I got this weird opportunity to go down to Fox and become the head of their games business.

I moved to LA, and it was only once I did that that I finally understood what I had been for my career as a video game maker, which was a creative executive. It was this term they have in Hollywood for somebody like me who helps creators go achieve their vision. We built the Fox business, which was acquired by Disney, who then sold it to Scopely. And so now, I am the Chief Business Officer at Scopely, which is one of the leading Western free-to-play mobile game companies.

TF: I believe you're a playwright as well, which means that narrative and drama are particularly important to you. Is that right?

Aaron: That is right. So during that entire period, I was also writing plays. My plays have been produced around the world, mostly in North America. Some very good reviews, some terrible reviews, but that's theater.

I've always had a healthy obsession with narrative and story-telling and the way in which it overlaps from linear storytelling, like in theater, and the ways are its totally different and unique like in the interactive form. I've experimented with ways of taking lessons learned from interactive storytelling and bringing them into the theater. I take a lot of lessons I've learned from the theater and bring them into video games. I do a lot of that right now at Scopely. But "narrative", as I've learned now over the years of doing both, is a much broader term than I think we often think of it as, which is somebody sitting by a fire and telling a story. It's a much more expansive canvas than that as video games have proven.

TF: You mentioned your enthusiasm for moving into free-to-play because of the size of the audience it allows us to entertain. Thus far, not very many, truly narrative-driven games have succeeded hugely in free-to-play. How do you expect that to change over the coming decades?

Aaron: So I disagree with the premise. Let's start there. I think there are not many games that are centered on a specific linear storyline, in which you are a hero who's going to go on a journey, and you enter the dark cave, and then you'll come out and return home at the end, transformed. There are not a lot of hero's journey stories in free-to-play. And those that there are have not been super globally successful.

However, there are lots of games with deep storytelling and world-building, and narrative. Both those that the game is creating by inviting you into this world or in the case of the narrative, stories that the players are telling themselves. Which I think is what video games have shown us: that the most powerful form of narrative in this next century will be the way in which people tell stories to each other as a community, based on things that are happening within a game. And there are many examples of free-to-play games that have achieved this.

When you and I first met you were playing a game called *Game of War* a lot. And I have now worked with a lot of people who made that game. And what we understood from the outside was *Game of War* was a narrative game in many ways. And, that was in fact what they were saying internally when they were making the game. The game was about the richest person on the server telling themselves the story that they were the best player on the server. And so, when you would watch the way that the game played out, there were heroes, there were villains, there were bad guys. People would have alliances that would break up. And then they would have to align with the person they hated more than anything in order to go beat the new kingdom...

People told themselves extremely elaborate stories in the landscape of that game, without there being an author. There was no author. Nobody sat down and said, "Okay Tim, you're the good guy this season." People authored that themselves as players. And I think this is an incredibly powerful form of narrative that is where things are going to go in the coming years.

TF: How do you imagine these sorts of user-driven narratives working in games where people across very different cultures play together?

Aaron: Lots of answers to that. Let's start first with a brute force answer, which is that the technology is already enabling people to talk to each other across language barriers with an instant translation that's increasingly good. And it is just going to get better and better. So, the community-told story in which, by way of example, you're the bad guy and I'm the good guy and we're mocking each other and we're challenging each other on the chat server and everybody's watching… The fact that you're challenging me in Russian, and I'm challenging you in Korean isn't going to matter, right? Because everyone will be able to read it in their own language.

But I think as we're also seeing now with what's happening in traditional scripted media, people are just more willing and excited to engage with content that is clearly something created by somebody from another country or another culture.

We've seen that recently, with the movie *Parasite* and the show *Squid Game* recently, both just gigantic global hits. And nobody's trying to convince themselves it was actually made in Germany. Clearly there are both South Korean products. And so, I think that the openness to narrative that comes from different places is rapidly evolving.

And I think in these kinds of user-generated narratives the barrier of language is just going away because of technology. But in these slightly authored or very authored narratives, I think there's going to be more openness to them globally now than there ever has been before. We are becoming a truly global society in a lot of ways.

TF: As a game designer or creative executive, how should a person think about building games for a world where people want to play the same game on very different devices or in very different settings?

Aaron: Well, I think about this a lot. I don't think anybody's done it on purpose well yet. I think there have been a bunch of folks who ended up doing it and have been happily surprised.

But there are a lot of people who have tried to design the thing that's going to be universally embraced that nobody ends up wanting, that or gets embraced in two countries and hated in other places. It's hard to do.

I think a lot of it is understanding things that are universal storytelling elements. And those are things like art design, or world design, or having very distinctive characters. So that when you see the castle in the distance, it's distinctive to your world, anybody can see it and know that's from a particular game. So moving away from the generic and making things that are distinctive to your game.

This is why I think, for instance, Marvel, which you and I worked on a lot, is such a powerful intellectual property. Because, yes, a lot of people have beloved childhood memories of it and those of us who do think that that's why it's so effective. But the truth is, it's much bigger today with people who never read a comic book when they were a kid. You can take any one of those characters and turn them into a silhouette and everyone knows exactly who that character is. Those characters have human archetype characteristics that everybody everywhere understands because all humans experienced uncontrollable rage at some point in their life, for example. Everybody understands the Hulk. Everybody feels that they don't belong sometimes and gets being Spider-Man. And immediately, you know them the second you see them, you know exactly where they're from. They're completely distinctive, they're distinctive from each other, they're distinctive from what else is out in the world and you understand them at a human level.

What I'm getting at with all that is, to be successful globally in enabling this shared narrative experience, you have to create an environment where people can make deep connections with characters, with places, and then tell their own stories with them. Either while they're playing or even outside of where they're playing as people have done with Marvel characters since well before there were ever video games. People have told their own stories about Spider-Man and imagined themselves as him. So think about that instinct and create an environment where people can do that with what you're building.

TF: What role, if any, do you imagine AI game masters can play in crafting bespoke narratives that will appeal to different players?

Aaron: It's a really fascinating question.

The truth is, I think I should ask one of my friends who is a brilliant game Dungeon Master. I think if you've done 10,000 hours
of DMing in your life, you start to see that there are patterns of
what people want out of these games. The kind of stories they
want out of these games, and sometimes they aren't even necessarily clear on themselves. If you said at the start of the game,
"Hey what kind of story do you want to tell?" They might say
something that's different from what they actually want. "I just
want to kill monsters and collect loot," they might say. But really
at heart they are deeply romantic and they want a love story.
And so the really good Dungeon Master starts to see the patterns of where this player's interest truly lies and starts telling
stories that give them the candy that they're really excited about.

And I don't know how many of those story archetypes there
might be. Let's imagine there's a thousand different kinds of
experiences that people want when they're interacting in the
story. I think AI can—with some human intelligence guiding
it—can recognize the patterns of how people interact with stuff
and start seeding specific stories to people based on the kind of
thing that they want.

Now, I don't know how far away we are from that. It's probably going to require an enormous amount of massaging by
humans to get it to a point where it actually feels good. It would
require authorship of what a good love story is, what a good
power fantasy is, what is a good thing that drives people. I think
with a fairly countable number of patterns you can get to the
point where you're giving people stories that are extremely compelling to them.

I think that in part because that's sort of what the class system
in most RPGs does. There aren't that many classes and you start
with this hierarchy and people go, "Oh, I want to be a cleric."
Well now your Dungeon Master can say, "Okay, I know what
you want. You want to be a supporter, you want to help people.
I know the story you want." And over 50 years of role-playing
games it turns out we don't need thousands of classes to be
able to tell stories that people like. So I'm reasonably confident

that with some really smart design, you can eventually get AI that's going to really help steer people into the kind of story lines they are most excited by. And that's pretty interesting, very exciting.

TF: Once you referred to our medium as a collection of different canvases. How do you see the canvases expanding over the next 20 years?

Aaron: So when I first worked on a *Sims* game, I thought of the *Sims* as a game about building some people, buying some furniture, building a house, watching the little people do things inside the house. I've always loved that game. I thought of it almost like a fishbowl or sea monkeys but on your computer. It's a terrarium. You're creating artificial life and you're watching it.

When I first made a *Sims* game, I said something like this in the people at Maxis and they're like, "No it's not what *The Sims* is at all. You're completely wrong. *The Sims* is a storytelling game. *Sims* is the most narrative game in the world."

And it turns out what the *Sims* is about for people is the stories they tell themselves in their heads about what their *Sims* are doing. "Oh, these two *Sims* are totally into each other, and I'm going to make them fall in love."

That narrative that the players impose onto the *Sims* – which is very internal-facing in that piece of software – that impulse has now exploded outwards. What I see when I look at the way my kid interacts with games, and everyone in my kid's generation is interacting with games…

Sometimes they aren't even playing the games. They watch videos of other people playing the games, telling their stories about the game they're playing. And then the kids are telling their own stories about that person's story.

Say they latch onto the characters of the people who are talking about themselves playing these games and they write fan-fiction about their characters in the games. They write fan-fiction about the actual streamers themselves. So there's all of this narrative activity happening, starting with the germ of the game. But it explodes into what is happening in the game, explodes into the stream of the person playing the game, explodes into the Discord or the comments section of people watching the stream, and then into fan-fiction about the stream and about the game, and then into Discord commentary about the fan-fiction. So people are writing fan-fiction, based on fan-fiction based on streams based on games. Each one of these is a different canvas that people are using to expand the game – the game itself, streaming, community, and fan-fiction. This is not exaggerating, this is really happening.

And then there are memes, tons of memes showing up that are based on fan-fiction that was based on the fan-fiction, that was based on the people who were streaming the games...

So this is where we are right now, this incredibly multi-layered deep referential language starting with games, but because there's something so compelling about the world of the game that allows for interesting characters to appear in the world and allows for interesting performance of playing the game. That's then creating all of this incredible depth of storytelling and interaction around this game.

So, I think where we're going over the next 20 years is that the folks who successfully tap into the human desire to tell stories, and enable all your players and all the people who know about your game – even if they've never played your game – to tell fun stories, create an environment that's rich for storytelling on any kind of screen or format... Those are the folks who are going to build immense IPs, and it won't look like what you expect it to. One of the most powerful examples of this right now is *Minecraft*. Certainly, not AAA graphics. Certainly not what anybody thought was going to be the biggest IP in video games. But *Minecraft* because it is such a brilliant set of building blocks that it also enables people to very quickly create stuff and make things, and it opened up layers upon layers upon layers of storytelling, in a way that *Call of Duty* doesn't. And that's what I believe will characterize the great storytelling games of the future.

CONCLUSION

How to Reach the World, Then Keep Them Playing

Throughout this book, as we explore the topics above, we will be focused on two primary goals. The first of these will be how we can get more people to play a game. The second is how we can dive higher engagement from players.

The observant may raise an eyebrow at techniques for monetizing players and increasing revenues not being mentioned as a primary goal. This is because, as a game maker, I truly believe that driving awareness and engagement are the hardest and most important things to do with the games we create in order to reach the world. When players love a game, they will pay for it, they will by merchandise associated with it, they will tell their friends about it, they will attend eSports events to watch it. In all these ways (and more!) players will fuel the financial growth of games that they love. Raising awareness in an increasingly crowded landscape, then building and operating games that drive deep and long-term engagement from players is the surest route to real financial success in the gaming business.

This is true today, and will be increasingly true over the coming decades.

NOTES

1 https://gamingshift.com/how-many-video-games-exist/.
2 https://www.statista.com/statistics/672141/electronic-arts-marketing-and-sales-spending/.

CHAPTER 3

The Evolution of Game Design

The Matrix has its roots in primitive arcade games...

– *William Gibson,* Neuromancer

This will be the hardest section of this book to write. And that irony isn't lost on me as someone who has described himself for almost 30 years as a game designer first and foremost. But I expect this section to be difficult because – fundamentally – I don't think the kinds of increases in technological capacity or population much affect the types of things that make games fun. It is not clear that games of the future will be meaningfully different from the games of yesterday from a pure game-design standpoint.

What do I mean?

Let's start by asking, "Why do people play games?"

If you ask users – which many of us have done throughout the years in formal studies, User Experience studies, in a thousand beer-hall or coffee-shop sessions listening to people talk about the games they love – they will give you a few different reasons. Gamers tell you that they like the escape, that gaming makes them feel a sense of mastery, that they enjoy the action, that it gives them something to do with their friends, that they love the feeling of getting to create things, and so on. There are a lot of different answers. Groups like Quantic Foundry[1] have undertaken wide-reaching studies to build out profiles of different gamers and recommend games they might like. Game designers and writers like Raph Koster have tried to

DOI: 10.1201/9781003291800-4

come up with theories that establish the common threads in each of these different motivations and so teach new game designers how to better distill a sense of fun. (At the risk of overly simplifying Mr. Koster's excellent work,[2] he believes that play and learning give players experiences that fundamentally change the player's neural connections, such that their minds are particularly stimulated by games that challenge them to learn.) But whichever theory or approach for validating why some players like certain games more than others, or why different games resonate with big populations of gamers, we have to admit that this was true two decades ago, is true today, and will be true in twenty more years. The human motivations that games appeal to haven't actually changed much in 20 years. And I find it unlikely they will.

Let's look a little deeper at a few of the main types of games which are popular and speculate on how they might evolve to deliver more of the fix they give the players who love them.

People play for the joy of small interactions that bring them a little smile: a perfect Mario jump, bounce, and sound effect. The satisfying click of blocks fitting into place, the sweet little expressions and sighs the Threes make when they are added together, the satisfaction of restoring a tiny bit of order by merging like objects and tidying a little corner of a make-believe space. The feeling of skill and domination from a perfectly aimed headshot that wins the match for your team. Goal scored. Achievement unlocked. Trophy earned.

QUALITY IS KING

But what separates those few games that capture and delight the imaginations of millions across the world and those – sometimes with identical mechanics – which sink into a dustbin of gaming history in a few weeks?

A lot of this comes down to beautiful and smooth integration of systems design, the presentation layer of User Interface that helps the user understand what is going on, a creative wrapper that provides context for the mechanics, and content that keeps a user learning, feeling challenged, and occasionally feeling triumphant. Many of the thousands of details that have to come together in a product in order to masterfully accomplish the above require great precision; animation is an example of such. The difference between a fighting game that feels responsive and great – like Street Fighter 2 Turbo – and one that feels plodding and just doesn't work is often no more than a few frames here and there. The same is true for audio, and other elements of scene design. Consider the beautifully crafted aesthetic of Bioshock, in which every drip of water reinforced a setting that was deeply thematically tied in with the art direction and narrative. Now think about the hundreds of generic and forgettable dungeons you've likely played through over time. The details are the difference; craftsmanship is about relentless attention to the nuance of the experience.

Consider the effort master game designers like Shigeru Miyamoto and his team put into determining precisely how high or far Mario should jump in each instance of a *Super Mario* game.[3] Think about the way games like *Halo* or *Goldeneye* finally made shooters work on a console controller through painstaking fine tuning of aim-assist, reticule feedback, and other features. Look at the attention to detail from the first moment a player starts up *Genshin Impact*, and the way the game proclaims in every pixel that it is bringing console quality open world to every mobile device.

And then the game needs to be free from undue frictions. Games that crash often, take a long time to load, or are buggy in other ways are unlikely to make it in so competitive a market. Publisher certification testing labs (as well as platform holder Cert labs) run top games through thousands of hours of automated and human-driven Quality Assurance testing to sand off the rough edges, and to catch every edge case problem that could negatively impact a user's experience.

All of the technical advancement in the world, including new interface mechanisms, advanced AI, stunning graphics, and much of what we're going to talk about through the rest of this book – none of that makes any difference unless the game is also a well-polished piece of work. This will not change over the next 20 years, excepting that the standards will keep getting higher every year.

WHY DO PEOPLE PLAY?

The first widely played games were games of skill like chess, checkers, and Go. At their heart, these games are a competitive mental exercise in tactics and strategy, featuring symmetric playing fields and zero randomness to effect the outcome. These are games about competitive strategy; the thrill is besting another player, and at advanced levels there are harder to define aesthetic conditions that describe a beautiful game well played.

Strategy games, both turn-based tactical games like *Phoenix Point* and real-time strategy (RTS) games like StarCraft are an extension of this branch of gaming. While they often remove much of the abstraction of a game like Go in favor of the audio-visual spectacle of watching a Zerg rush of alien insects overwhelm an opponent, they fundamentally appeal to similar user motivations.

Similarly, team-based tactical games like *League of Legends, Defense of the Ancients,* and *Honor of Kings* take the strategic competition element and couple it with some level of dexterity based reaction in real-time play. More focused on tactics than strategy, and delivering much more visceral call-outs to player motivation ("Penta-kill!"), MOBAs of this sort have grown in popularity, aided by effective real-time synchronous play. By adding teams of three to five players on a side, they incorporate many of the satisfying elements of social team play that make team sports popular.

Most eSports fall into this general category of motivation, coupling tactical effectiveness, Twitch gameplay that requires a certain level of manual dexterity, and team coordination. While the games present themselves in a different way, *Overwatch* and even *CounterStrike* call upon the same player motivations.

Many sports games are adjacent to this category of player motivation. Sports games mostly test team tactics, light manual dexterity, and a deep knowledge of the intricacies of particular game rules. And by wrapping these with representations of teams and stadiums and individual athletes that players know and love, sports games are able to tap into a broader social conversation about a particular sport, the season, and the players themselves. Madden is a sales arm of the NFL, and the NFL helps sell copies of Madden in a beautiful symbiotic relationship that is mirrored in almost every popular sport across the world.

Leaning more heavily into the adversarial thrill of combat and victory and the visceral sound and fury of virtual murder, many shooters do away with most of the strategy and many of the nuances of tactics and team play that drive eSports. *Call of Duty* zombie mode, for example, lets a player feel like a badass for machine-gunning hundreds of grotesque human opponents. Expressions of power and skill through violence are a tremendously popular motivator for players, and will likely continue to be; this speaks to something deep within the psyche of modern humans, likely because those who were less motivated by such passions were slain by those who were throughout history.

Similarly, since humankind first wandered out of our caves and looked with a sense of wonder at the horizon, some people have been driven to explore. Many adventure and RPG games, from *The Legend of Zelda: Breath of the Wild* to *Skyrim*, fulfill this fundamental human need to explore and discover new things. Of course, few games only appeal to the desire to explore – most open-world games also feature the thrill of combat, tactical mastery, and the like. And this point speaks to a truism in game design – most great games appeal to several adjacent motivations their target users have in common. Does Chess benefit from adding exploration? Well, the beloved *Final Fantasy* series has driven hundreds of millions of sales across more than three decades by appealing to these two motivations.

Narrative driven games, from early text adventures like *Zork* to vast branching epics like *Mass Effect* and *Persona* have often combined a sense of exploration with the context of a world, characters, and a story that keeps users coming back. Add in a dash of bloody visceral combat and you've got a masterpiece like *Ghost of Tsushima*, appealing to users' motivations across three different axes.

Some games have endeavored to strip away some of the action elements and focus on pure dialog. Games like *Emily is Away* by Kyle Seeley exercise branching narrative in a nearly pure form and speak to player motivations that are more subtle. More overt versions of the same, like the host of dating *Sims* and romance cultivation games popular in Asia allow players to engage in relationship fantasy fulfillment. I suggest that this category of player fantasy fulfillment is one that is most ripe for disruption as we begin adding better conversational AI to games.

Appealing to a completely different player mindset, the need for a relaxing, soothing way of creating order, many puzzle, match 3, and merge games allow players to enter a machine zone state similar to whittling or knitting or the classic card game Solitaire, in which their fingers are engaged in a repetitive action while their minds are free to wander. Some of these games – like *Overcooked* – add in more frantic time elements, and even multiplayer, which pushes players to cooperate effectively. This is another example of synchronous multiplayer adding a new social dimension to an old favorite activity and birthing something new.

Music and rhythm games tend to focus on puzzle-like pattern matching, but also speak to many people's innate love of music. When coupled with a narrative context, strong licensing, and amazing presentation games like *Rock Band* can add in deep social interplay between players in real time, and also fulfill the fantasy of being a celebrity; millions of people love the idea of an adoring crowd applauding when they perform. So it is no surprise that games like *Dance Dance Revolution, Guitar Hero*, and dozens of great of Karaoke games have delighted millions.

For some, the thrill of combining elements, making new things, and sharing them allows them to feel a sense of mastery and creativity. Many games allow players to discover and combine recipes or even create things from simple building blocks which can reach the complexity of cathedrals. Games like *Shop Titans* combine this with a light RPG layer, and a heavy focus on social shop-keeping mechanics. Others like the popular *Dwarf Fortress* go dep into crafting and construction using deep world simulation belied by simple text-based graphics.

Games about creativity and crafting are often referred to as User-Generated Content (UGC) games, in which their chief appeal is that anyone can create playspaces or full adventures. *Minecraft* is the best known of these, followed very closely by *Roblox*, which goes beyond just allowing people to work with existing blocks and instead introduces scripting and even programming abilities so that users can create and monetize their own full games. Lovely games like Aquaris' Wonderbox similarly allow players to build their own adventure games and distribute them to other players around the world. This broad category of User-Generated Content games continues to benefit from tools which make it ever easier to create and share; as Pay to Earn becomes more common, these kinds of games and game creation kits will grow ever more popular. Indeed, some developers, like HypeHype (bankrolled by *Clash of Clans* publisher Supercell[4]) are focused on creating tool suites that allow users to create sophisticated games just using their mobile devices. And this speaks to a core motivation millions of gamers share with most game developers: They want to create experiences to share that other people will enjoy as a way of celebrating the joy video gaming has brought them in life. Indeed, broadly, one of the themes we will continue to explore in this book is the way in which the world of video game development is changing. Everyone can now be a game developer.

What to do with the incomplete, partial, and highly subjective list of game types and motivations above? Aren't there a hundred more game types that don't fit well into the above? What about maze evasion games like *Pac-Man*? What about beautiful mechanical explorations of tone like *What Remains of Edith Finch*? What about games that are little more than core toys, like *Fruit Ninja* or many hypercasual games?

Zooming out, the answer is this: There are a finite set of motivations that drive people to play games. Some groups, like the superb market research group Quantic Foundry have undertaken deep studies across millions of

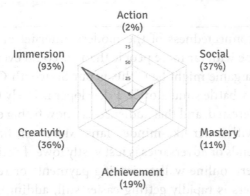

FIGURE 3.1 Quantic Foundry, a market research team, allows game makers to conduct studies to determine what motivates gamers to play particular games using behavioral models like this. (*Image Credit:* Quantic Foundry.)

gamers to come up with a system of formal classification for gamer motivations (Figure 3.1).

There are a lot of valid ways to analyze and describe what motivates a particular type of player to love a particular type of game. But perhaps the most important point I'd like to make here is this:

Game motivations have been largely unchanged for 40 years, because core human motivations have not changed much over the centuries. However, as new technology allows us to build new ways of connecting players, and allowing them to express themselves more easily, we will see emergent new patterns which result from the interplay between traditional gamer motivations, distributed ability to create and share, and massive social populations of gamers online.

Let's go deeper down this rabbit hole.

A FEW THINGS ARE DIFFERENT...

By looking at these examples, we can see many of the player motivations that game designers have tapped into haven't really changed in a long time. Some few new genres have emerged which brought more types of gamers into the fold, but even most of these have parallels that existed in earlier generations. So what's different now? What will change over the next 20 years?

I believe there are four main forces that will continue to expand gaming audiences, and allow for deeper connections to games from more people. Let's look at each in turn.

DEEP SOCIAL

The mass interconnectedness of the modern internet allows us to play games of any type with far more people than we could even ten years ago. However niche a game might be ("This is our Sixteenth Century Iberian Peninsula cavalry battle simulator!"), a developer is likely to find an audience who are interested, and that audience can now be big enough to allow for social play with other like-minded fans. Moreover, finding and connecting with friends or adversaries is just vastly lower friction than it once was. With modern online wallets, issuing payments or receiving tribute from other players is rapidly getting easier still, adding a dimension of social economies to games that have existed on BBS games or the *World of Warcraft* Auction House for a long time, but are now truly possible in a mass-market way. Coupling gaming with social networks, always connected devices in billions of pockets around the globe, and widespread migration of most every aspect of people's lives onto the cloud makes many kinds of multiplayer gaming far easier than it once was. What's the first game that will have one billion concurrent users playing together in some way? I'm not sure, but I know this is possible now and simply was not even ten years ago. Mass social gaming will be the biggest change in the future.

VISUALS

As a purist game designer, it may often be easy to dismiss the role of visual fidelity and the levels of immersion that enhanced production values offer. And while there are only a few elements of core toy or game systems design that change as a result of bigger screens, better graphics, there are a few. (Mostly having to do with the need to establish visual hierarchies of information and other "UX/UI" design techniques to help players understand what to do without being overwhelmed by scenes of great visual complexity.) But we should not dismiss the importance of visuals in driving widespread adoption of games. Consider the number of people who were attracted to playing the original *Pitfall* from Activision in 1982, as opposed to the number who chose to go on adventures for more than a decade with Nathan Drake of the *Uncharted* series from Sony Interactive Entertainment and Naughty Dog (Figures 3.2 and 3.3). Is the core player fantasy the game appeals to that different?

The *Uncharted* series delivers an incredibly high-fidelity user experience (Figure 3.3).

With the exception of a rich narrative wrapper that connects the jumping, swinging, and action derring-do, the biggest difference to the core

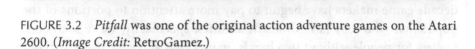

FIGURE 3.2 *Pitfall* was one of the original action adventure games on the Atari 2600. (*Image Credit*: RetroGamez.)

FIGURE 3.3 Image from *UNCHARTED 4: A Thief's End*. © 2016 Sony Interactive Entertainment LLC. (Created and developed by Naughty Dog LLC.)

user fantasy is in visual fidelity. Similarly, when mobile games began to approach console levels of graphics around 2014, the user base exploded. Immersive visuals make games more appealing to more people. This trend will continue to drive interest in games from those who have ignored them in the past.

ACCESSIBILITY

Accessibility is another major area of improvement for game hardware and software in the last 20 years. Few remember the complexity of creating your own boot disks to be able to play Origin PC games like *Ultima VII*, but suffice to say it took enough knowledge and effort to make playing these seminal PC RPG games beyond the reach of the mass market. Consoles, Steam, mobile phones, and new interface models like the Wii or the Xbox Kinect all made gaming approachable for millions of people who do not think of themselves as technical. This has always been a particular strength of the console products coming out of Nintendo. As hardware and software creators reduce the friction required for those without the time, inclination, or knowledge to engage in "tech support" just to play a game, the gaming population has multiplied. This trend will continue. Moreover, over the last decade game makers have begun to pay more attention to portions of the population who may have different abilities; specifically, we've seen controllers for people without two hands, games that allow for those without hearing, with reduced visual ability, and other thoughtful approaches to ensure that the whole population can play. Larger populations mean different abilities, skills, ages, cognitive states, etc. Allowing different onramps to the same game can engage more players. Only in high-end competitive modes do input models have to have a level of symmetry to be fair. And while this has been considered true for a long time, is it?

Beyond the hardware, the science of User Interface and User Experience design within software has evolved hugely, making the standards for ease of use for gaming software much higher. Games are made to be much easier to understand and lower friction now. Collectively, these have helped bring gaming to the masses. Increased accessibility encourages more people to play games; this trend will continue.

CAPABLE DEVICES EVERYWHERE

As a game designer, the reason I made the move from AAA console to mobile-first game development in 2013 was because of the sheer number of players who suddenly had gaming capable devices in their pockets. Between 2010 and 2020, more than six billion people adopted smartphones into their lives. Thanks for sustained push by Apple, Google, Samsung, Huawei, Xiaomi, and a few other handset manufacturers, almost the entire world can now play video games.

The market now reflects this switch – and while mobile phone gaming taking the lion's share of the gaming business was certainly news over the last few years, what I believe is more important than the dollar values in play is the way widespread (ubiquitous, really) mobile smartphone adoption has made gaming so much more egalitarian. Everyone really is a gamer now, and while that may not change the core of player motivation or human experience much, it does allow for a significant change in the way game designers need to think about the future of game design.

CROSS PLAY AND DEVICE AGNOSTICISM

The era of particular games being only playable on specific hardware is on the wane. While platform exclusives like *Halo*, *The Last of Us*, or *The Legend of Zelda: Breath of the Wild* may continue to be used to sell high-end gaming hardware for the wealthy for a little longer, there are many signs that I coupling of hardware and software exclusivity will soon be a thing of the past. Indeed, we can already play *Halo* on a Windows PC, play *Mario Kart* on an Android phone, and play top Android games on emulators on the PC. Cloud gaming will further reduce the need for a particular game to be played on a particular piece of hardware. *Fortnite* showed the industry the way for device-agnostic cross-platform play. We will talk about this at far greater length elsewhere in the book, but increasingly designers should consider their designs as specific device-agnostic. Or, perhaps put more clearly: Every game should strive to be playable on any given device in the way that will yield the best experience for the users. Cross-platform play does not necessarily mean that game clients on each device need to operate at parity. I expect by 2025 the notion of any tentpole video game being available only on a particular device family will seem terribly outdated. By 2035, I expect that the kinds of ubiquitous inputs many games need to feed their hunger for data on the user will have all but ended any concept of device specific play. For games to always be with a player, they need to be everywhere the player is, able to interact with the player on a phone, a television, the bathroom mirror, their earbuds, and so on. Gaming ubiquity benefits from access to a full ecosystem of connected devices. The design implications of this will be profound.

AI AGENTS

The last major element of gaming that I expect to drive far greater adoption over the coming decades is the more widespread use of high quality Artificially Intelligent Non-Player-Characters (NPCs) in games. Again, there is little fundamentally new in the role these characters will play in the structure of games themselves. Players have made friends and plotted against with fictional characters in games for decades. At their simplest level, adding *persona* to game pieces (King, Queen, Rook, Pawn, Jack of Diamonds) has been used to give narrative context to game mechanics for hundreds of years. Deeper emotional resonance and meaningful choice in interactions with NPCs has been a mainstay of RPGs for a long time. But the depth and facility NPCs can command in games is right on the cusp of a massive transformation. Rescuing a princess who blows you the icon of an eight-bit kiss in *Super Mario Bros.* may be thematically similar to a virtual lover who a player wins over through performing in game feats. But with conversational level Natural Language Processing, photo-real visuals, bespoke character creation parameterized against a database of that particular player's preferences, and potentially long-term play together that lasts months or years… Well, the depth of attachment, emotional resonance, and the ability for NPCs to motive players and hook them deeply is just about to enter a new phase. The tale of Joel and Ellie from *The Last of Us* is moving; but when Ellie is asking you personally to help her every day her story will be more gripping still. We have tasted the merest sip of what the application of machine learning AI technologies to NPCs can offer. Adaptive bespoke AI characters will transform gaming more than advanced graphics have. We'll talk a lot more about this in coming chapters.

VR, AR, IMMERSION, METAVERSE

We've talked a little about the importance of visual fidelity, which has mostly referred to how graphics on a two-dimensional screen look (even if what's being rendered is a viewport into a simulated 3D world). But there's a deeper layer of immersion based on visual fidelity that is (and has been perpetually for almost two decades) right around the corner. And that's more immersive displays which provide twin stereoscopic viewports into a 3D world. These days, that's mostly referred to by the highly inaccurate shorthand acronym "VR" which stands for virtual reality.

The first mass-market VR headset was the Nintendo Virtual Boy, released in 1995 to lackluster sales. The core notion of these devices is that by rendering a scene twice from two different cameras, displayed on two screens with a small offset from one another we can give users a stereoscopic viewport into a 3D environment which allows a perception of depth in the same way humans perceive real-life 3D space. While the reality of widespread adoption of this technology has continually lagged expectations of those who are excited about a virtual reality future, it is improving and rapidly. Today's high-end consumer VR headsets are a long way from the Virtual Boy.

Some of the major improvements include:

- Head tracking, which allows the user to smoothly look around the world by moving cameras within the 3D simulation based on movements of the user's head in real life.

- Framerate has improved dramatically, so that displaying two screens each at 60–120 Hz is common. While this is not quite the same level of perception that most human eyes can achieve,[5] it is close. Higher framerate for VR headsets tends to help reduce headaches and visual fatigue.

- Resolution has improved a lot as well. The Nintendo Virtual Boy displayed at 384×224 pixels per screen; 2021's HTC VIVE Pro2 displays at 4,896×2,448 pixels. Improved resolution leads to dramatically greater immersion in the 3D scene.

- Wireless headsets are becoming more common. Being attached to a PC through cables is awkward and makes it hard for players to move around freely, which is one of the promises of VR gaming.

- Shared spaces in software applications let multiple users wearing VR headsets feel as if they are together; this helps reduce one of the significant downsides to immersive display mechanisms. Wearing a headset that blocks out your vision of the rest of the world can be deeply uncomfortable, particularly with other people in the room.

There are dozens of other improvements that VR headset manufacturers and the game makers who create content for them are focused on. There is simply no doubt that this technology is becoming cheaper, better, and lower friction. Recently, John Carmack gave a superb keynote talk[6] on the technical complexities still to overcome and some of the promising approaches. This should serve only as a reminder that there is a terrific amount of IQ focused on making immersive VRs and the software they run better. Between gaming and other enterprise solutions, VR applications are estimated to generate over $50 billion per year by 2030.[7]

And yet, the number of people willing to strap on a headset and block out the rest of their world remains quite small. ("Attach a TV to the end of your nose," as cynic visionary Elon Musk put it.)

I believe, in part, this is a socially driven constraint. Sitting on the couch playing games with friends is simply a very different experience than everyone sitting in a room but unable to see one another. For this reason, I do not expect VR headsets to completely replace other types of screens for gaming, no matter how good they get. When I'm sitting at dinner with my family, I may want to play a game – we all might want to! – but we still want to be able to look up and see one another on occasion.

There are a few applications for which deeply immersive VR headsets could be quite useful though.

There are more than a hundred million people across the globe in nursing homes or long-term care facilities. Many of these people are no longer ambulatory and cannot venture outside of constrained physical spaces which are often not particularly nice. As we saw in our section on demographics, the population of many countries in the developed world will be experiencing an unprecedented "elder boom" as their societies average age gets older. VR in nursing homes and care facilities could well provide a means of escape for multitudes of people. What is the value of being able to see and hear the spray from a ship's deck, or walk once more in a sunny meadow when you will never again be able to do so in real life? Almost incalculable, I should think.

In a different use case we can imagine, some situations are very difficult to train for. VR can serve an immersive training ground for doctors, first responders, undersea welders, and many other professionals. "Serious Games" as they are called, have long pushed our ability to use games to teach or simulate complex scenarios for training purposes.[8] Particularly with high-stress situations (firefighting, combat, reactor repair, etc.) the greater the level of immersion we can provide in training, the better prepared for the real event these trainees can be. Serious Games like these may be an ideal use case for VR.

And then, the sheer amount of personalized data that social media has collected on billions of humans could be used to create bespoke social spaces which could become extremely compelling in VR. For example, imagine that Facebook stitched together enough pictures of your childhood home, and the people who once inhabited it that you could tour again spaces – and visit with people – who may otherwise only exist for you in memory. Couple this with the kinds of highly sophisticated AI agents we will discuss in a coming chapter, and it is quite possible to image being able to tour your grandmother's house and carry on a conversation with her while she sits in that rocking chair you remember so well…

It is possible that comfort with deeply immersive displays and the resulting isolation from real life may be more palatable to new generations who grow up with greater access to such devices earlier. Will kids who grow up with this technology embedded into glasses or contacts from an early age no longer have a need for dedicated external displays? Perhaps. But I doubt it, actually.

It may be briefly useful to contemplate where we are on the timeline for this technology, particularly because "VR glasses" or embedded contact lenses have been a mainstay of future facing science fiction movies for a long time.

When could we have RayBan-weight wireless VR glasses that could play a game like *Skyrim*? Perhaps 2025 at the earliest, and that seems optimistic. But even then, these would not be mainstream. A billion pairs of them sold by 2030 sounds improbable. So I do not expect widespread consumer adoption of "VR glasses" before 2035.

An even better bit of sci-fi imagination involves contact lenses or circuitry embedded directly on a user's cornea, which can augment their regular vision, or provide fully immersive high-resolution imagery. So when might we start to see contact lenses with this capability? I expect this to be a while. Even in 2022, displaying at high resolution on a clear pane of glass is limited, and not particularly high quality. Companies like ClearView Innovations are developing such technology, but most use cases even in high-end casinos or residences are limited. To perfect this technology, miniaturize it, provide power and input without bulky wires? 2028 at the earliest perhaps? Then to make it safe with integration into a human biology? 2035? So then even in this optimistic scenario we should not expect any such display technology to be widespread by 2040. Sorry.

AR AND REAL-WORLD GAMING BLENDS

Still, while fully immersive VR headsets are improving rapidly, a number of companies are betting on a technology called Augmented Reality (AR) which let you see the real world, just with digital visuals overlaid.

For the last few years, AR has mostly been a function of smartphones, which use their camera function coupled with 3D rendering software to allow game makers to display 3D objects, characters, and UI elements over the top of the camera scene. Combining clever sense of depth, multiple cameras, precision location awareness and a variety of other techniques has allowed some truly innovative gaming applications of AR technology.

To date though, only a few games have had widespread commercial success using AR.

Pokémon Go, built by Niantic using technology from Google Maps, and characters and Intellectual Property from Nintendo's *Pokémon* Company, is the obvious and most well understood example of this tech. *Pokémon Go* took the world by storm, driving staggering profits and helping Niantic push some of the underlying technologies they created to new heights. Ask most gamers if they can name an "Augmented Reality" game and they would call out *Pokémon Go*.

This area of gaming is ripe for further exploration and development. We can easily imagine additional datasets provided by wearables, cameras, drones, or other tracking services which provide additional layers of meta-awareness of how a player and their view fits into the real world. (Several of these have considerable consumer privacy implications as we will explore later.) Coupling these kinds of technologies with the inherent design elements of real-world spaces could be used to gamify experiences like exploring a theme-park, touring a new school campus, or even shopping. Now imagine these kinds of AR experiences driven by AI gamemasters to drive deeper social connectivity than we have seen to date in AR games by determining who is present, assigning teams that would be fair, proposing game modes that would be well suited toward a particular playspace or player set.

Augmented reality games, relying on real-world datasets to form the game itself are one of the newest and freshest elements of game design to appear in a long time. We should expect massive evolution here over the coming decade.

VR & AR COMBINED MAKE... THE METAVERSE?

No discussion in the winter of 2022 would be complete without a bit of a discussion on "The Metaverse." In what has rapidly become one of the most overused and overhyped buzzwords ever to echo through Silicon Valley, almost every game, tech, and media company is suddenly expected to have a "strategy for the Metaverse." But... What is it?

Metaverse descriptions began in early dystopian cyberpunk fiction as a concept for an interconnected and diverse set of shared digital online experiences as seen in Neil Stephenson's *Snowcrash* or Ernest Cline's *Ready Player One*. By 2021 though, the notion of the Metaverse has somehow morphed into a collection of ill-fitting concepts including DeFi (Decentralized Finance, like blockchains) NFTs and other digital goods, Artificial Intelligence, Virtual Reality, Augmented Reality, gamification, and generally anything that involves being online with other people. Collectively this is also sometimes referred to as "Web 3.0." But the hype train is real enough that companies like Facebook have recently even changed their name to Meta, and various corporations are falling all over themselves to be the ones who define and control... whatever it is. Mostly, so far, it seems to involve fairly cringey videos of unappealing virtual avatars sitting around virtual conference tables or colorful non-spaces pretending that they are doing things people in real life mostly try to avoid (like having meetings or high fiving their bosses). It has been widely pointed out that the conceptual nature of a Metaverse is inherently opposed to a particular company establishing a curated environment with a limited set of user possibilities.

As the godfather of 3D game spaces, John Carmack said:

> I doubt a single application will get to that level of taking over everything. I just don't believe that one player—one company—winds up making all the right decisions for this.

Dean Takahashi, veteran games industry reporter further predicts at the start of 2022:

> Over time, it will become interoperable with easy transit between worlds, open source standards, and trade agreements. Standards always take a long time to establish, but they eventually happen when enough of the power brokers conclude that working together is better.[9]

But all of this is tied up in gaming, which seems to be one of the use cases humans actually want to participate in, as evidenced by MMORPGs and the popularity of *Roblox* to allow millions of people to create 3D spaces and experiences for one another. In practice, it is possible that the Metaverse will remain mostly, well, meta: a conceptual mental space each of us engage in as we navigate our real-world spaces, looking at our phones, thinking about what friends in some game world did last night, walking past a hologram of some long-dead celebrity dancing in a bank lobby to promote high-interest crypto-currency savings accounts, and occasionally strapping on a head-mounted display to confer with others or explore some higher-resolution virtual space for recreation.

A number of great companies are building out new sets of tools, technology, and offering funding for developers – including game makers – to develop content and experiences in line with their ideas for what the Metaverse might be. Indeed, as of the winter of 2022 it seemed that every company from Walmart to Samsung had rolled out a demo of how consumers could interact with their brand in some virtual space. Let's take a look at a few groups doing interesting things that might give us some hints into what the future of games might be.

NIANTIC AS METAVERSE

Game company Niantic, creator of the incredibly hit Augmented Reality (AR) game, *Pokémon Go,* has quietly built a suite of tools designed to allow other game makers easily develop high quality applications using AR and real-world locations as a way of organizing data.

> Niantic, makers of *Pokémon Go,* launched a new platform for AR developers called Lightship. The company is taking the set of iOS and Android AR tools out of beta and offering worldwide access, with a model that's initially free to use for all developers through to summer 2022.
>
> John Hanke, Niantic's CEO and formerly the leader of the Google division responsible for Google Maps and Earth, said that his hope is that Lightship will attract developers who share the company's values for the use of AR, particularly as we approach mass market AR glasses.
>
> Hanke is ardent in his belief that AR tech will lead to a "real world Metaverse," a particular spin on the Metaverse idea that is more about layering digital information over a user's surroundings than it is about entirely immersing a person in virtual environments.
>
> *Amanda Silberling,* Tech Crunch *November 8, 2021.*

There are several really exciting elements of Niantic's vision. First, when AR first appeared on Apple and Google operating systems most of the games built with it felt gimmicky. Yes, it was very cool to be able to see characters race across your kitchen table toward their foes if you held your phone just right. But the joy from these applications was mostly quite short lived. Games certainly didn't play any better because of the addition of a real-world camera, and most of these applications were processing heavy enough that they drained users' batteries very quickly, which has long been a kiss of death for mobile games.

Niantic's *Pokémon Go* was different for a few reasons. Building upon their innovative location based game, Ingress – which let users capture sectors of a map based upon the real world – *Pokémon Go* combined optional AR views which let users see cute iconic creatures dancing around in the real world when they looked through their cameras. It also encouraged very lightweight social play, driving users to Pokestops where they ended up making friends with other *Pokémon* fans. Of course, the addition of Nintendo's phenomenal license didn't hurt either, and *Pokémon Go* introduced hundreds of millions of players to AR gaming between 2017 and 2022. This established Niantic's brand as synonymous with real-world AR overlays and games that take place using real-world maps. *Pokémon Go* was accessible, understandable, got users out and walking around with their friends and families, and helped the world understand what was possible with AR gaming.

In the several years since its launch, Niantic has not rested on their laurels. Lightship and the technology Niantic has continued to push the envelope on what developers can do to include real-world mapping information and overlaid 3D graphics atop images taken by the cameras on their smartphones. Their Lightship technology allows for large scale multiplayer experiences, advanced techniques for deriving information from the world around us, such as collision data, awareness of what objects captured by the camera are in real life, and fast access to map data from everywhere in the world down to a very granular level.

Niantic's publishing and partnership teams are active in reaching out to the games industry as a whole. Over the next five to ten years we should expect to see hundreds of new experiences and games using variations on real-world locations and Augmented Reality that combines 3D characters and objects set against camera captured backdrops.

Niantic's vision for the Metaverse amounts to an augmented way of looking at the real world; and there is much compelling about this vision.

ROBLOX AS METAVERSE

Years before the rest of the world started talking about the Metaverse, California-based *Roblox* quietly set out to allow anyone to build their own games inside the *Roblox* system. Using straightforward but powerful tools that make game making accessible, the *Roblox* platform currently has 47 million Daily Active Users (DAU)[10] and almost ten million developers who have built out experiences for the platform. Currently *Roblox* runs on most mobile devices, PCs, and on some Xbox devices.

It is worth noting that *Roblox* supports neither AR nor VR currently. *Roblox* is taking a different approach, pushing hard on social connectivity and good tools. The company has focused on strong analysis of the social graph that describes users' relationships with one another, avatars that can move freely from one experience to the next, and a lot of energy put into moderating content. A global economy by which users can buy and sell and trade virtual goods, entry to experiences, give away prizes, and the like allow for a rich and emergent economy in the game already.

In many ways, developers and other technology companies alike should look to *Roblox* as an example of a Metaverse that exists today. Without AR, VR, crypto-currency support, or almost any of the other hallmarks of the buzz-fueled "Metaverse" of current media, *Roblox* has delivered against a vision of the future with unerring clarity.

And since anyone and everyone with a PC and a modicum of technical skill is welcome to jump in right now and create new experiences, *Roblox* is one of the best examples of the future of gaming today.

TENCENT AS METAVERSE

Despite significant setbacks in their domestic market as a result of Chinese regulators recent war on gaming, Tencent remains a mighty force across the ecosystem. As *The Economist*[11] puts it:

> Tencent may be the best positioned of any company to win the race. It is the world's biggest publisher of games and one of the biggest forces in social media and e-commerce. It invests in or operates many of the most popular multiplayer online games in the world. It owns a minority stake in Epic Games, the creator of *"Fortnite"*, a game which Tim Sweeney, Epic's founder, has called a possible vehicle for a Metaverse. An edited version of the game was allowed a test run in China, but Epic gave up on that trial in November.

With massive amounts of capital, their own popular social network (WeChat), and global partnerships that span the entire business, we should expect Tencent to continue to command hundreds of millions of users and play the most significant role in Chinese and other Eastern versions of Metaverse gaming.

EPIC'S FORTNITE AS METAVERSE

Fortnite is one of the most popular games in the world. It started with a zany Battle Royale premise, in which 50 players are parachuted into an island world to build things and shoot one another. But very quickly, *Fortnite* expanded to allow users to craft their own worlds they could invite friends into. The Epic team has promoted large concerts and social events within the game, and Epic is racing to get from the 60 million Monthly Active Users (MAU) they boast today to a billion players.

Backing all of this is Epic's phenomenal toolset and engine, called Unreal, which has set the standard for 3D rendering and content creation for two decades now. Beyond being used to build hit games, Unreal is also used for pre-visualization of shots in major Hollywood films and television shows like Lucas Arts Disney+ hit *The Mandalorian*.[12]

While *Fortnite's* number of users is incredibly impressive, it is ultimately Epic's Unreal Engine – which allows game makers, and almost anyone else who wants to craft characters and environments to do so – that will have the most profound impact on shaping how game makers think about gaming over the next ten years.

NVIDIA AS METAVERSE

Beginning as a 3D hardware acceleration company building consumer products for PC gamers in the mid-nineties, Nvidia has grown to be one of the world's foremost advanced chipmakers for graphics chips, but also for AI chips. Nvidia is one part consumer hardware company, one part business to business chip-maker, and one part R&D powerhouse, whose practical advances in GPU parallel processing have significantly advanced the state of the industry for real-time 3D simulation and graphics fidelity.

More recently, calling their vision for the Metaverse the "Omniverse," Nvidia has released a new suite of tools for programmers and content creators which seek to facilitate creation of Augmented Realities, 3D spaces, and Artificial Intelligence systems which make use of deep learning neural networks.[13] They have also released tools to facilitate the simple creation of 3D characters to be used as avatars. They have recently added more sophisticated tools for content creators, allowing for seamless animation of characters based on just the input of an audio track,[14] as well as tools for allowing multiple users to edit and create within a scene simultaneously. All of these tools target a level of device agnosticism that allows content or technology created upon them to be at home on mobile phones, PCs, or consoles. Interoperability between scenes, settings, and experiences has been considered as well, which is an important consideration for any truly "meta" Metaverse. The application for understanding real-life spaces relies on open source technology developed by Pixar initially, but also a host of proprietary Nvidia systems associated with rendering, scene and 3D asset creation, and physics simulation.[15] As we will discuss in coming chapters, several of these elements are going through massive and rapid evolution in the next few years, and will likely lead to huge increases in the quality of a variety of games.

Further, in November 2021, Nvidia announced that they intended to build a "digital twin" for the Earth. Using a technique they have pioneered in conjunction with assorted companies (like BMW), Nvidia will build a scale replica of a space, attempting to model and replicate a real-world physical environment (like a factory, for example) in as close to perfect detail as they can manage in order to allow for detailed design and planning. In an ambitious extension of this technology, Nvidia announced they were going to build E-2, a supercomputer dedicated to storing a 1:1 replica of the topology, weather patterns, and simulations of other physical, thermal, and other characteristics of the Earth. This project is described in such terms as to feel a bit overwhelming in its ambition:

> We're going to go build that digital twin of the Earth. It's going to be gigantic. This is going to be the largest AI supercomputer on the planet. It's going to bring some of the brightest computer scientists, the brightest physical scientists and climate scientists on the planet to go and use that computer to predict how the Earth will change over decades
>
> *Said Jensen Huang, CEO of Nvidia.*

He further added, "*If we build the digital twin of the Earth, we will get the Metaverse for free.*"[16]

On some level, unlike Facebook and Microsoft, Nvidia seems keen on arming creators of the Metaverse in much the way they have game makers for the last 20 years: With formats and software tools which allow the creation and sharing of assets, and the hardware and software to effectively organize and display them. Will any incarnation of "The Metaverse" likely be branded Nvidia? No. Will almost all foreseeable incarnations of Metaverses likely rely on software, hardware, and architecture Nvidia has had a hand in developing? Yes.

FACEBOOK AS METAVERSE

Despite numerous ups and downs in its PR campaign to win hearts and minds of the public, there is no doubt that Facebook has been a massively transformative force both on Western civilization and on the internet over the last two decades. The very embodiment of the phrases "social network" and "social media," Facebook has been connecting people to their families and long-lost friends for a long time. Facebook provided the first look at more casual social gaming to hundreds of millions of people in the early part of this century and became a huge component of how we think about online targeted advertising, viral coefficients for product adoption, and a host of other concepts which define the modern digital space.

In 2014, Facebook bought Oculus, one of the early successful VR head-set companies for $2 billion, but little became of this acquisition for some years. Then in October 2021, Facebook's founder and polarizing CEO, Mark Zuckerberg, announced that Facebook would be transforming itself into a Metaverse company. "I believe the Metaverse will be the successor to the mobile internet, and creating this product group is the next step in our journey to help build it," said Zuckerberg in a Facebook post. They also released a suite of tools called Horizon Workrooms, seemingly targeted at allowing people to meet in a shared VR space.

Facebook is so invested in this concept of leading the Metaverse that they have changed their very name to Meta, and have committed to hiring 10,000 staff in the EU[17] before 2025 in order to bring about some variant of the vision Zuckerberg promoted.

Based on Facebook's (sometimes contentious, sometimes symbiotic) relationship with game makers, we should expect that a Facebook driven Metaverse has some common tools for allowing game logins, potentially some concept of a shared wallet. (Remember that Facebook also has toyed with their own crypto-currency, initially called Libra, then Diem, for some years now. This project has been a regulatory mess of starts and stops, but we should not rule it out.)

While Facebook is not exactly the most trusted name in technology at the time of this writing, they have a number of elements required to bring about some vision of a Metaverse: Billions of users, true cross-platform experiences, high-quality authentication, an established VR hardware unit with a track record of success, a foothold in legitimizing crypto-currency, thousands of smart engineers, a giant war chest of money, and relation-ships and unparalleled insights into almost every game publisher in the world, and potentially more consumer data that could be used to custom-ize the experience for users than any other company in the world. We should not be too quick to rule out Meta's ability to put the meta in the Metaverse.

MICROSOFT AS METAVERSE

There's almost no important part of the technology business Microsoft hasn't played a big role in shaping over the last 40 years. As the creator of one of the three big consoles (the Xbox) and the masters of the global PC ecosystem, Microsoft – more than perhaps any other name – defines technology and has always stood for gaming. From a ubiquitous Solitaire game that shipped with every copy of Windows in the nineties, to Forza to Age of Empires to *Halo,* Microsoft games and platforms have pushed the boundaries of visual fidelity, social connectedness, and mass-market accessibility for complicated technologies for longer than most humans on Earth today have been alive. And while Microsoft's backend cloud computing technology, Azure, doesn't have the market capitalization that Google Cloud or Amazon Services has, it still powers massive amounts of the backend for the global internet.

Microsoft's innovative HoloLens technology promises a new standard for AR and Mixed Reality (eventually). The HoloLens recently landed a $22 billion dollar contract from the US Army.[18] At the moment, the HoloLens appears to be more focused on targeting training, industrial, and military uses than those suitable for gaming. However, since Microsoft also owns *Minecraft* and teased *Minecraft* running on a HoloLens as early as 2015, we should not be surprised when consumer level HoloLens technology focused on productivity and entertainment begin to appear. Microsoft currently offers developer editions of the HoloLens which integrates into Unity game engine. I would expect this to be sometime around 2025 (Figure 3.4).

FIGURE 3.4 The US Army has invested $22 billion dollars in Microsoft's HoloLens technology. (*Image Credit:* United States Army.)

However, their current talk around "Metaverse" is more focused on productivity and connectivity applications than games. "Mesh" for Microsoft Teams is their most recent example of this, allowing people's virtual avatars, which are currently severed tops of a cartoon torso, to stand around a virtual conference table (featuring virtual empty coffee cups sitting on the table to give the appearance of a real conference table?) and having the conversation they would otherwise be having over Zoom or in person.

And while anyone would be a fool to rule out Microsoft as a player in any field of technology, thus far they have delivered little that would seem to compel developers (or the public at large) to participate in this view of what a Metaverse could be.

However, as the purveyor of the Operating Systems, office productivity tools, server software and standards, one of the great consoles of the last 20 years, and as – as of this writing – the most valuable company in the world, with a market cap of $2.49 trillion dollars... Well, all game makers will continue to live in the world Microsoft created for a long time.

Whatever Metaverses we build over the next 40 years, they would be remiss not to include statues of Bill Gates, Paul Allen, Steve Ballmer, Satya Nadella, Phil Spencer, and the other master architects of Earth's technoverse.

METAVERSE WRAP UP

And what to make of all of this? A few thoughts:

For any Metaverse to be worthy of the name, it by definition cannot be controlled by a single entity.

It seems essential that many people are able to create the worlds we will collectively share.

And this last point is the notion I believe directs us toward one of the most important predictions about the future of game development over the next 20 years: Everyone will be able to be a game maker.

There are dozens of companies and groups not listed here who are doing things that want to be described as "The Metaverse." Decentraland hosts parties and virtual shopping centers branded by corporate giants, selling NFTs emblazoned with corporate logos.[19]

A single type of gameplay experience will never capture everyone's imagination, which means lots of different spaces and rulesets will need to be able to coexist with some common elements. Beyond that, there is a lot more than just gaming to the Metaverse, but... As the New York Times put it in a recent headline in which they interviewed Microsoft Xbox boss Phil Spencer, "To Understand the Metaverse, Look to Video Games."

And while, at the moment, each of these different companies and a hundred more are building different spaces with different parameters, features, and limited to no ability for users to seamlessly move between them, this will change. As veteran industry journalist, Dean Takahashi predicts[20]:

> Over time, it will become interoperable with easy transit between worlds, open source standards, and trade agreements. Standards always take a long time to establish, but they eventually happen when enough of the power brokers conclude that working together is better.

Let's look at some of the interesting elements of this coming world.

USER-GENERATED CONTENT

We've mentioned User-Generated Content, but let's take a little closer look at some of the reasons games which incorporate this type of player contribution is exciting and why I believe it points the way for game development over the next 20 years.

From the earliest days of personal computer gaming, software like *Adventure Creator* or Spinnaker Story Machine allowed users to build their own interactive narratives or games. Later, games like Neverwinter Nights and other complex RPGs started dressing up and publishing the tools their creation teams used to make game content, and in so doing they managed to build thriving communities of creators who stayed with the game for years longer than they might have otherwise. As mentioned earlier, this trend has only grown as the tools have improved, as more people gained access to powerful PCs, and as the gamer population exploded.

And now, thanks to game making platforms like *Roblox,* everyone who is so inclined can be a game maker.

Gaming itself can now be considered an act of creation for millions, rather than an act of consumption. This is a fairly profound difference in the way a game (or game tools platform) is designed, and also signifies as much of a shift culturally in the way games are perceived as the rise of home cameras, and later smartphone cameras did to linear video media. If every player can now be a game maker, what are some interesting outcomes we can expect over the next two decades?

First, *Minecraft, Roblox,* Wonderbox, and many of the other platforms that exist are amazing, but still fairly primitive. Adding deep AI assistance, voice control, more and better libraries of content and behaviors to pull from will all advance the kinds of things users can create rapidly. Moreover, as generations of gamers who view gaming primarily as an act of creation rather than consumption grow up, we will begin to see the emergence of new kinds of games being made, with far more localized and diverse elements in play. As game making becomes a hobby for far more people than it is a profession for, we will see some of the constraints that are dictated by a need to generate commercially successful ROI begin to dissolve for some – resulting in even more experimental and indie games, and a far richer canvas of experiences.

Why will people make their own games? They will make games they want to play, to achieve fantasy fulfillment they cannot get elsewhere, to impress their friends and peers, to make money, as teaching tools, as ways of getting back at enemies, and for all the same reasons people have created art or literature or music over the centuries, as a means of creative expression.

And because the ways communities form around games – commercial or hobbyist ventures – and the communities themselves can create content or their own spinoff stories and games, the nature of User-Generated Content is about to get very self-referential and meta.

The internet is filled with "fan fiction" in which amateur writers create and publish online narratives involving characters they love. Twilight fan fic had a massive following, as does almost every other major brand. And, of course, so do characters from video games. But where this starts getting a lot more interesting is that amateur game content creators who have authored UGC are now the subjects of fan fiction themselves. Dream SMP, an invitation only *Minecraft* server hosts a community of 2.7 million[21] who write fan fiction about the people who create drama on the *Minecraft* server, and still others write fan fiction about the fan fiction writers.

Can we imagine a Choose Your Own *Adventure creator* for fanfic content sets? With millions of dedicated readers and creators, all interested we can definitely imagine those tools finding fertile ground. And because the content that appeals to fan communities is very hard for publishers to replicate internally because the creators are the only ones who decide authenticity of their favorite characters, in jokes, etc. A few community focused staff and influencer advocates can keep the content relatively within bounds. And fan fic keeps licenses and characters relevant even between tentpole releases from the IP holder. When a fan downloads the

Marvel Cinematic Universe Choose Your Own Adventure Kit, Marvel, Disney, the fans, and the actors themselves all benefit.

In the future, everyone will be able to create games about their favorite characters. By making fans themselves creators everyone wins.

MODS AS UGC

And then, there are game mods. Long ago, hackers would decompile or hex-edit pieces of games and release modifications ("mods") that let players change the way the games played. Starting with MUDs, MMORPGs created healthy mod communities by allowing third party creators to build new UI elements, scripts that would automate tedious tasks in game, and so on. Soon whole games started being modded, sometimes quite heavily. In perhaps the most famous example, fans modded Blizzard's hit RTS *Warcraft 3* to create a multiplayer battle arena called *Defense of the Ancients* (DOTA). DOTA became so popular that a young upstart company called Riot Games built their own clone, improving a few complexities of the original, and *League of Legends* was born.

And modding has not slowed down since; anywhere there is a popular game, fans will download and attempt to hack, decompile, and mess with the source code and content. Most of these efforts never go anywhere, but some of them create whole new genres (Auto-Chess being a currently fashionable example). Again, as tools, programming languages, and the population of tech-savvy gamers increase, we should expect some of the most interesting gameplay systems, modes, and content to come from modding communities.

THE WORLD WANTS TO PLAY FOR FREE

Most people on Earth cannot afford high-end PCs, or the newest PlayStation console with a 4K television, high speed internet, and a subscription to the online service of their choice before shelling out another $70 USD for the latest *Call of Duty*. There are millions who can, and this is a great business, but it is inherently for the well-off citizens of a few developed countries. But there are billions of gamers who expect their games to be free to play. In general, the question of how best to monetize entertainment to delight the maximum number of users and derive the greatest amount of revenue is one of the more interesting evolutions of the entertainment sector over the last two decades. A person could now spend every waking minute of a hundred lifetimes just watching free content and listening to free music on YouTube. For this reason, to my mind, the evolution of "free-to-play" gaming, with all of the good, bad, and ugly means of turning these games into a viable business is one of the most interesting areas of game design over the last decade. Completely optional In App Purchases (IAP) can allow every user to contribute at a level they feel comfortable with to a degree that the game adds value to their life. And for the more than 95% of users who never pay anything for their gaming, In App Advertising (IAA) has provided a way for game companies to build successful businesses and pay all the staff and server costs required to build and operate this entertainment. Free to play is the undisputed present and future of gaming for the majority of the world.

This does not mean that all games released will be free to play; many may deliberatively have a very high initial price to enter. A "minimum bet" if you will. Think of this like a golden VIP room in Vegas; you've got to show up with a balance before you're allowed in. Indeed, most elite competitions in most every game and sport is already this way to a degree; a team doesn't walk into the Superbowl or World Cup event without millions and millions in training and entry fees established over decades. The same will likely be true of large gaming player alliances and so on. (Imagine an online Poker Top 1000 Clients Syndicate, 2034. One million ETH bets could be common. Even getting a first-circle Twitch view could cost box seat prices.) Exclusivity will always have its adherents, and we should expect elite echelons of the gaming world to follow suit.

Overall though, game designers on all mediums need to continue to evolve their thinking to incorporate some of the systems designs that have led the mobile and PC free-to-play sectors to dominate the market in recent years. All games of the future need to be thought of as "software-as-a-service" that can continue to engage users daily for months or years. This requires a fundamentally different design, production, and business mentality than retail product development of yesteryear. While SAAS designs are not always completely aligned with "free-to-play" designs, there is significant amounts of overlap that game designers of all genres and business models would be wise to study. If you want to reach the largest number of gamers, your game needs to be free (at least initially). And since the cost to build games is ever increasing, the study of some free-to-play mechanics is essential.

APPOINTMENT MECHANICS

One of the more compelling elements that free-to-play games have introduced to the world of game design comes in the form of "Appointment

Mechanics." Because free-to-play games are constantly desperate to score a monetization opportunity, they are forced to care a lot more about user engagement than traditional boxed retail products needed to. (Once a game publisher had your $70, they were unlikely to make another penny from you off that particularly game. This doesn't mean that game developers and publishers didn't care about driving user engagement; highly engaged users tell their friends, don't resell the game DVD, and are eager for the sequel.) But for free-to-play games, keeping users logging in many times a day, and spending as much time in the game as possible means the difference between commercial success and failure. After all, users who aren't playing cannot spend or see an In App Ad.

And so game designers formalized a collection of so-called Appointment Mechanics which encouraged users to check in every day, every few hours. And because many free-to-play games were initially mobile first where session times tend to be shorter due to real-life interruptions, the timing, tuning, and pacing of a number of game systems evolved to suit. Recognizing that many of these same systems could have compelling effects on players in premium console games, we've seen this design trend migrate from free to play. Nintendo's beloved 2020 hit, *Animal Crossing: New Horizons*, made extensive use of appointment timers to keep users harvesting and trading fruit and other resources, and in so doing led to users who became habituated to making the game a daily part of their lives.

Because habituated users stick with a game for months or years, spend more, and tend to engage with the game community in positive ways much more so than users who are more casual in their affection for a particular game, we should expect to see Appointment Mechanics continue to migrate into every genre and type of game in the coming years. Game developers want players who play more often; well-designed Appointment Mechanics are a great way to habituate players for any type of game.

EVERYTHING IS AN RPG

Progression systems that give a player ways to measure their advancement by incrementally rewarding them for completing in game tasks have been common in games for decades. Traditional pen and paper Role Playing Games (RPGs) like the original *Dungeons & Dragons* by TSR introduced the concept of players earning experience points, leveling up, improving statistics that influenced how effective they were at performing in game actions. Then the dungeon master could throw new challenges at them which were numerically even tougher, and the player performing roughly the same actions again ("I swing my sword at the dragon!") were given new context because on the inflation of the numerical values.

Action games mostly ignored these kinds of game-design systems for a long time. (Mario doesn't get any better at jumping over barrels in the original *Donkey Kong* no matter how many times he does it, and the barrels don't become more lethal, etc.) Earlier this century this started to change.

When *Call of Duty: Modern Warfare* by Infinity Ward came out, they introduced basic RPG level up mechanics to the online multiplayer parts of the game. Now, every kill gave a player some XP, enough XP allowed them to level up, which unlocked a new perk that made them better. I view this as a watershed moment for gaming because the simple merger between RPG progression system tropes and high-action first person shooter mechanics so obviously worked and drove far deeper engagement in the multiplayer mode. Now, of course, *Call of Duty* wasn't the first shooter to have experimented with adding RPG progression systems into their game, but because it was such a massive hit, it drove widespread awareness of these RPG systems among gamers who would never have picked up and rolled a 20-sided dice. In the decades since, the use of leveling up and other RPG mechanics in all types of games has become common.

Moreover, "gamification" of everything from airline loyalty programs to the app for the Economist has brought similar RPG systems into mainstream use. I expect this particular trend of game systems design to continue becoming ever more pervasive in coming decades, because it is simply such an effective way of giving new meta-context to repetitive actions and behavior which would otherwise get dull.

If there is a more effective treadmill than RPG progression systems for getting gamers to perform the same action over and over without getting bored, I've never seen it.

As an added bonus, these types of systems are magnified by social systems that characterize modern multiplayer games and most games of the future. What's better than getting a few more kills and leveling up your character? Leveling up your character so that everyone else can see that you just advanced.

GACHA, NEAR MISS, FOMO

For a long time, gamers have been excited to open treasure chests and see what reward waited inside. In Japan, vending machines sold little toys in plastic shells, and the buyer couldn't be sure what they might get until they bought one. The sound the machines made sounded like "gacha!" and so the name stuck. Gacha is now used as a shorthand description for almost any kind of random reward mechanic, also commonly referred to as "loot boxes."

Now, just opening a box to see what is inside is interesting, but when combined with audio-visual sizzle that builds anticipation, lets a player see what they might win, then lands a moment of release upon the reveal… Just before offering a player the chance to open another mystery box or crystal… Well, that ends up providing a very compelling experience that gets users excited enough to spend a lot of time opening boxes, mystery crystals, and the like.

In her insightful 2012 book, *Addiction by Design*, researcher Natasha Dow Schüll explores the design and psychology behind slot machine games, of the sort which have come to dominate the revenue for Las Vegas, Macau, and Maltese casinos over the last 20 years. There are dozens of techniques that game makers use to deliver dopamine hits when the wheels of a slot machine spin, from well-timed claxions and bells, to systems which stimulate the FOMO of a "near miss" to mechanics that encourage the "just one more" mentality that keeps punters pulling the metaphorical lever and remaining in a mental "machine zone" for hours at a time.

These same techniques have proven so effective at driving outside spend, and just capturing user's attention and engagement that they have become ubiquitous in many free-to-play games. Indeed, as we will discuss later, some countries have even begun to regulate the way gacha systems can operate.

There's nothing inherently malevolent about the use of techniques that are informed by psychological triggers that get humans excited. Game designers will continue to refine, improve, and make use of these techniques in games of all types over the coming decades. Collectively, I believe these represent a great way of making game reward systems more compelling to players, and we are likely to see this design trend become more commonplace in games of all types.

REAL-MONEY GAMING AND WAGERING

People have been playing Poker, Pai Gow, and other games of skill and chance online for real-money stakes for about 20 years now on the web. Real Money Gaming (RMG) is a hugely profitable enterprise, which nearly all of the big entertainment (casino) conglomerates have embraced. In 2021, this was estimated by Google-KPMG to be a $1.1 billion per year industry.[22] Many of these same companies also run "Social Casino" games, in which players play only for in-game currency which cannot be exchanged outside of the game for other types of "real-money" currencies. This has been ruled not to constitute "gambling" by several courts. Various governmental regulations on gambling are one of the biggest differences between the two types of casino games, but the ability to freely distribute applications on the big first-party app stores is the other. Today, you cannot download and play an RMG casino game on Apple Store or Google Play, but hundreds of millions of players a year play Social Casino games.

Beyond these kinds of casino based games, social or otherwise, formalized systems for wagering on the outcome of games is playing an increasing role in the gaming business in some markets. In India and South Asia in particular, a number of platforms have arisen which allow players to place a real-money wager on the outcome of a game of skill. (A MOBA like *League of Legends*, a shooter like *Free-Fire*, or Tic-Tac-Toe, the principle works the same.) Companies like WinZO from India are rapidly creating superb businesses using this model.

For a small ante-up entry fee, each player can join a game; then the winner or winning team takes the majority of the pot, the house (platform) takes their share and on to the next round. This mechanism for monetization is particularly interesting for a few reasons. First, it is largely game agnostic, and can sit at a layer atop the individual games themselves. This works for almost any "fair" competitive type of contest. Second, it allows players of highly different levels of disposable income to participate, so they are not left out of the competition just because they cannot afford the game. Think of this as the equivalent of different stake level tables or rooms in a casino. Third, because each individual cash outlay can be very small, this feeds into a "sachet pricing" model for consumption of goods and services which is popular in emerging markets where disposable income and access to credit are limited. Finally, the act of wagering on the outcome of a game drives further retention and engagement in the game by giving context and real-world value. While right now most of this action is in emerging markets like India, we should expect this model to become ubiquitous across the gaming landscape. There is no competitive game in which players and gaming companies cannot benefit by allowing a layer of real-money wagering to sit atop.

PERVASIVE COMMUNITY

Another of the ways in which always online populations have contributed to a shift in game-design thinking over the last few years is the sense of pervasive community surrounding a game or world, which are "always on." The significance of this to game design will assuredly increase in the coming years. What do we mean here?

Games exist in the minds of each of player, and when the player base reaches a critical mass distributed around the world, the game never stops. Conversations about the game are always ongoing, chat channels are abuzz 24 hours a day, for years at a time. And this buzz – this conversation – continues onto social media channels, where the latest reveals or marketing videos or patch notes or conversations about the same are ceaseless. The act of running, monitoring, maintaining, and hyping a game never stops now for any game operating at scale. And as games become brands or larger elements of a social zeitgeist, we need to constantly think of ways for more users (who may not even be players) to get involved. If you doubt the importance of this, go through this thought exercise: Imagine a player who purchased a game or some in game assets for $20. A paying customer, but one who never talks about the game to a friend, never posts on a forum, or similar. Now imagine a player who downloads and plays a game for free, but never deposits or spend a penny. But imagine that this second player runs a Twitch stream with 30,000 viewers daily, drops a weekly YouTube game review followed by two million. Which of these two players likely has more impact on the product's bottom line in a year? Community matters, and this means giving users who may not be hardcore about the game itself to exist and participate and contribute.

There are a dozen valuable places to engage community, from a simple Facebook page or Discord channel to incentivizing Twitch Streamers. But the ones which I believe are the most interesting and likely to continue to expand are by giving players actions they can take inside a game world which are separate from the core loop or mechanics of the game itself. Indeed, these kinds of non-gaming game-adjacent experiences are likely to form the basis for an interactive Metaverse that spans across games.

THE NEED FOR SOCIAL SHEPHERDS

As games have become deeply social and game communities have become bigger, one of the biggest areas of change we've had to adapt to as game makers is the need to protect our players from one another. As we've all learned by now, the seeming anonymity of the internet doesn't always bring out the best in people. Making sure in game chat is safe and free from toxicity, keeping users' accounts secure from hackers, removing inappropriate content, silencing trolls that seek to grief other community members, and a preventing and responding to a host of other online social maladies now requires squadrons of dedicated community members for almost every game. And it also requires battalions of content moderators for the major social networks that run the modern internet.

A New York Times article from December 2021 reported that according to the CEO of Discord, a popular chat app among gamers, 15% of the company's employees are dedicated to Trust and Safety.[23] And Discord takes some pride in being a bit of a "wild west" where server hosts are expected to largely police their servers themselves. For larger organizations like Instagram, WhatsApp, and others, there are thousands of people employed globally. Racist invective, threats, pornography, animal cruelty, scammers, lurkers, creepers, pervs, and every other kind of misdeed are regular problems for all forums on the internet, and games are no exception.

Most game publishers now have a "Trust and Safety" department dedicated to addressing just these kinds of business challenges. AI is playing a major role here already as well, identifying prohibited content and flagging it for human moderator review. Coming up with clear and transparent policies for warning players of prohibited behavior and taking action when necessary has significant costs – both financial and in human capital. (Content moderators have a very taxing job sometimes!)

As gaming communities get bigger and more socially interconnected, all of these challenges will become more pronounced and important. The need for social shepherds to ensure in-game and game-adjacent communities are healthy will grow over the next 20 years.

There are many opportunities here as well. Games have a great chance to look at player onboarding to make sure that new players are shown what good behavior looks like up front. There are opportunities for games to incentivize veteran players to help mentor and provide guidance to new players; such efforts could have very positive results on games. AI can help here as well, by pattern detecting certain types of behavior that is associated with deleterious or toxic players and introducing curbs to protect against it. Setting standards for letting players decide what types of interactions they are willing to allow with other players can go a long way here. So could voice chat with disguises so players' ages and genders and ethnicities can be easier to hide. Real-time filtering for hateful speech will continue to improve.

I expect that in coming years, we will see a Social Ranking Score (as explored in *Black Mirror*) become a sought after, carefully guarded, and hacked part of a player's online identity. Could this become as important as a credit score eventually? Maybe. As your online identity becomes an ever bigger part of how you see yourself and how the world sees you, it may become critical for it to be measured and protected.

In the next 20 years, we will see game makers and publishers need to devote an increasing amount of brainpower and capital to ensuring that player experiences are safe and rewarding, despite the mal intent of other players.

Q AND A WITH JEFF MAHER

VP Trust & Safety, Roblox

Roblox is an online platform that hosts immersive virtual experiences. Users customize wildly adaptable avatars and inhabit the virtual space, play games from other users or their own creations. The community dates from 2004 and succeeded by catering to children and young people, giving *Roblox* a prescient perspective on the safety, security, and privacy issues that loom over the internet today. Jeff Maher has worked there since 2017 and is currently head of Trust & Safety for *Roblox*.

Q. What's the biggest challenge you face today?

Jeff: Striking the right balance between privacy and security, which of course all social platforms struggle with. Most of the private sector is placing user privacy over security because it's a way to hold onto users and, to some extent, abdicate responsibility for your content. But *Roblox* wields a heavy hand in community moderation in the name of security and safety. The role we're trying to fulfill is to enable positive experiences online.

Q. How did you become the head Trust & Safety at Roblox?

Jeff: In my five years at *Roblox*, I've been fortunate to have some broad experience. I was head of analytics, then head of growth, and started teams devoted to growth marketing and product experimentation. In all those positions I faced a persistent challenge familiar to all online platforms: bots and spam polluting our user data. With some incredible engineers I launched a dedicated Bots & Spam team, which led to me running all of Trust & Safety.

Q. There's probably no aspect of internet life getting more scrutiny today. What does your job entail?

Jeff: User safety is absolutely paramount for us. The way we see it, when you unpack the word "safety," you get four major vectors. User safety is, broadly speaking, account integrity – seeing that our users are authentically who they claim to be, not bots or aliases. Number two, content safety, is about making sure *Roblox* assets are safe for our community members – elements like audio, images, or 3D mesh. Then there's communication safety, which focuses on the quality and appropriateness of all communication- primarily text and voice. Finally, we also work on behavioral safety, which covers abuse reports and flagging toxic behavior across our product.

In each of those four areas, we have amazing leaders who run large operations teams dedicated to moderation and customer support.

Q. There are about three billion gamers worldwide, and more joining. How has the entire world interacting online, gamers or not, made platform providers and content creators think differently about safety?

Jeff: What interests me is, online spaces are so new. We don't have well-defined rituals and standards for how to treat each other in virtual spaces. How to interact. In virtual worlds we don't have the benefit of thousands of years of cultural traditions and social norms telling us what is okay and what's not. We're defining the rules as we learn to occupy the space.

There are some positives to this state. A lot of social reflexes and biases in the real world that some might consider discriminatory don't necessarily exist at the same intensity online. But some of the social pressures that would normally discourage bad behavior, directly or indirectly? Those don't exist either.

We're thinking through how to establish *Roblox* cultural norms, and to what extent they ought to mirror norms in the real world. But as more people join the internet, greater need will emerge over time for platforms to do more to make sure everyone knows the rules of the space.

Q. Yet you and Roblox don't cope with bullying or hate-speech issues in nearly the volume faced by other social platforms.

Jeff: Because it's not tolerated on our platform. But on *Roblox* the real difference is the manner of expression. In a 3D environment you're able to express yourself in much richer fashion compared to lines of text, memes, gifs, or even short bursts of video – the languages of those other platforms. It's harder to walk up to someone else's avatar, or character, and tell them off or start a fight.

One of the unique things about so many people visiting *Roblox* immersive environments is, they pretty quickly take visual cues about how to behave. In this respect, we're closer to the real world than text- or emoji-based platforms where flame wars break out. If you and I were to meet in a foreign country, it would be really clear what environment we're in. In a café or on a farm we've never visited before, we can look around and understand the expectations. We'd see a lot of unspoken things telling us how to interact.

For the most part, you can figure out how to act by watching other people around you. And that's how richer expression works in favor of *Roblox* community harmony, where we want people to feel safe enough to express themselves.

Q. You formed a Bots & Spam team at Roblox, and we've seen the impact bots can have in social media discourse. And we expect that in coming years, non-human agents online will become increasingly sophisticated and indistinguishable from humans.

Jeff: If they aren't already!

Q: How do you think about the world of trust and safety when you're deal-ing with so many synthetic actors?

Jeff: The insight I arrived at with bots was, we should prioritize harm reduction. And not every bot is by definition harmful. So, if bots are good at imitating people, but you're good at moderating and stopping harmful situations, how much do you care if it's a bot or a human? Where's the harm, and how do we make sure that it's always minimized or eliminated. Certainly transparency about when you're dealing with a bot would help.

Q. It raises some good philosophical questions.

Jeff: Sure. Should bots be required to identify themselves when interact-ing with humans? Even when they're benign, or might qualify as community features, should we limit their interaction with humans in some way? Already in the world of online customer service, AI-enabled chatbots are everywhere. Perhaps there's a safe way to have them populate our community, too. I look for-ward to trying to work through these problems in the next few years.

Q. Back to the question of regulating the behavior of real people. Online anonymity seems to encourage people to act differently. It's been suggested that doing away with it would make the internet more civil. India is moving in this direction, rolling out a digital ID requirement. Will anonymity wane elsewhere?

Jeff: It's already happening internationally. Korea has a real-ID system, mostly used in PC games. China has WeChat, authenticated using real names. I think a lot of the West kind of gets away with preserving social-platform anonymity because Facebook and Google logins are connected to your real identity, and they have a high-fidelity understanding of who you are. It's the data basis for algorithm-based advertising.

It's tempting to conclude that verifying everyone would result in more appropriate behavior. But I don't think getting rid of anonymity would drive as dramatic a reduction in toxicity as people believe. It's certainly a piece of the puzzle, but not the whole puzzle. Twitter released an interesting study about hate speech during the World Cup, which said most of the bad speech came from people who are verified users. And everyone has an example of some problematic relative on social media who makes extreme comments using their full name.

That said, I do think that in the next 10–20 years, we're bound to see less anonymity on the internet. If a business knows who you are, it can provide offers and services you're more likely to appreciate. You can host safer community experiences, because with more verification, you can hold people accountable if they behave poorly, or because you know their age.

That goes for *Roblox* too. Given more identity information, we could unlock better experiences for people. The more you know about users, the more you can use that information for good, especially when it comes to keeping them safe. I think it'll always be optional, but no matter how much data we might leverage, we won't ease up on moderating the environment and making clear what's not okay.

Q. *From the company's earliest days you focused on the needs of children. How does that experience help now?*

Jeff: Our role in children's lives is always top of mind-even as we age up or become age agnostic on our platform, we know kids will continue to engage with *Roblox* experiences When you've been solving for the hardest use case for a long time, making safety and security for kids our first priority, over time that priority becomes integral to your approach. I think that puts us in a better position to deal with today's challenges compared to a platform that stuck with a more hands-off, user-beware strategy – and now might be struggling to implant better safety standards.

Q. *Some say rising public concern about internet privacy means a comeback for so-called "walled gardens" online – that is, protected environments that are theoretically safer. Do you agree, and would you call Roblox a walled garden?*

Jeff: I really wouldn't. *Roblox* is community-powered and wants to remain that way. The problem with walled-garden environments is, sooner or later they become more subject to the laws and edicts from the platform authorities than the community itself. On *Roblox* everyone can create and share their own experiences and content. Almost anyone can join *Roblox* and be an experience-maker. That's wonderful for our users, but it doesn't align well with a centralized approach.

Q. *It's an incredibly complex game environment you describe – and you're assigned to moderate it and keep it safe. It's only going to grow more complex. How do you think about this problem?*

Jeff: I think *Roblox* would say we're not limiting ourselves to gaming in a traditional sense. We're a human co-experience platform. We've been surprised over and over by the incredible creativity of the *Roblox* community. Things we wouldn't traditionally label as games become very popular experiences on *Roblox*. In many ways, this is the magic of *Roblox*, and it's what keeps us coming back to extend the platform.

What will our users build next, and how will we make sure their contributions stay safe and appropriate for an increasingly diverse community? It's a problem without an end, and we believe it's much bigger than developing rules for games. It's something much closer to a full, virtual human experience.

A huge challenge, but one my colleagues and I are passionate about working on – now more than ever.

NON-GAMING ACTIVITIES IN GAMES

Anyone paying attention to the gaming space over the last few years will have noticed a strong effort by a few companies to bring non-gaming activities, like virtual concerts, into their games. Epic's *Fortnite* is the best known example of this to date. In late summer of 2021 Pop icon Ariana Grande hosted a concert experience in *Fortnite* called the Rift Tour.

In this time limited event, *Fortnite* users on PC, Xbox, PlayStation, or their mobile phones were able to log in and dance, surf, and explore beautifully crafted and highly dynamic soundscapes while a giant avatar of the performer sang and gyrated high above them like a goddess. Around the same time, the pop band Coldplay performed a set in a virtual online interactive space called Joytopia, sponsored by auto manufacturer BMW.[24]

Shortly thereafter, *Roblox* hosted *World Party* in conjunction with Electric Daisy Carnival, a massive Las Vegas EDM dance festival held every year. With a giant virtual festival ground, *Roblox* allowed users of all ages from around the world to attend a "live" and virtual music festival of the type previously only available to adults with significant disposable income. In their words:

> In partnership with Wonder Works Studio, creators of the top experience Overlook Bay, EDC on *Roblox* will feature five 'party all-night tents' inspired by this year's festival theme with over 50 artists — including Kaskade, Zedd, Alison Wonderland, Kygo, Louis the Child, Slander b2b2 said the sky, Rezz, Loud Luxury,

DJ Snake, Alan Walker, Phantoms, Wax Motif, Oliver Heldens, and Benny Benassi — streaming their performances across virtual stages.[25]

Wave, an Austin, Texas based company has long been a proponent of similar technology, but focused on more immersive events (called "Waves") which span platforms and can be accessed from other worlds, like *Roblox*, but also YouTube, Twitch, and customized for VR headsets. One part trippy animation visualizer, one part electronica concert, one part video game, these Waves provide a good insight into what shared entertainment experiences of the future will be for millions.

The appeal of this kind of event should be immediately apparent. While some of the excitement of physical presence will clearly be lacking, so was the debatable pleasure of standing in long lines for porta-potties. For parents, a sanitized version of a festival atmosphere allows children to explore and enjoy without the risk, and in a time of endemic disease millions of people who may not feel safe in crowds can experience some of the sense of participating in a communal event. Finally, and obviously, while even the most well run festival ground can only accommodate a few hundred thousand guests, a virtual event can scale almost indefinitely. For users, tech companies, festival promoters, and the performers themselves, this is a winning partnership. We should expect these sorts of events to regularly – without fail – be significantly better attended than the "real-world" versions thereof. And, of course, these types of events can allow every online fan to have personalized, bespoke encounters with their favorite celebrity stars; imagine online contests allowing a winner – or a concert in which every single fan – got to see a beloved KPop idol serenade them personally while everyone else in the virtual space appeared to be watching and applauding. Now imagine selling NFT "photos" of this special celebrity meeting for the fan to display in their online home alongside their NFT ticket-stub. Does this capture the joy and energy of Woodstock or the first Lollapalooza? Perhaps not... To generations that didn't grow up with this kind of interaction; but likely these sorts of experiences will increasingly supplement real-world large gatherings.

What does this have to do with the evolution of game design? Because giving people ways to engage the world and game software without having to necessarily participate in the core loop or the primary activities the game provides can massively expand the audience for a game. Creating a "sandbox" in which users can create and find their own fun has been a fundamental design element of highly social games, particularly some MMOs for 20 years now. But the increase in player diversity, device input models which aren't at parity (keyboard and mouse vs. touchscreen input, for example), and the ascendancy of free-to-play gaming makes the "sandbox design" mentality more important now. This will continue to increase in value as games become less about showing up and doing a particular thing and more about providing a social space for players to get together.

For years, social games have gone out of their way to give different players different ways to engage. Early party-based MMORPGs allowed for support classes like healers. More nuanced ones like Star Wars Galaxies sought to allow players to be traders, dancers, and cooks, as well as delivering more traditional fantasy fulfillment by letting players be bounty hunters or Jedi. Even hardcore pay-to-win games like *Game of War* allowed for some players to act as "bankers" for an Alliance, eschewing combat altogether. The more social a game is, the more important it is to allow for people to play in different ways; many players will be there primarily (only!) for the social connection to alliances or guildmates.

With games that are deeply social, in which we are trying to attract a wide array of players, it can be very useful to allow players some level of customization of a home space. MySpace got this very early on in the social networking game. Games followed suit shortly thereafter. From early social games like Habbo Hotel to early MMORPGs like *Ultima Online* (or the more recent incarnation of a similar experience, *Shadows of the Avatar* by Lord British and team) allowing players to build and show off their own home area is a great way to encourage them to engage with the game. *Farmville* did very well by applying basic Appointment Mechanics, simple player to player gifting and trading, and the ability to visit other users' farms.

It would appear that Meta, Facebook's entry into creating shared 3D virtual spaces, is likely to capitalize on this game-design standard. While on some level this could be seen as little more than an extension of MySpace or Facebook home pages into a 3D environment, I believe there is more to it. By allowing players to build out a space which is uniquely theirs and encourage visitors, game designers can mimic critical human desires and fantasies which are separate from the core loop motivations of many games, but fit nicely inside many. Player Avatars, companions, voices, home areas, calling cards, etc. should all be customizable. Bespoke content tailored for and by each player in the way that social media backgrounds are will end up being a huge part of games for millions. Indeed, this is likely one of the areas it will be the easiest to get large gamer populations to pay for.

As interconnectedness and AI agency increase we will see the ability to craft player home spaces with realistic avatars of characters, loved ones, heroes or celebrities they admire. With increasingly immersive ways of engaging with these shared personal spaces, we will see a great deal of emergent social behavior. Add player driven trading, sales and display of NFT assets ("Check out my framed NFT ticket from when I attended the *Roblox* EDC 2026 festival!") and the ability to display them in virtual spaces within games or more overarching Metaverses, and we will begin to see new types of player-created economies and perhaps even games which emerge from the combination of these elements.

Q AND A WITH GAGAN AHLUWALIA OF GLOBALSTEP: THE FUTURE OF SERVICES

Gagan Ahluwalia is the CEO of GlobalStep, a production services firm that supports the entire game life cycle from its studios in North America, Europe and Asia.

TF: Hello, Gagan. What do you believe the future holds for the gaming services business?

Gagan: So Tim, as I look at it, the first thing I try and always put in my mind is to ensure there is some kind of an analytical framework to be able to analyze the situation properly.

For me, I look at your question about the future through these frameworks: What are the platforms of the future? What are the enabling technologies of the future? What are the economic models of the future for gaming? And then, what is it that a services company needs to do support partners in this world?

So, let me take them one by one. First, the platform. As you're looking 20 years into the future, I definitely feel that the Metaverse is going to play a very big role in the platform of the future. That kind of brings us to the question, "How would I define the Metaverse?" And today, there are as many definitions as there are the people who think profoundly about it.

So as I look at it, very simply, I would regard it as the tissue that connects the virtual and the real worlds. So, one implication of that is all the hardware, you know, the consoles, the headsets, whatever ways that we have in the real world of interfacing with the virtual world. Then there is networked technology with great connectivity. There is all the hardware that makes every user experience, and the manifestations of that experience possible.

Another way that I look at the Metaverse is, potentially, a way to connect different universes, so you can have a world in one game. If you are a studio with 15 games, potentially, the Metaverse is a way to connect all of them and bring them into one ecosystem. Something that we are not very great at as an industry, but may potentially evolve to is many different universes sharing a common Metaverse or the Metaverse being a platform in which many developers without the resources to create their own complete worlds can participate.

And things will get connected inside one closed ecosystem of multiple worlds or an open ecosystem of many different independent worlds inside a Metaverse... The connectivity, the portability, the transferability between these are all issues that we don't deal with today, which will become very important in the coming years.

Just the scope and the magnitude of what we are looking at is immense. I would say that, for me, the enabling technologies required are, to a large extent, AI-based. They are based on data science, automation, predictive analytics, and a lot of things that we are spending time doing manually today. We will rely on these enabling technologies, and we will be spending our time on the next level issues, next layer challenges.

The third thing that I look at in the framework is the economic model.

Tim: Tell us your thoughts on the economics of the future of the games business and these Metaverses.

Gagan: So, you know, our initial framework was pay-to-play. That was the consumer-packaged-goods model. From there we evolved into the games-as-a-service and subscription models. Of these, the dominant one has been the free-to-play model, which relies on immense player engagement and the stickiness comes over time as players invest more and more time and money into a game.

The challenge still remains, that all that money and time that's invested in a game is only in that game. If that game sunsets tomorrow, that's a lost chunk of time and money from a player standpoint. Which gets us to the third model, which is play to earn. Right now, this is reliant on NFTs. There is a reliance on players potentially owning assets that they either buy or they mine or they create through gameplay.

This creates some interesting parameters: If you look at the overall platform, "Who captures the economic rent of the Metaverse? The economic rent of the game? The economic rent of the artifacts of the game?"

So all of that economic model will shake itself out. But nonetheless, if you just look at some games and see, you know, how things are shaping up. Let's say farmers in *Axie Infinity* or *Cryptokittes*... So, one potential model, is that you buy in to gain assets. Or you mine them, you embellish them, you grow them, you can potentially sell them.

So how is the game economy going to make money? There's the old traditional model, but in a new model where someone's paying a lot of money to invest into a game that they can potentially pull out of a game. And then there is the transfer of assets within game that you may sell to someone else, or you may even sell it outside the game to someone else. And that's the transaction fee model.

So, one thing that becomes very different is that now a lot of money may be held within the game, which is not potentially revenue to the game but are assets held within the game. Is that going to be a banking model or a stockbroker model? And there are connotations to both of them. Then in the gameplay experience, when real transferable money that can both enter and exit a game becomes involved, trust becomes a very, very important factor.

There is the underlying trust of the technology. There must be an underlying trust of the economic model, the framework. The level of trust in the reliability that the money is an investment and you can take it out and it hasn't been required until now.

So this is the intersection, I feel of entertainment, a regulatory environment that has connotations of the banking environment we will encounter. And I feel that for a services company there is also a significant investment needed in R&D.

If I have not got the experience to develop a game using blockchain technology... From the outside, it may be very hard for me to envision all the test cases. All the ways to test it. And for the production company of the future, the company must have a brand that lends credibility to the game economies, as it becomes involved with the game economies.

So this is the framework that, I think, as I end up to the future that I see has to be taken into account in fashioning and shaping the response of the capabilities that we at Globalstep feel that we need to have. And it's a very evolving scenario, but this is the framework that I'm using.

Tim: I very much appreciate the thesis you've described. You have an extremely clear vision of what you believe is coming. What are the specific areas of expertise that services companies, like Globalstep who are leaders in the space, should focus on over the next five years to prepare them for the coming 20?

Gagan: So, Tim. The first thing that I feel we have to prepare for is understanding that everything has been done in the current model of work. That it we will need to transform and transition to AI-based technology, to predictive analytics, and to automation. So specifically, what does that mean? Today, we have...

There are probably millions of defects in the database. I think that through data science and predictive analytics it is absolutely possible to come out with – in an automated fashion – with all the test cases that need to be deployed with minor tweaking on things that are very new game specific.

And all of those things, if those inputs are fed in properly, is one specific thing that can be automated. Predictive Analytics on time to completion, time to market, development efforts. So, these are all technologies that have to be put in place in the next five years.

And with the amount of data that's available, better and more intelligent connectivity between player experience and game evolution and game development.

So, if there's an existing game, how does the game development roadmap evolve based on what we learn about player preferences? And how can that be intuitively automated and fed into the product evolution roadmap? I think that this is something that in the next five years will have to happen.

Then there is the project that you actually embarked on, I think three or four years ago. If you know the test cases, why not program them into your game engine code? So that, as you are coding, you are testing for what the game is supposed to do and the outcome that this code is supposed to produce.

I think all of these things that are talked about will become mainstream and they will totally and profoundly change how it would have been done today inside of game companies.

Tim: Is there anything else that you would like to add to game industry professionals or for those who are just starting to get their foot in the door? Any message you would like to convey to games industry of the future?

Gagan: So I think that what we define as an immersive experience... The definition of that is ever-evolving and ever-changing because the environment in which that immersive experience occurs is always changing.

A very simple example, you can have game artifacts and now you have an avatar. Across you may even be using it for a future Zoom meeting. And using all of your assets – maybe clothing, maybe hats, whatever.

So the fusion of the real world and the virtual world and the entertainment experience is an evolving definition. And at the end of the day, everything that we've discussed is important, but we have to remember that what it feels like and what's at the heart of it is an engaging, immersive entertainment experience. And that is the basic economic model. And that's the fun fact.

As we go through everything changing around us, we have to recognize that in our industry, this is the constant, unchanging fact. The core of the experience must be engaging and immersive entertainment. And how that unchanging principle evolves and how we relate to it, will separate the winners from the losers.

EDUCATION AND GAMING

Another area of convergence between gaming and other types of digital interaction which we should expect to blow up is the intersection between gaming entertainment and education. Since Math Blaster by Jan Davidson in 1983, educators have recognized that making learning more entertaining by couching it within games can help increase student engagement. But in a world where "gamification" of everything from treadmills to insurance policies has become popular the opportunities in education are still nascent. The Covid19 pandemic of 2020 threw students around the world into online only education before the education system was ready for it. (The technology of tens of millions of simultaneous Zooms held up well, but the ability for teachers, curriculums, parents, and the students themselves to make the most of this was limited in most countries to say the least.) However, it is clear that we now have the ability to offer education remotely, digitally. While not all of the impact of a great teacher-student relationship can be realized with full remote learning, the advantages for millions of students without access to safe classrooms or qualified teachers is clear. And AI teachers aren't yet a reality, but they assuredly will be over the coming decade. Couple these factors with heavy gamification of educational curriculums and software platforms which make them accessible to students on all the devices and networks they are already using, and there's a real chance for gaming and education to combine forces to dramatically improve the way we educate young people the world over.

Indeed, some game and toy companies have already pivoted into this space with some promising early results. One of these is Sphero,[26] once better known for building the BB8 home robot companion toy. Now Sphero is focused on an application and education system which promises to use home robotics to teach and educate young people on STEM type educational initiatives. Other companies are following suit.

Many of the systems designs common in RPGs and the notion of intent-driven design and UX optimization could pay huge dividends to education. Gaming and education have long flirted with partnership, but over the next two decades we should expect to see many of the bright lines between the two become blurred.

WRAP UP IN THE FUTURE OF GAME DESIGN

The reasons people play games do not change much because they speak to core human needs, desires for expression, various types of fantasy fulfillment, and ways to idle away the time pleasantly. However, the changes to our connected ecosystems and cross-genre applications and recombinations of some particular design techniques show us the way toward game experiences that can engage and connect millions of gamers who might not have been interested or able to participate in decades past. As these technical, social, economic, and design elements are combined, we begin to see the world not as a collection of individual games, but as a canvas of game experiences. As the democratization of tools allows millions of players to begin to create their own games, objects, characters, and playscapes we can see the outline of a true Metaverse canvas begin to take shape.

NOTES

1 https://apps.quanticfoundry.com/.
2 https://www.amazon.com/Theory-Game-Design-Raph-Koster/dp/1449363210.
3 https://www.nintendo.co.uk/Iwata-Asks/Iwata-Asks-SUPER-MARIO-3D-LAND/Vol-1-SUPER-MARIO-3D-LAND/7-Advanced-Players-Do-the-Long-Jump/7-Advanced-Players-Do-the-Long-Jump-217120.html.
4 https://www.pocketgamer.biz/news/77601/frogmind-rebrands-hypehype-supercell-invests-15-million/.
5 https://www.pcgamer.com/how-many-frames-per-second-can-the-human-eye-really-see/.
6 https://www.youtube.com/watch?v=BnSUk0je6oo.
7 https://www.gamesindustry.biz/articles/2021-11-08-vr-to-be-a-usd51bn-market-by-2030-says-globaldata.
8 https://www.vrdirect.com/blog/vr-for-training-hr/five-companies-that-are-using-vr-for-training/.
9 https://venturebeat-com.cdn.ampproject.org/c/s/venturebeat.com/2021/12/31/the-deanbeat-predictions-for-gaming-2022/amp/.
10 https://www.morningbrew.com/emerging-tech/stories/2021/12/10/roblox-s-metaverse-is-already-here-and-it-s-wildly-popular.
11 https://www.economist.com/china/2022/02/04/building-a-metaverse-with-chinese-characteristics.
12 https://www.unrealengine.com/en-US/solutions/film-television.
13 https://venturebeat.com/2021/11/09/nvidias-omniverse-adds-ar-vr-viewing-ai-training-and-ai-avatar-creation/.
14 https://venturebeat.com/2022/01/04/nvidia-unveils-free-version-of-omniverse-for-millions-of-creators-and-artists/.
15 https://venturebeat.com/2021/11/09/nvidias-omniverse-adds-ar-vr-viewing-ai-training-and-ai-avatar-creation/.
16 https://venturebeat.com/2021/11/19/the-deanbeat-building-the-metaverse-for-free/.
17 https://itone.lu/news/facebook-to-hire-10000-in-eu-to-help-build-the-metaverse.

18 https://www.forbes.com/sites/moorinsights/2021/04/06/why-microsoft-won-the-22-billion-army-HoloLens-2-ar-deal.

19 https://venturebeat.com/2022/01/06/samsung-takes-a-stab-at-its-own-immersivc-metaverse-store/.

20 https://venturebeat-com.cdn.ampproject.org/c/s/venturebeat.com/2021/12/31/the-deanbeat-predictions-for-gaming-2022/amp/.

21 https://www.theverge.com/22338418/dream-smp-youtube-minecraft-fanart-fanfiction-video-edits-fandom.

22 https://economictimes.indiatimes.com/tech/internet/covid-19-lockdown-accelerate-online-gaming/articleshow/75640044.cms

23 https://www.nytimes.com/2021/12/29/business/discord-server-social-media.html.

24 https://www.youtube.com/watch?v=TMWvFxs_YIM&t=21s.

25 https://corp.roblox.com/2021/10/electric-daisy-carnival-becomes-first-music-festival-roblox-metaverse/.

26 https://edu.sphero.com/.

CHAPTER 4

Web 3 Gaming

Crypto, Play to Earn, NFT

> It was difficult to transact legitimate business with cash in the Sprawl;
> in Japan, it was already illegal.
>
> – *William Gibson's* Neuromancer, *1981*

Thus far it's all been pretty straightforward. Draw a line through all of the critically important or top grossing games over the last 20 years, then squint and extend that line another twenty into the future. Add in a dose of speculation and extrapolation, and there we have it. But there is a new force in gaming that has taken hold of popular narrative and imaginations over the last year, and we need to explore it. Because many people seem to believe this will change the future trajectory of finance, human society at large, and certainly gaming.

About a decade ago an anonymous creator (or creators) who went by the pseudonym Satoshi Nakamoto published a whitepaper on the concept of blockchain technology, and along with it the idea for Bitcoin. As of the beginning of 2022 this person's identity is still unknown. Blockchains are a mathematical concept designed to address the problem of trust in networks, in which any link along a network could potentially be compromised. By distributing copies of updates to a ledger to each node of a network nodes which are attempting to introduce a datapoint that doesn't match others will be revealed to be false. The resulting decentralized ledger is the fundamental principal behind modern crypto-currency, decentralized finance, and Non-Fungible-Tokens (NFTs).

According to many, this allows individuals to engage in transactions with the trust of the ledger, rather than having to trust in corporations or governments to verify identity or the veracity of a trade. The degree to which this clever new paradigm for thinking about trust in a networked environment will truly revolutionize the internet, gaming, finance, and society remains to be seen. But it certainly has generated a massive amount of hype, huge rafts of investment in new technology, and to many it points the way for a new era of software, including games.

As a quick word of warning: This section is likely to satisfy almost no one. If you are already well steeped in chains, NFT assets, staking currencies, and the rest then these explanations will probably seem unbearably trivial; within a few years this may well read like a 1990 mainstream press article trying to describe the potential of the Web using phrases like "information superhighway." If you're a traditional video game maker or new to the space, then this section is likely to read as cloyingly full of jargon and arcana. In either case, given the incredibly rapid evolution of this area of human enterprise, this section will likely end up being (hopefully) charmingly dated within a few years. Such is the risk of discussing the cutting edge in print.

CRYPTO-CURRENCY, DECENTRALIZED FINANCE, NON-FUNGIBLE TOKENS, AND GAMING

From Blockchain, Bitcoin, Etherium, Tokenomics, BOO tokens, governance tokens, Axies, staking, Spookyswap, gas fees, compounding farms, thousands of different crypto-currencies, multiple layers of the chain (both "on" and "off"),.jpg files of 8-bit apes going for millions of dollars' worth of tokens, and a whole new vernacular to learn… Well, you can be forgiven for not exactly knowing what to make of it all. Frankly, in 2022 the world of crypto-gaming is very complex, and intentionally disorganized. Add to it a certain type of day-trader mentality and an incredibly rapidly evolving space, and many game makers and gamers cannot help but wonder if this is really something their games need.

There are a few arguments which are most commonly used to explain why a world of NFTs is valuable to gamers. First, there's an argument that players will prefer games in which they can "own" digital assets (their kingdom, a magic sword, etc.). The idea is that because them taking possession of an asset is stored on a decentralized ledger they aren't reliant upon whatever game company pays for the servers to maintain a record of that ownership. And this is true, for whatever value that has. Then, provided the rules of a game allow it, they can sell that asset to another user, or buy assets from another user rather than having to grind for them in a game or pay the company who made the game for them. This could be true if the game economy were set up that way. (Which would also be the case in any more traditional models; there's nothing in this design that requires decentralized ledgers.) Decentralized ledgers are seen as extending product life, because there's no way a single company or creator can decide to wipe the servers. This is true… Excepting that unless all of the game and client code exist in this fashion, there still is someone running it. This is where the Distributed Autonomous Organization (DAO) argument usually comes in, arguing that the community themselves can own and run the game using smart contracts. I do find it likely that some games will be created in this fashion, though it still relies on some actual humans doing the actual hard work of building and maintaining the game. (A Kickstarter page alone does not make a game, even with lots of funding pledged; individuals still have to build it!)

To summarize, enthusiasts believe that blockchain games can allow users more control over their digital assets and can free games from the tyranny of control by their creators. And they may even be right, so long as the software is created with this in mind. And provided we can solve some of the challenges with distributed ledger security, regulation, energy efficiency, scalability, and speed of this new tech.

Games like *CryptoKitties* and *NBA Top Shot* by Dapper Labs have generated a lot of interest and made a lot of money, creating a 2021 gold rush into the crypto-gaming space. Most of what is sold, and most of what people find interesting about these games are in the concept of NFTs. Indeed, this has provoked enough interest that corporations outside of the tech space, like shoe manufacturer Nike who recently has begun preparing to protect their trademarks and consider selling virtual apparel as NFTs.[1]

At the moment, the true volume of users engaging with the cryptocurrency space remains fairly low. On December 22, 2021, for example, fewer than one million active users engaged across the world's seven top blockchain currencies.[2] And many of these are likely bots. This puts the total number of humans engaged in this space still lower than would be required to be a top 20 mobile game, at least by volume. There are two ways to interpret this data. The first would be to proclaim that this is really a nice fad, popular among so called "cryptobros" and few others. The other way to look at it is that this represents a nascent space, ripe with opportunity.

Certainly human's relationship with currencies has changed over time in the gaming space. For example, in 1985 arcades ruled the gaming sector, gobbling up millions of quarters so users could play games like *Pac-Man*, *Centipede*, and *Yi-Ar Kung Fu*. But go try to play any modern game using a quarter today and you won't get far. The COVID-19 pandemic pushed many societies to take another step away from accepting physical currencies, moving to touchless credit transactions. And many of those who are bullish on crypto-currencies believe that the death-knell is currently sounding for government issued fiat-currencies. Is it possible that purely decentralized crypto-currency could become the primary (or only) mechanism for transacting with game economies within the next twenty years?[3] Yes. That's possible.

Studios like DapperLabs, based in Vancouver, British Columbia in Canada creators of *CryptoKitties*, and *NBA Top Shot*, games which were early experiments in gaming on blockchains have seen their valuation soar into the billions over the last few years. Zynga, Square-Enix, Ubisoft, Electronic Arts have all declared their intent to integrate NFT and blockchain systems into games. Suddenly there are few game companies who are not at least evaluating how to approach this wild new world powered by innovating mathematics, the hope for a different social order, and a strong appetite for cashing in on a new gold rush.

Since most of the games which make use of these technologies and currencies attract users based on the promise of earning crypto-currencies through play, let's start there.

NFT BASICS

If you were in the games business in 2021, you couldn't help but suddenly be bombarded by stories and true believers declaring that "NFTs" were the future of gaming. This is based on a trend that has been building for a couple of years but really entered the mainstream vernacular in 2021. While at the time of writing it remains too early to tell if these predictions will prove true, there is certainly some level of directional accuracy to them. Digital assets have been the backbone of free-to-play game economies for almost a decade now. So what's different? Where is this trend likely going?

Blockchain technology has been around about a decade but has truly risen to a place of prominence (and massive investment) within the last 36 months. Decentralized finance and currencies and contracts stored and executed on chains which use variants of these innovations are multiplying at an incredible rate; indeed, many people believe that this technology will introduce the next step of human social evolution, transforming societies as profoundly as the shekels of Mesopotamia, widely believed to be the first portable unit of currency used in generic value exchange. Deep discussion of blockchain, crypto-currencies, decentralized finance, and its impacts are well beyond the scope of this book. (Plus, you've got loads of other places to read about all that.) So, let's focus on how it is impacting, and may impact games and game development in the future.

NFT stands for non-fungible token. An NFT represents a unique digital asset – an image, an audio-clip, a 3D model, or similar. An NFT is a token which can be owned, traded, bought or sold. A ledger of the creation of the asset, each transactions and the history of ownership is stored on a blockchain. Typically, people use different crypto-currencies (Ethereum, Fantom coins, or hundreds of others) to trade NFTs. Often the NFTs have built in contractual transaction conditions by which the original creator will earn a portion of the sale. Digital artwork and other digital assets are traded on marketplaces like OpenSea, Paintswap, or many others. The original digital asset can live on a chain itself, or the NFT can simply be a reference to a file on a server somewhere. Effectively, an NFT is a way of verifying ownership of an asset which could otherwise be replicated an unlimited number of times, and in so doing ensuring scarcity of the original.

Mooncats are an example of a collection of early NFT assets. In practice, these allow users to buy ("foster"), sell, name, and trade cute cat icons that exist only in limited amounts (Figure 4.1).

FIGURE 4.1 Mooncats are an example of a popular and cute early NFT. (*Image Credit:* Mooncatrescue *by ponderware.*)

For games, this allows for a user to buy, win, trade, or create something that then has perceived value (resulting from scarcity) that can exist within the game. For many users, this scarcity creates the perception of additional value. When coupled with marketplaces that allow users to trade these items (either for in game currency or some external currency), this allows for digital only assets with potentially very high value. Many of these NFTs can also be sold on external marketplaces outside of the games, further increasing their perceived value.

From a total estimated value of roughly $3 million in June 2020, the total market value of all existing NFTs has grown to an estimated $14 billion by October 2021 according to the Economist, which magazine auctioned off the art for their cover story on NFTs in late October 2021.

NFTS AS THE FUTURE

There are many people who believe that NFTs are the future of gaming. Newsletters like Bankless tout the superiority of NFTs as a way for players to take control and ownership over game economies, all with a certain "fight the man" mentality that suggests that buying digital assets which are associated with a distributed ledger is somehow associated with overthrowing corporate tyranny. In November 2021, Electronic Arts CEO Andrew Wilson said, "NFTs are an important part of the future of our industry," but further cautioned that it was "really early" and "a certain amount of hype." But with millions of dollars of venture capital investment pouring into the space, led by well-respected VC firms like Andreessen Horowitz (aka a16z), there is almost no leader in the games industry who is allowed to ignore this trend completely at this point.

NFTS AS SNAKE OIL OR DIGITAL DUTCH TULIP CRAZE

Not everyone is convinced that NFTs are actually the wave of the future though. As the amount of real capital tied up in tokens – either in games or in simple standalone tokens – has increased into the millions, there are plenty of voices decrying these as a scam. (Comparisons to the "Dutch Tulip Mania" are rampant, in which speculation on the value of some fashionable tulip bulbs in the 1630s in Holland reached astronomical levels before crashing back to the well tilled soil in which they were planted. This is widely regarded as the first "speculative bubble.") Others suggest darker forces than mere speculation, accusing the markets themselves of perpetuating widespread fraud or being used primarily for money laundering.

(For example, a recent article by *Nature Magazine*[4] performed an analysis of 6.1 million trades of 4.7 million NFTs total, and concluded that the top 10% of traders have traded 97% of NFTs. This argues somewhat persuasively that a lot of NFT trades are wash sales intended to artificially boost prices.)

The argument against NFTs is generally based on the notion that they have no tangible value, and exist only as entries in a database. Then, since the sale and purchase prices of these assets are publicly tracked, while the identity of the buyers and sellers are largely anonymous, critics suggest that a small number of bad actors are regularly buying up the value of their own assets, then selling them to a sucker for a price far higher than would have been otherwise realized. (This practice is known as "wash trading" and is mostly illegal.) Since the entire world of crypto-currencies and NFTs is presently still almost completely unregulated by design, it is likely that many of these criticisms are accurate. Environmental concerns over the power used to drive the computing power that verifies ledger transactions on complex chains like Ethereum form a second common complaint. The third complaint seems to be able to be summarized as, "You're trying to sell us jpegs! That's bullshit."

Still though, many things (including digital assets sold in games for a long time) have value only because others impart value to them. And so, NFTs are very probably here to stay for a long time, though they are likely to morph into arenas – like games – in which the value of the tokenized asset has some context inside of a different meta-system. In other words, a magic sword whose owner receives great powers inside a multiplayer game is more likely to retain value than an image of an eight-bit cat, because it allows the owner to do something others cannot inside the artificial construct of a game, rather than just to have bragging rights.

For this reason, I suspect that while many people may cool on the idea of simply owning NFT images, NFTs in the context of some games will likely remain popular from now on.

AXIE INFINITY

One example of a blockchain driven crypto-currency fueled game that has taken the world by surprise in the last year is *Axie Infinity* by Sky Mavis, a game development studio based in Vietnam. *Axie Infinity* allows players to purchase creatures called Axies – *Pokémon* style characters – each of whom are a semi-unique NFT asset. Players purchase these Axies using the popular Etherium crypto-currency, then raise and battle them against other players. The creatures can then be traded on open markets. Within 12 months of being founded, the game had raised enough venture capital from celebrated investors like Mark Cuban and Andreessen Horowitz to qualify for a $3 billion dollar valuation in early 2021.

Moreover, as an indicator of how fast this space is evolving, recent articles suggest that *Axie Infinity* could deliver $1.2 billion dollars a year in gross revenue.[5] This would put it above top grossing games like King's *Candy Crush Saga*, though not quite at the heights of the new eight-hundred pound gorilla of cross-platform mobile gaming, *Genshin Impact* (which reported over $340M gross in September 2021 alone).

Now, this kind of annualized run rate presumes a lot. First, it presumes that users will retain over time and continue spending at this $2,000 per user level annually; this is a big presumption. Second, this revenue per user is reported in USD, but unlike Candy Crush this is money spent in crypto-currencies. Specifically, users are spending AXS, a custom crypto-currency they buy into using Ethereum, Bitcoin, or other currencies. As you can see from the 2021 YTD chart below, this currency experiences incredible volatility. This concept is important because (as detractors are quick to point out) Pay-to-Earn gaming inherently combines some of the high-octane elements of day trading with whatever thrill the game itself offers; users' earnings are subject to high volatility and have something of the flavor of a fad driven stock craze or pyramid scheme (Figure 4.2).

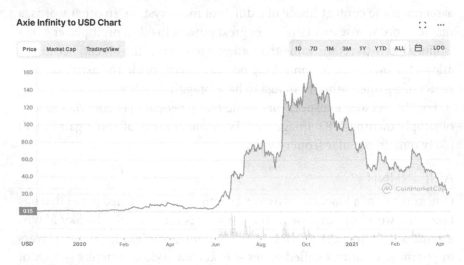

FIGURE 4.2 The currency value of games like *Axie Infinity* can be subject to great market volatility. (*Image Credit:* Coinmarketcap.com.)

PLAY TO EARN

More interesting than the rapid increase in value though is the way players from emerging nations – the Philippines in particular, have flocked to the game as a way of earning revenue, causing a number of journalists to speak of the game as the first major example of the new "Play to Earn" economy.

While *Axie Infinity* is a relatively simple train & battle game mechanic (think *Pokémon*), we can easily extend the core concept into other game design models. The general notion provides an interesting roadmap for player driven game economies of the future, and works like this:

There are two primary economy design models that seem well suited for Pay-to-Earn economies in games. In the *Axie Infinity* model, which is the most common today, players can purchase or play to win prizes or digital goods which can then be sold on a marketplace. By investing time, money, or both, they hope to generate assets of greater value that can then be sold to another player for more.

A second model involves the same core idea, but also allows players to pay one another for in game services.

Players participate in games at a high level of play to win either bragging rights or prizes which have real cash value. Because these games can be multiplayer and sometimes require coordinated team play to win, wealthy players – or just those from geographies where they have access to far greater disposable income than other players in poorer countries – may choose to spend to become more powerful. By building up and then selling items, or by offering their in-game services, gamers with access to less disposable income may find that gaming can generate more money per hour than other jobs available in the region.

Let's imagine a hypothetical example in which a person in Lagos, Nigeria, where the minimum wage is less than $75 USD per month begins playing a popular free-to-play first-person shooter game on their mobile device.

High-quality Samsung, Huawei, and Xiaomi phones running Android operating systems are the most common devices in Nigeria today, all more than capable of playing most popular shooters beautifully. And while bandwidth is quite spotty throughout the country today, we can expect at least 5G in all the major cities within ten years. With unemployment in the country hovering around 30%, finding time to play is seldom a problem. And with a population expected to double from 200 million in 2020 to 400 million by 2040, the number of young gamers will soon be significant.

Before long, our hypothetical player is VERY good at the game, and is farming out his services as an in-game bodyguard, expert sniper, and mercenary for hire. For less than $0.50 an hour USD, this player can be hired to join the squads of players with more money but less skill. By so doing, they can earn more than a standard wage in a country where jobs that pay like this are in high demand.

Gamers in wealthier markets have already proven to be more than comfortable spending in this fashion even to advance themselves in games with no real-money prizes. (Chinese gold farmers changed the economies of several popular Massively Multiplayer Online Role Playing Games in the late 90s.) When competing for top prizes the desire to pay for skilled online companions becomes even greater.

The allure of this type of gaming has already proven popular for tournament style games like *League of Legends* or DOTA, where eSports tournaments with large cash prizes have stoked the fantasies of millions of gamers in much the way that fantasies of excelling at basketball and becoming the next Michael Jordan have motivated generations of inner-city ball players (Figure 4.3).

The rise of crypto-currencies allow players to more freely engage in buying and selling in-game assets and services. The key here is that the in-game assets or payments can be made in a currency which can easily be exchanged for other currencies; crypto-currency wallets make this much easier and more decentralized than it once was. Moreover, these kinds of asset exchange marketplaces take much of the responsibility and accountability for addressing problems with money laundering, fraud,

FIGURE 4.3 While Web3 games started out with simple 8-bit graphics and little gameplay, they are rapidly taking on many of the characteristics of popular games on other PC and mobile platforms. Games like *Mighty Action Heroes* combine collectable characters and in game items sold as NFTs with multiplayer action RPG gameplay and strong visuals. (*Image Credit*: Mighty Bear Games.)

chargebacks, and the like off the plate of the game developer and publish. This reduced friction and the ability to allow users to take currency in and out of the system without having to manage these kinds of financial and regulatory complexities suddenly opens up a wide array of game design possibilities to developers.

We should expect that "Play to Earn" economies increasingly become a largely untracked mechanism by which wealth is transferred from wealthy countries to gamers in poorer countries. Indeed, in the case of *Axie Infinity* (and a rapidly increasing number of other new games) this is happening at scale with Etherium for gamers in the Philippines today.

In a world of four billion gamers distributed across countries with very uneven levels of disposable purchasing power, we should easily expect a billion or more players to game "professionally." Indeed, building carefully designed social game economies which allow for players to pay for services rendered could well guarantee high levels of player engagement across very large populations. This is the most likely route toward building the first "one billion daily active user" game, which has long been a holy grail for game designers.

INTERVIEW WITH SIMON DAVIS "THE MIGHTY BEAR OF SINGAPORE"

Simon Davis is the co-founder and CEO of developer Mighty Bear Games, based in Singapore.

TF: Tell us who you are and about your background in the games business.

Simon Davis: I am Simon Davis. I've been in the games industry since 2004. I was originally a musician by training. I was teaching guitar and went through a particularly lean period with my students not being available for lessons. I come from a bilingual family and I applied for a job in localization for video games in my hometown of Brighton, in England. I ended up getting a job at a company in 2004, which was meant to be a six-week job. It's been 18 years now, and I'm still making games.

I've done everything, from audio and composition, writing dialogue, localization, QA. I started in project management roles, I've been an external producer. I've been an internal producer, designer, product leader. I was briefly in charge of online technical operations for a major AAA publisher because I was the least unqualified person there at that time. Primarily, I'm a product leader. And today I'm the CEO and co-founder of Mighty Bear Games.

TF: What type of games is Mighty Bear focused on these days?

Simon: Mighty Bear focuses on creating accessible multiplayer experiences. So we take games which have been proven hits with more hard-core audiences on PC and console. And we reimagine them in a way which is accessible to more mainstream consumers.

TF: When you talk about mainstream, do you mean deeply-mass market, like hypercasual? How do you think about the audience you are trying to target and why?

Simon: For us, it's a function of thinking about the broader gaming audience. I think hypercasual is an interesting space but it's not really what we do. For us, it is more about creating shared social experiences, so when we think about the audience, generally, players from the age of seven or eight upwards, like some of our Butter Royale players. These are games that people can also play with older members of their family. We get a lot of emails from members of our community who play together as a family, and that's really cool.

A lot of the studio are young parents, and we made a conscious decision early on that we didn't want to create games that had a heavy emphasis on violence or gore or any kind of negativity. I don't really pass judgment on games like that. I play them myself. But we believe that the content we create has an influence on the environment that we are in. This also affects studio culture. If someone is looking at decapitations eight hours of the day, that affects how they interact with colleagues. We wanted to have a positive studio culture first and foremost, so that influences the kinds of products we create.

TF: Your studio is based in Singapore. Southeast Asia has rapidly emerged as one of the most interesting parts of the games industry. Can you tell us about game development in the region?

Simon: Yes. Southeast Asia, by many measures, is the world's fastest-growing smartphone market. I think Singapore has the highest smartphone penetration rate in the world. That means that consumers behave fundamentally differently here than in the US where people tend to still be PC or console players first. This region is mobile first. People here tend to be a lot more comfortable adopting new mobile technologies, like mobile payment wallets, for example.

It's interesting because we're basically at the cutting edge of mobile in this part of the world, so I think we get a taste of what is coming in Europe and America, just five years early! It's also an environment which is lower cost so that you can experiment, try new things much faster with much lower risk.

Also, as you know, the region is diverse. If you include India, which many people do when they talk about South Asia, there are more than one and a half billion people here. Which is an absurd addressable market on our doorsteps. One of the things I would say though is that people talk about Southeast Asia as one homogenous market. And that's not really the case.

Between Vietnam, Cambodia, Thailand, and the Philippines, they all have very different tastes. It's not easy to create a game that resonates well across all of those markets. Generally, you want to pick one or two and focus on those and then hope it will grow outwards. One example of a game that has done well in the region is *Mobile Legends: Bang Bang*, which is made by a Chinese Studio called Moonton. That game has very high levels of engagement in Indonesia alone. And it has expanded to do well in many places. It's been a really impressive case study in how to succeed.

TF: When you think about the way that Southeast Asian markets will evolve over the next decade, what do you imagine?

Simon: It's a great question. I think from the business perspective, there are two trends. The one that has people excited at a most basic level, is that the revenue per user is going up. People are becoming wealthier, becoming more comfortable with mobile payment wallets, the economy is growing, so it's going to become a much more valuable market. There's no question there. And demography is playing a part. The region is very young, and many people are just coming into working age.

I think the other thing which is much more interesting though for the next few years is that Southeast Asia is already at the cutting edge of Web3. And I think that the amount of experimentation and innovation in this space in Southeast Asia is unparalleled. Most successful Web3 and play-to-earn games are all coming out of Vietnam right now, with the Philippines as a primary market. It's very much a Southeast Asian phenomenon. Global hits are really coming out of Southeast Asia for the first time.

TF: You've had a lot of success with building games for subscription services like Apple Arcade. How do you see subscription service gaming platforms evolving over the coming years?

Simon: In terms of audience and adoption, I think subscription will only increase in relevance and importance. Apple, Microsoft, and Sony have been there for a while. Nintendo has its subscription service now. Netflix just showed up with game offerings. Strategics are shifting to this kind of subscription recurring-revenue model, and they have to keep adding value with new games.

From a developers' perspective this is good because if you have experience shipping games on subscription services you are going to have more options. For studios that are not really set up for user acquisition and don't run online publishing operations, subscriptions are a very good choice. The services themselves will have to become more aggressive with one another, to determine who lands hits. And that means it is going to be the developers and consumers who win in the end.

TF: What do you imagine lives at the intersection of subscription services and Web 3.0?

Simon: That's a really good question. I think that Web3 by its very nature is opposed to something like a centralized subscription service. It's not really a business model that fits well with Web3.

TF: Could you imagine membership to a subscription service being a function of a smart contract?

Simon: Yes, It could certainly be designed that way. I suppose, if you look at the most successful NFT offerings that is essentially what they are. Bored Ape Yacht Club is a club and membership has its own benefits so long as you hold that NFT. I think that could be the intersection of Web 3.0 and subscription models.

TF: Over the next 20 years, we're going to go from three billion gamers over the world to about four and a half billion gamers. What opportunities do you think we have as developers to imagine new ways of delighting these players?

Simon: I think as the audience gets bigger there is also an opportunity for us to be more inclusive. The world's population is not getting younger. We have older and older gamers with different challenges of mobility and perception, and I think that as the addressable market gets older we are going to have to think about these topics much more.

I also think one of the challenges we need to think about are the opportunities in reaching markets that haven't traditionally been gaming markets, like certain parts of Asia, sub-Saharan Africa, Latin America even. How can we create content that resonates with them?

I think just doing the same content for everyone in the world is probably not going to play. I know we've traditionally done that as an industry, but it doesn't work as well as what people are starting to do with tailoring content for a particular region.

Singaporean publisher, Garena, with *Free Fire*, for example, is doing really interesting stuff in Latin America where they create localized offerings for major regions like Brazil and Argentina. By really understanding the influencers in a particular market, and creating events and content for that specific market you can really engage players.

In the future, I think developers who are successful will be more inclusive, and they'll take the time to understand the market. Which I think is a good thing. Honestly, people should have representation. They should be able to play characters that look like them. The games people play should be relatable.

CONCLUSION

Wrap Up

Imbalances in income across the world coupled with tremendous distribution of computing power and bandwidth allow for the exchange of goods and services – transactions – between citizens of different countries to happen easily in ways that were all but impossible even 20 years ago. The rise of new types of currencies available to anyone with an internet connection, which exists outside of the ability for governments to easily regulate further enables peer-to-peer transactions between citizens of the internet. This has implications far beyond gaming (as the early use of Bitcoin on black-market trading sites like Silk Road showed.) But because online gaming is now the most popular global hobby in the world, there is significant area for overlap between these types of technology.

Crypto-currencies, NFT digital assets, and the ways in which games will use them are still very much in their infancy. Even the basic regulatory questions of digital rights ownership, taxation on digital assets, and fundamental questions about trust, safety, and legality are still murky. But their potential is undeniable, particularly when viewed through the lens of a truly global population of gamers with little in common except for their access to the internet and a shared love of gaming.

NOTES

1 https://www.cnbc.com/2021/11/02/nike-is-quietly-preparing-for-the-meta-verse-.html.
2 https://www.statista.com/statistics/730838/number-of-daily-cryptocurrency-transactions-by-type/.
3 https://www.nytimes.com/2021/12/10/opinion/cash-crypto-trust-money.html.
4 https://www.nature.com/articles/s41598-021-00053-8#MOESM1.
5 https://chaindebrief.com/axie-infinitys-1-2-billion-annualized-revenue-overtakes-candy-crushs-2020-total-revenue/.

CHAPTER 5

Devices and Platforms

T HE MOST SUCCESSFUL, AND the most lucrative, products are those
that help us with tasks which we would otherwise be unable to complete. Our limited working memory means we're bad at arithmetic, and
so no one does long division anymore. Our memories are unreliable, so
we have supplemented them with electronic storage. The human brain,
compared with a computer, is bad at networking with other brains, so we
have invented tools, like Wikipedia and Google search, that aid that kind
of interfacing.

– *From* If a Time Traveler Saw a Smartphone,
*by Tim Wu (*The New Yorker, *2014)*

Computers have come a very long way since the days of punch cards. Once
big enough to fill a whole room, they are now pocket sized and so very
powerful. Let's take a look at the major devices people play games on, and
ways we can expect the technology to evolve.

MOBILE DEVICES

In 2011, when writing about social and mobile gaming, I observed that
the war for gamer attention on consoles and the PC had an exciting new
entry with mobile gaming on Apple devices. It was clear then that the
sheer number of devices and their accessibility would shake the founda-
tions of the old order of console and PC supremacy. These predictions led
me professionally to make the move into the world of mobile gaming that
year. Google's more open Android platform quickly caught up and then

DOI: 10.1201/9781003291800-6

blew past Apple, at least in terms of total addressable market – number of phones in the world – and as the sophistication of mobile games grew, so did the audience.

By 2021, it is beyond clear that for most of the planet, video games are played on mobile phones. While consoles and PC gamers are still legion and loyal, particularly in mature markets like the United States, Europe, and Japan, the revenues from mobile gaming dwarf those from all other mediums. And remember that the majority of mobile game players never monetize through In App Purchases, so that these numbers significantly underestimate the number of total users.

By 2021, this had become even more pronounced, with mobile gaming delivering $93.2 billion in gross revenue, compared to $50 billion from consoles and $36 billion from PC games.[1] Indeed, in October of 2021 Apple's cut alone of the gaming market alone was estimated to have been in the ballpark of $10B in 2020,[2] based on a total of more than $45B spent on the iOS App Store. This exceeds Microsoft, Sony, Nintendo, and Activision's take during that time period. And Google was not far behind, with far more users, but a lower per user revenue[3] due to their primacy on lower cost phones and dominance in emerging markets. Mobile gaming was the undisputed king by 2020. And this trend and gap will continue to become more pronounced over the coming decades.

PLATFORM AGNOSTICISM

More than this, thanks to the cross-platform play that games like *Fortnite* popularized, mobile, console, and PC gaming are beginning to merge. So-called Cloud Gaming, first made mainstream by Google's efforts with Stadia, will further push the notion that gaming can be largely platform-agnostic. This trend will continue such that within a few years, most gamers will expect to be able to play their favorite games on whichever device is most convenient at the moment, switching between a mobile phone while on the bus on the way home, higher fidelity dedicated gaming hardware when in their living room, perhaps using a dedicated controller, then finishing out the day on a PC laptop in their bedroom at night. Gamers will expect progress, friends, and the investment in time and money put into their games to persist with their account regardless of the device they are playing on at any particular moment.

These days, most modern middleware technical stacks for building games support PC, Xbox, PlayStation, Nintendo Switch, Apple and Android operating systems, and even common virtual reality display and input devices. From a technical standpoint, there is little which is overly complex about this; as software developers, there are really only a few challenges. The primary buckets of engineering and design work tend to be:

Optimizing front-end User Interface screens and menus for each major device category touch screens, mouse/keyboard, or a controller takes a lot of work, at least to make the UI and User Experience design feel right and flow smoothly.

Control-input specifics need to be carefully tuned, particularly for games with frame specific level action controls, like shooters or fighting games. Achieving some level of parity such that multiplayer games feel fair can be quite challenging.

Optimizing visual fidelity for different 3D graphics chipsets and target display outputs can be quite technically complex and usually relies upon degrading the visual experience in the least notable ways for different device families. Doing this in a way that it doesn't give an advantage to some players over others can be challenging.

But the more complex and thorny obstacles to cross-platform play and parity tend to stem from business models, data connectivity, and legal avenues.

- Who owns friends lists & other valuable user data?

- How do Personally Identifiable Information or other regulatory user protection (COPPA, GDPR etc.) concerns mitigated across different platforms?

- When a user buys something through an In App Purchase on one platform, do other platform providers get a cut? What stops the developer from offering lower prices on one platform and biasing spend toward one partner or another to curry favor?

- How are advertising responsibilities and costs sorted out, if at all?

There are plenty of answers to each and all of these types of questions, but there are few answers that please all of the companies and regulatory bodies involved all of the time.

GAMING ECOSYSTEM OF DEVICES

Increasingly, mobile devices are able to share data with one another via Near Field Communications (NFC) or shared Wi-Fi connections. This allows a variety of devices on the gamer's person or in their home to potentially provide information to the game or receive game information as inputs. The obvious and most common use case here is for home speakers which can automatically start playing the music and sound effects from a game on the user's phone when they enter the room. Shifting display from the mobile device to other screens in the home has been available (if rarely used) for a few years. It will become more automated and common place. Other use cases for this kind of iOT sharing are still primitive today. Imagine a game that talks to a smart lamp in the room and adjusts the color of an LED to match the ambient lighting hue and temperature of the in-game environment, for example. We should expect other use cases (which could be used to provide additional levels of immersion, or more interestingly allow for easier social play between nearby users) to become increasingly common.

While technology companies like Microsoft, Amazon, Google, and Samsung are developing different ecosystems, one of the more compelling visions for the connected home and device families recently comes from the Chinese manufacturer Huawei. With a coherent vision of how laptops, tablets, mobile devices, speakers, earbuds, VR glasses, treadmills, scales, watches, lamps, and an array of other consumer devices will connect and communicate with one another, all unified by a custom (proprietary) Operating System called Harmony and run by a massive AI backend, this R&D and manufacturing giant is beginning to show hints of what this connected device ecosystem could look like in a few of their showrooms around the world.

Of course, with each of the major tech giants competing for consumer dollars, the inherent fragmentation of different device families promises to be a headache for developers. The trick will be coming up with use cases that will actually make games better in some real way. Often these kinds of connected systems end up feeling a bit like a solution in search of a problem, designed to encircle consumer's wallets rather than anything actually built with a vision for how to make life – or games – better.

So what are a few game development use cases for connected device ecosystems?

FORM FACTOR & FOLDABLE

What constitutes a mobile device for gaming is also changing fairly rapidly. From the original iPhone – which popularized the modern notion of a "smart phone," characterized by a touch screen rather than dedicated keypad, Wi-Fi connectivity, and third-party applications distributed via a manufacturer-curated "app store" – to the current incarnation of devices we've experienced a number of incremental device level improvements. (Bluetooth, Near Field Communications, improvements in screen resolution and resilience, significant improvements to camera technology, battery life and charging time to name a few.) At the same time, processing power, dedicated GPU power for driving 3D visuals in games, and the amount of available RAM have improved rapidly. (The original iPhone, released 15 years ago in 2007 boasted 128 MB of RAM. The high-end phones coming out in 2022 regularly ship with 8 GB of RAM, more than a 60 fold increase over a decade. Most other hardware components have seen similar improvements.) It's easy to extrapolate from there: Imagine the level of simulation and visual fidelity available with a terabyte of RAM on device. Imagine with more than 20TB of RAM, which would be common by 2040, were this measure to continue to increase at current pace. This would allow common mobile devices to easily fuel extremely advanced displays, run very complex simulations, and manage high-fidelity inputs and outputs from an array of connected devices simultaneously.

But perhaps the more significant sea-change has been the rise to dominance of the software ecosystem on these devices; while "apps" may not have replaced the web, they have definitely emerged to be a parallel and equal mechanism by which humans engage with the online world. This is even truer for populations in emerging market nations, where PC access never reached the same level of adoption as mobile application has over the last 20 years.

Mobile Devices as More Than a Phone: Watches, Glasses, Wearables

Recently, foldable devices and experimentation with a variety of form factors continues this evolution, and while few of these technologies have fundamentally changed the way gamers interact with their devices, every year has brought improvements which make gaming more accessible and integrated into users' lifestyles with lower friction. Imagine all of these advances continuing, and the result is that more people carry and use more high-quality gaming devices with them more of the time. Imagine "phones" capable of playing better games than we've ever made before which can be wrapped around a user's wrist or embedded into the fabric of a jacket. More time for gaming anywhere and everywhere.

This mechanism of distributing software – games! – extends to other devices now, like smart watches, or Ray Ban's recent mass-market smart-sunglasses. Basic "VR" displays on headsets, which are driven by phones are becoming increasingly affordable and high quality as well. While the interfaces for these devices are still fairly primitive and of limited use for gaming, we should certainly not expect this to remain the case. Expect that greater integration between devices allows for natural, high-resolution, high-framerate displays, which can easily be folded and put into a user's pocket when not in use.

But the use of smart glasses just as easy to use display mechanics likely only covers use cases for the next few years, perhaps through 2030. Consider though some of the other capabilities that more advanced version of Google Glass or 2022's Ray Bans could accomplish:

If smart glasses can record everything you see for years at a time, starting when a person is a child, perhaps, then the sorts of Artificial Intelligence we talk about throughout this book can use it to easily search back through conversations. In jokes or themes that arise could easily be tagged and brought back in games. By 2035, we should expect that people a wearer once saw could easily be captured and mapped to an NPC character in a game using many of the techniques we will talk about in Chapter 13.

Imagine also, that these events in a wearer's past were recorded along with biometric data gathered by their smart watch, or smart dermal patch. (Or even small connected subcutaneous implant devices similar to Norplant – a commonly used chemical birth-control delivery system from last century.) Biometrics could track interactions that made a user's heart race – like the first time they saw that person they had a crush on – and that made their heart sink – like when those bullies from school came around the corner. Collating this data with the people seen visually by the glasses would allow AI to create NPCs in games which were likely to provoke a strong emotional reaction in the user. Imagine the cliché princess in need of rescue in a tower… who looked just like your first high school crush.

The combination of bespoke content drawn from a user's environment over the years, collated with knowledge of the emotional impact those moments had on them (as revealed by biometric data which would have even been imperceptible to other humans present at the time) could be used by AI to work into storytelling. While we are likely still 15 years away from each of these technologies being stitched together and used by autonomous game directors, most of the basics exist today. We'll discuss this kind of thing more in a dedicated chapter on AI.

CONSOLES

Dedicated gaming consoles hit their peak at the beginning of the century with the Sony PlayStation 2, which currently holds the record for the largest number of units sold, at 155 million. Since then, Microsoft's Xbox, Sony's PlayStation, and a variety of Nintendo offerings have continued to leapfrog one another in graphics capability, controller quality, online social connectedness, and broad integration into the entertainment landscape. (From DVD support for watching movies to Netflix integration allowing streaming of same, consoles have tried to continue to add to their value proposition by being the center of living room entertainment.)

While the device hardware keeps getting better, advancements in the OS and software have been uneven. The types of games that continue to move units on these devices has remained relatively static over the last two decades: Each year has a few great first-person shooters (*Call of Duty, Halo, Battlefield*), a category leading game for each major sport (*FIFA*, Madden, NBA), a few tentpole narrative driven adventure games (*Uncharted, God of War, The Last of Us*), and a smattering of RPGs (*Final Fantasy, Dark Souls*). Music and fitness games experienced a crescendo 15 years ago with *Guitar Hero* and *Rock Band* turning living rooms across the United States into impromptu parties slash concert halls.

Digital distribution of games over high-bandwidth connections now allow users to bypass the retail channel and deliver a greater portion of the profits from sales to console manufacturers and game publishers. This has also allowed for a wider array of lower-sales volume games built exclusively for digital downloads. XBLA, PSN, and Nintendo Switch have allowed smaller or indie game developers to bring games for niche audiences to these platforms as well, resulting in a huge number of very high-quality titles. Still though, given the relatively small addressable market for console gaming, the space remains a winner-take-all landscape.

And while the above paragraph could come across as overly dismissive of the advances made in the console space, it should not. Many of the advances made first on console games form the backbone behind the engineering required for some of the more widely adopted advances that we discuss in this book. For example, the Microsoft Kinect which used an advance camera sensor mounted near the television accelerated a number of complex Computer Vision (CV) concepts to effectively track a player's dance moves or exercise postures in a yoga game. Advanced relatively affordable consumer-grade application of this kind of CV technology that can be used by many devices in the future for advanced frame-over-frame tracking of multiple users' movement in 3D space. Imagine a swarm of high-resolution-camera equipped micro-drones all feeding footage of a dance floor into a CPU that converted each dancer's movement into near-perfect avatar expressions in an online dance party game which rated users from clubs – and their living rooms – around the world, simultaneously. Such a worldwide simultaneously dance competition with real-time entry fees, voting, prizes, and the like would not have been possible with some of the advances made in early century console games.

And of course, this is just one example. The art and science behind advanced simulated lighting models, from raytracing to Physically Based Rendering (PBR) to toolsets to facilitate the creation and optimization of advanced shaders for describing the surfaces comprising objects in 3D scenes would not have come nearly so far so fast without the mass-market adoption of consoles which pushed these technologies. Indeed, the arms race for ever more visually compelling content in console gaming has fed back into the film and CG animation industry; the Unreal Engine is regularly now used to facilitate movie-making, rapidly supplanting older bespoke tools and techniques. The skills and training required to create content with all of these technologies for console gaming has led to better CG for movies, the explosion of high-quality content for mobile games, and a widespread understanding of 3D graphics programming and artistry. As on some level MUDS and the Atari 2600 begat *World of Warcraft*, so did *Farmville* and the Xbox 360 beget the drones and advanced optics fueled mass-social games of 2040.

MULTIPLATFORM

The most interesting recent development in the console market is the recognition that allowing people to play games on different devices and across device families gives more gamers what they want, increases user base and revenues, and does not seem to unduly cannibalize sales on any particular device. Indeed, based on a September 2021 analysis of Epic's industry leading *Fortnite* suggests that adding mobile support brings new players into a PC and console game's ecosystem and adds incremental revenue.[4] It appears that players often start on a mobile device and then migrate to other platforms if they have access, not the other way around. These kinds of studies appear to be rapidly setting executives' minds at ease, leading to a broad thawing of the platform exclusivity approach that has characterized console developers like Microsoft, Sony, and Nintendo for the last two decades.

It seems a near foregone conclusion now that the next ten years will see most major game publishers push to bring their products out on as many different platforms as possible. This approach allows brand marketing dollars and initial product development budgets to be amortized far more efficiently. And while supporting each additional platform well does add incremental costs to development and live operations of a game, the incremental revenues this approach drives generally makes it worth doing for many games.

Extrapolating on this trend, I believe we should expect to see wide cross-platform support between mobile, PC, and console games become the standard over the coming decade. The bigger question in my mind is if dedicated gaming hardware (consoles) will remain a viable business as mobile hardware and input/output models become increasingly sophisticated.

PC GAMES

For many gamers, particularly in North America and Europe, the only "real" games are played on a personal computer or laptop with a high-resolution monitor, using a mouse and keyboard as the primary input devices. This mindset has been known as the "PC Master Race" mentality by adherents, and there is no doubt that many superb high-quality works are released primarily or exclusively on Valve's Steam distribution platform. For certain types of games that trend toward the more hardcore player, PC gaming remains the only game in town.

PC remains the undisputed home for MMORPGs like *World of Warcraft*, some shooters, particularly with free-to-play business models, tactical and strategy games like Bulgarian Developer Snapshot Games' superb game *Phoenix Point* (Figure 5.1), real-time strategy games, and deep fantasy role-playing games like Russian developer Owlcat's *Pathfinder: Wrath of the Righteous*. Most games at these levels of sophistication require users to download the game and play it on a local machine with high-end dedicated 3D hardware acceleration hardware. These games are usually played in a chair, sitting upright, a few inches from a large screen, and typically invoke fewer sessions per day with far longer session times than mobile or console games.

FIGURE 5.1 *Phoenix Point* by Snapshot Games is a PC first product, and a great representation of the turn-based tactics genre. (*Image Credit:* Snapshot Games.)

There are an estimated 1.85 billion PC gamers across the world as of 2020.[5] This number has roughly doubled over the last decade. We should continue this trend to continue, accounting for more hardcore games like the ones just mentioned, but also accounting for more casual web-based gamers, PC forward social MMO games like the massive *Minecraft* (already aggressively cross-platform) and *Roblox*. Moreover, NFT and crypto-focused games are largely web (and mostly PC) based right now. As this is an area where we expect to continue to see massive growth, this will likely swell the ranks (and alter the definition) of PC gamers. Expect 2.5 billion people to play games on these kinds of devices by 2040.

SETTING AND CONVERGENCE

One reason I've mentioned form factor (size of screen), posture and location (in the pocket, on the desk, mounted across from a couch), and input device (touch, keyboard, controller) in this section is that increasingly, these remain the primary difference that matters for different kinds of games. As hardware and software improve on all types of devices, game designers will be increasingly encouraged to think less about what is possible, and more about how they want players to engage with the games, which is as much about envisioning a user's setting while they are playing your game, as it is about anything else. Three friends drinking beer on the couch and playing *Madden* is a very different experience than a solo player running complex boss raids in an MMO on an ultra-wide monitor and a gaming chair in a darkened bedroom. And both of these are very different than a pensioner matching gems while riding the metro bus home from the grocery store.

Let's look now at a few of the hardware and software elements and infra-structure considerations that may increasingly drive device convergence and make this matter of considering set and setting more important.

Battery technology may not be improving at the breakneck speed of CPU power, but it is getting better. This allows more sophisticated compu-tation, better cooling systems with high-end GPUs to run longer on more mobile devices. While heat remains a serious problem for games that push visual fidelity or complex simulations, battery power has traditionally been a bigger obstacle over the last decade. This is slowly improving. These improvements will help everything from mobile phones to free-range VR headsets, to wireless controllers, to drones. And while there are a number of environmental, geopolitical, and supply-chain complexities associated with creating increasingly sophisticated batteries, according to Forbes,[6] in 2020, companies poured more than $8 billion dollars into R&D efforts focused on battery technology. We should expect these to improve dra-matically by 2040.

CLOUD GAMING

At the same time there are significant efforts underway to reduce the importance of localized data storage, processing, and calculation and simulations. Collectively, this different approach is referred to as "Cloud Gaming" and is more or less analogous to the movement we saw on PCs between 2000 and 2020, in which software and data moved from being installed and managed on a local PC to being managed "in the cloud." At the most extreme example, this can allow any PC or mobile device to become what computer systems designers used to refer to as a "dumb ter-minal", used for user-input and display, with all of the processing being performed across a network by dedicated machines. Effectively, this trans-fer of input and visual information while the game is played elsewhere allows users to use more bandwidth but give up the heat, power, and cost of on device CPU and GPU processing. The net impact could be better games, provided you have sufficiently high-bandwidth and low-latency connection (Figure 5.2).

The most public example of Cloud Gaming over the last few years came in the form of Google's Stadia platform. Players were offered a monthly

FIGURE 5.2 2020 Google Stadia advertisement showing the cross-platform promise of Cloud Gaming. (*Image Credit*: Google.)

subscription package of around $10 per month for a collection of games they could play on any device with sufficient internet connectivity. After a brief foray into internal development, Google abandoned their high-profile Stadia Studio in 2001.[7] While the technical promise of the platform largely delivered visual quality equivalent of any platform on the market, the licensing complexity and lack of exclusive "must-have" content from any top-tier developers has largely impeded widespread adoption of the platform to date. However, just as Google's short-lived initial experiment with "Google Glass" AR glasses should not be taken to mean that such devices will not ever succeed in mainstream markets; neither do I believe Stadia's initial experiment should cast a pall over Cloud Gaming. Google has proven to be a company that can afford to take a very long-term view on technology R&D.

Not to be outdone, Microsoft has also launched Cloud Gaming initiatives serving PC players into some test markets where they have struggled to sell dedicated hardware. And given the popularity of a few games in the Xbox portfolio and the ubiquity of the Windows platform globally, this approach is likely to win converts. This move is particularly interesting because it comes from a brand which has been associated for the last two decades with specific console hardware. The implication here is that we will see Microsoft, Sony, and perhaps even Nintendo move toward a world where their brands stand for certain types of gaming experiences which are divorced from specific hardware. Given that for years gaming consoles have been sold either at a loss or with very thin margins (profits are usually calculated from the attach rates of average number of games per user) this may end up being a boon to the companies that have long been at war in this hard business. We might also expect to see dedicated cloud server chipsets, graphics or AI capabilities, or other software differentiation that allows for product- or brand-level differentiation. Could a "console" be sold just as a dedicated controller, a few specific games, and the promise that the games a player gets access to will be more impressive than the competitors'? Perhaps.

Overall, my estimation is that Cloud Gaming, while nascent, is likely to become a standard in coming years. The tech is good, the promise is there, and as global bandwidth increases, we should expect this underlying solution to largely take over more traditional models. Particularly in some emerging markets where access to high powered consoles and PCs will remain very limited, Cloud Gaming is a way of delivering first-class gaming experiences to anyone with a smart phone; and that's almost everyone.

Moreover, there is no reason to believe that players would be forced to pick one solution over another; they can have both. Imagine that their device detected the bandwidth and latency they had available, the available battery power and heat signature, or even what they were going to do in the game and switched between local processing and cloud processing seamlessly. While I'm on the train playing on my phone with a full battery charge over a cellular connection, we bias toward local calculation, reduced graphic complexity, and so on. Then once we get home and have great dedicated internet connection and an 8k resolution display, we switch to running most of the game simulation on the cloud. While this would prove a little complex today, it is quite likely the way we could architect software solutions in coming years.

ON BANDWIDTH

This last part speaks to one of the complex variables that game designers and developers must take into account: Across the globe, players have a huge variability in network speeds (latency), bandwidth volume (capacity), and reliability. Currently, fixed-position bandwidth across the world varies between 1 and 300 mbps. (Mobile speeds are a bit slower, between 1 and 200 typically.) South Korea and some Scandinavian countries tend to be the fastest, while Africa and parts of the Middle East are generally the slowest. (And of course some places have hardly any connection at all. Think of those dark spots on the NASA satellite views we looked at earlier.) These speeds are changing quite rapidly as true fiber broadband begins to appear in some cities and as mobile infrastructure providers begin to roll-out 5G connections in developed markets. Of course, the speeds quoted here are for widely accessible residential or personal connections. Many universities, businesses, and well-heeled individuals have connections which can be dramatically faster using dedicated lines (Figure 5.3).

Since the days of the 300 baud modem (Modem Wars!), games have hungered for more bandwidth. As discussed in our section on "Cloud Gaming", there is a clear opportunity to use increased bandwidth to off-set some of the challenges with physics and thermodynamics which complicate our ability to continue to increase the fidelity and sophistication of games on mobile devices. And even for fixed-position devices, like PlayStations, increased bandwidth aids in rapid distribution and content updates for games. Higher bandwidth allows us to make multiplayer games more immersive, add features that allow for a greater sense of telepresence

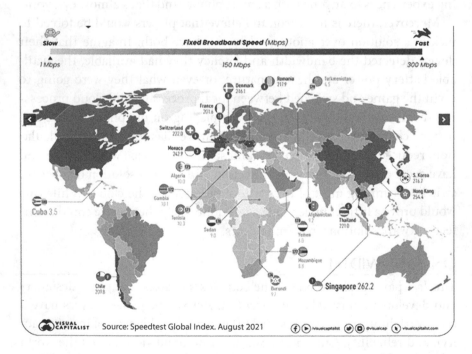

FIGURE 5.3 Average residential broadband speed by territory, October 2021. (*Image Credit*: Visual Capitalist.)

for players, and – perhaps most importantly over the next 20 years – allow us to begin to support a huge increase in the number of connected devices that can form the gamer's ecosystem by providing additional inputs and outputs. Games want more bandwidth.

So how should we expect this to evolve? There are three main ways the available bandwidth can increase: large-scale infrastructure projects can use modern technologies like optical fiber cables, which can transmit a great deal of data rapidly over physical lines, and wholesale upgrade of cellular towers can enable 5G and eventually 6G technology,[8] which packs more data into radio waves for increased cellular connectivity. Faster and more sophisticated switching systems can increase the speed of transfer on these technologies. And we can continue to develop improved software and logic for compressing, decompressing, and otherwise handling data at volume.

None of these approaches are without challenge. Infrastructure projects have high costs with long payback windows. (Consider the logistic construction difficulty of tearing up miles of city to lay down newer, better fiber optic cables.) So these take big capital outlays deployed against long-term potential gain; these kinds of projects are seldom a delight to shareholders. And even when the spine of an urban area can be wired in this way, there's a "last mile" problem of getting these lines patched into every apartment building or dwelling within the area. This ends up falling to millions of owners, strata counsels and the like, so it takes a long time to reach widespread distribution. Some similar problems affect upgrades to cellular networks. And regulatory complexities around distribution of available bandwidth, etc. further slowdown these efforts.

There are some promising new technologies that may foretell new approaches to increasing bandwidth and lowering latency for gamers. Visionary Elon Musk's Starlink company has deployed thousands of low-earth orbit satellites in 2020 and 2021, allowing high-bandwidth and low-latency connections established by small non-fixed location satellite dishes. This technology is a massive improvement over previous satellite internet connections, which had very limited bandwidth, latency which made action games unplayable, and ceased to function during atmospheric storms. Starlink and similar technologies by a few competitors are actively bringing high-quality internet to millions of largely rural locations; moreover, since the only hardware required is a small portable dish that looks at the sky, this technology is very difficult to regulate. This allows millions to evade government censorship. As Musk puts it, "Regulatory bodies can shake their fists at the sky." If nothing else, this technology can be used to connect millions of new gamers, and as it is in its infancy, it promises to upend much of the existing telecommunications market, resulting in better games for lots of people.

Separate from low-orbit satellites, other companies are pushing to alter networking for gaming in a different way: by offering dedicated networks which are built for (and reserved for) gaming and game-like applications which rely on low latency. The nature of the internet is that it was never built for low-latency, fast address resolution, and other characteristics which are ideal for gaming. Companies like Subspace[9] are building out parallel "internet" style networks with gaming-dedicated fiber optic cables and dedicated bespoke hardware in major cities. While it is early to tell if this is necessary or ideal, it is encouraging to know that even with existing terrestrial technologies there are many opportunities to improve gamers' experience.

STREAMING SERVICES AND THE CONVERGENCE OF LINEAR AND NON-LINEAR MEDIA

Beyond the physical complexity of getting bandwidth in place and devices into users' hands, delivering content to users requires a complex patchwork of agreements, subscriptions, contracts with providers, regulators, and so on. In many ways, the true complexity behind creating a "platform" only starts once the gross pieces technology are sorted out. How do you get content into homes and onto devices once the hardware and mechanics of the software are in place?

Some of the groups who are the best at solving this collection of problems are streaming services, which are rapidly replacing Cable TV as the way people consume content (Figure 5.4).

Hundreds of millions of people around the world subscribe to various services, from Netflix to Disney+. These services have local pricing, payment models, and customer service apparatus in place to handle millions of users in several territories already. And the big players are currently focused on rapid expansion into Eastern Europe, the Middle East, Africa, and other regions they've not yet solved.

Moreover, looking at the top streaming services, there is already huge overlap with the biggest consumer entertainment brands in the world. Disney owns Marvel, Star Wars, LucasArts, Fox, National Geographic, and many other brands. The temptation to deliver video game content will be high once the streaming services are all in place; indeed, we can already see Netflix making forays into the gaming distribution space.[10] Others will too.

Worldwide Streaming Subscriptions Q2 2021 (m)

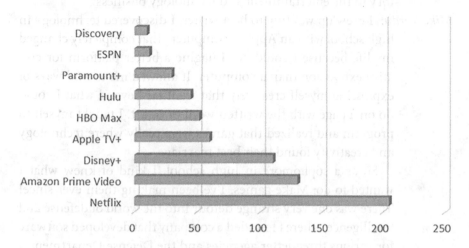

FIGURE 5.4   (*Image Credit:* TF, Data from *The Economist*, December 2021.)

It is quite easy to imagine the convergence of Cloud Gaming and the major IP Subscription Services being the real future of game distribution by 2030.

INTERVIEW WITH MIKE VERDU: THE FUTURE OF PLATFORMS

Mike Verdu has run studios for companies at Atari, Electronic Arts, and has led companies like Zynga and Kabam. He served as the Vice President of AR and VR Content for Facebook, and currently is the Vice President of Games at Netflix.

TF: To start with, can you tell us who you are and tell us about your history in the entertainment and technology business?

Mike Verdu: I grew up wanting to be a writer. I discovered technology in high school with an Apple 2 computer. That completely changed my life because I could not imagine a better platform for creative expression than a computer. It allowed me to find ways of expressing myself creatively that went far beyond what I could do on a page with the written word or in art. I taught myself to program and realized that games were really where technology and creativity found their best marriage.

So as a sophomore in high school, I kind of knew what I wanted to do: Make games. I've been making them ever since! There was one very strange detour into the world of defense and intelligence, where I founded a company that developed software for various three-letter agencies and the Defense Department. I wound up selling that company, and in the end convincing the management of the acquiring company to fund a new gaming venture, which was when I took a hobby and turned it into my career. I have made games ever since. Adventure games, RTS games, role-playing games, first-person shooters, games on Facebook, strategy and role-playing games on mobile devices. And then dabbled with VR at Oculus (now Meta), where I wasn't so much creatively involved as overseeing the teams that we're picking the hits.

TF: You've had a phenomenal career of focusing on both content creation and also software creation. How do you see the future of game development blending these two different distinct disciplines?

Mike: The future to me is a collection of trends that will transform not just the way games are made but the way we think about them. When I reflect on my own career and my sense of where things are going, I believe we need to think about game worlds as systems that can be extended and expanded. Game developers need to embed tools for creators from the start. Because like it or not, we are now partners with our players in the most profound way. You see it in a lot of games that are popular in 2021, but I think it's a trend that will continue.

People will also interact with games on a spectrum of engagement. We need to give people the option to spectate on one end of the spectrum and create full games on the other end – and allow them to engage anywhere in between. So that means thinking very deeply up-front about the tools that you use to create your game worlds and systems, and also the tools that you give your players to give them agency.

Another trend is designing specifically for VR and AR because the language of interaction in those spaces – either blended with the real world in AR or completely artificial worlds in VR – is something new. We're still learning the grammar of AR and VR. You have to worry about comfort, the science of locomotion, and the way the user interfaces will work when you are in hands-free AR-VR experiences. The problem space goes beyond the world of controllers or touch screens as input devices... your hands could be the primary input devices or farther in the future, even your thoughts. These are all profound changes to be wrestled with.

The other thing I would point to is harnessing machine learning and procedural content generation to take some of the heavy lifting out of the raw asset creation in game development. I don't think the era of $500 million first-person shooter games is going to go for much longer. These are like the last of the dinosaurs. In the future, we will create very powerful tools for procedurally generated content, and then inject them into worlds that are defined by systems and that are very robust in the way they're expressed. And, oh by the way, these can also provide the assets for linear film and TV production as well as games.

And the last trend that I think people need to be aware of is interoperability. Players are going to come to expect that the things they use and own and the ways they express themselves in one game are actually going to transfer to others, whether it's your avatar or attributes or objects you acquire. There's a whole interesting world of transferable, portable, interoperable systems that will be at the root of this transformation. And at some point, all of these trends will converge into something like the Metaverse. I worry about the level of hype that is associated with that concept in 2021, but it will sure as hell be a thing by 2040.

TF: In a world where everyone can create content and games, how do we let players around the world find and learn about the games that people have created?

Mike: I believe streaming is going to play an enormous role in the future of gaming. This is actually a key enabling technology – because there's no way you can put all the computing power that you need for a high-fidelity virtual reality world or AR experience on your face. So really, the only way we're going to give people access to high-fidelity AR/VR experiences is to stream them into the devices that people wear, whether it's through your phone up to glasses or even a very light processor configuration that you might be able to have in the frames of your glasses. But I think the hardware that is on your face or even on your body is going to be mostly dedicated to capturing inputs and sending them upstream, and capturing the stream from the cloud and integrating it with the experience that the player is having. Because it's required to enable the full potential of AR and VR, streaming is going to bleed into every manifestation of games and interactive experiences on all devices.

You see some glimmers of what the future will bring with Microsoft's success with GamePass and xCloud. It's a movement, finally, toward streaming as a mainstream way of experiencing content. There will still be a variety of business models. Free-to-play isn't going away, but subscription is going to be a thing. So are creator economies where players pay creators for cool experiences and virtual stuff.

TF: In a world where there's far more great game content than any human can ever consume, how do you see the role of AI-driven recommendation engines in helping people find games and content that they love?

Mike: Algorithmic discovery is absolutely the future. There are some companies, my current employer included, who do it really, really well. The fact that you can get a personally relevant and satisfying selection through the filter of personalization or recommendation is incredibly powerful. We just can't sort through the millions of millions of choices that are offered to us even now, when you think about the millions of games there are on the various mobile app stores. There's almost a tragedy of the commons happening there, where there is not a lot of trust on the part of players in the undifferentiated sea of content or the early forms of algorithmic game discovery that exists now. Performance marketing is filling the gap, with ad targeting substituting for awesome recommendations. However, recommendations will get much better, and thus players will trust more, and paradoxically the narrowing of choice based on personalization will lead to much more discovery of new and cool experiences!

And so, over time, I do think that we will move away from the world where companies are just paying Facebook and ad networks to move players from one game to another and toward a world where there's a lot of intelligence and finesse in the way the algorithms are connecting you to content that you'll enjoy. I think this is one of the most important trends out there.

TF: Over the last ten years, we've seen content that is based around popular intellectual property like Marvel, or Star Wars, or James Bond, take the lion's share of consumer attention. In a world where everyone is creating content and games, how do you see the role of IP and IP owners changing?

Mike: I am very excited about the role of IP in the future. I don't think that the beloved characters, worlds, and stories that we think of as franchise IP are going to disappear any time soon. However, I do think that forward looking companies will open up the ways that people interact with their IP. I see a day where enlightened IP owners will open up their worlds as places where people can create – where players and creators can actually generate their own expressions of these beloved worlds and characters. Over time, those IP holders that don't open up will be left behind, with their IPs becoming calcified and perhaps not as widely followed or accepted.

But at the same time that you have large IP holders opening up their worlds for people to play in, you're going to have all this exciting new IP being generated by democratized game creation, and that's so damned cool. It's been a dream of mine to let everybody create and express themselves in this amazing interactive medium that is gaming. Democratized game creation started with mods and a subset of players willing to use editors that came with game engines to make cool new stuff. And now it has progressed with platforms like *Minecraft* and *Roblox*. UGC is one of the most exciting trends and it's going to continue. There will be lots of great new worlds, stories, and characters introduced, and those will live side by side with the big established IPs that big companies own.

And I believe that in the farther future, new IPs will actually start small, originated by players, and get adopted by big companies and then grown and nurtured and turned into IPs that are broadly accepted. This has happened with book publishing. Look at how authors that are self-published have spawned empires around their IP. Twilight started as fanfic and there are any number of examples of well-established beloved IPs that had their origins in the creator economy.

TF: What advice would you give a young person who had just picked up their first PC and wanted to make a name for themselves in the coming world of game creation?

Mike: My advice to young people who want to get into the game industry has been fairly consistent through the years. And I would give much the same advice going forward.

This is an industry that's really about passion and creativity. And you don't generally get into making game as a job or a way to make money. You do it because you're compelled to do it. Because there's something in you that drives you to create, express, and contribute something to the medium. The tools for doing that are being democratized. And so there are many different venues where people can show what they can do and make experiences that can attract an audience and show something fundamentally new or innovative or interesting.

What I used to tell people was, make some art, or a little prototype, or contribute to a mod that a team is developing. Use a game engine to show off something interesting. Give the world some evidence that you care, that you have the talent, that you have willingness to invest the hard work that's needed to make something that somebody else would enjoy. In the future, fast forward 10–20 years, I think that the advice is the same but the platforms and tools that will be available to creator will be different – and much more robust.

To get into the industry, you have to show that you have some talent and are willing to do the hard work to get other people to engage with something that you've made. That process is becoming easier and easier over time. You will have many ways to connect with players. When you do, you'll not only find you have a career path in gaming, but that there is no bigger thrill than to connect with people through this medium!

WRAP UP

Wrap Up on Devices and Platforms

The device does not define the game. While once every game had to be individually programmed and painstakingly optimized for the specific chipset and capabilities of a particular piece of hardware, we left this era behind some decades ago. By 2022, powerful toolsets and freely available tech stacks make the mechanics of getting a game to run on a huge array of consumer devices a straightforward affair. Almost all games can now be multiplatform, or even played across platforms. The choice of which piece of hardware or which distribution mechanism to debut a new game on should largely be a business choice today. And going forward, players will expect many – most – games to be playable on whatever hardware is most convenient for them at that moment, with information on their progress, their friends, their investments carried seamlessly from one operating system to another.

The arms race of increasing processing ability, increasing amounts of accessible RAM, improved hardline and wireless bandwidth with reduced latency will continue to the benefit of gamers everywhere. These will afford us the ability to create new interface, input, and output mechanisms. The advent of cloud computing and rapid increases in the number of connected devices around the world will allow many of these input and output sources to be joined together in an ecosystem which will allow bespoke experiences impossible today and only dreamed of as the stuff of science fiction 30 years ago.

Devices do not define the game, but the coming connected ecosystem of smart devices of incredible power will facilitate gaming that is more accessible and emotionally impactful for billions of players around the globe.

NOTES

1 https://www.gamesindustry.biz/articles/2021-12-21-gamesindustry-biz-presents-the-year-in-numbers-2021.
2 https://www.gamesindustry.biz/articles/2021-10-04-apple-estimated-to-earn-more-from-gaming-than-sony-microsoft-and-nintendo.
3 https://www.gizchina.com/2021/10/01/apple-app-store-beats-google-play-store-users-pay-billions-of-dollars-yearly/.
4 https://naavik.co/themetas/fortnite-activision-zynga.
5 https://www.statista.com/statistics/420621/number-of-pc-gamers/.
6 https://www.forbes.com/sites/rrapier/2021/02/06/funding-for-battery-technology-companies-exploded-in-2020.

7 https://www.theguardian.com/games/2021/feb/02/google-stadia-closes-in-house-game-development-studio.
8 https://www.highspeedinternet.com/resources/6g-internet.
9 https://venturebeat.com/2021/10/26/subspace-will-launch-its-parallel-and-real-time-internet-for-gaming-and-the-metaverse/.
10 https://about.netflix.com/en/news/let-the-games-begin-a-new-way-to-experience-entertainment-on-mobile.

CHAPTER 6

Input and Feedback Mechanisms

Look how his hands move on the controls, he told her. In those worlds, left-handedness does not impede him. Amazingly, he is almost ambidextrous.

– Salman Rushdie, Luka and the Fire of Life

Ultimately, gaming devices are just computers with input and output feedback mechanisms. Then the logic and craftsmanship of the game play out in software. For the last 40 years games have been played on keyboards, mice and keyboards, joysticks, controllers of increasing sophistication, touchscreens, plastic guitars and other arcane custom peripherals, and on rare occasion, voice inputs. For a while, touch-screen phones, controllers, mice and keyboards will continue to drive user inputs into games. But direct speech input and other, more nuanced mechanisms of communicating with games will become standard within the next ten years, probably less.

A decade ago, touch-screen gaming was a tiny fraction of the industry and controllers were all. Within the next decade, people will be mostly communicating with games through basic speech, as Natural Language Processing makes computing and gaming vastly more accessible to the world. Eye tracking will become a common way of knowing where a user's attention is and what they want to do.

DOI: 10.1201/9781003291800-7

167

But other ways of tracking user input, attention, mood, stress-levels, and physical presence will become standard. Strong levels of machine-learned AI interpretation of user inputs will make control of complex characters more intuitive. Higher quality visuals will make it more appealing for users to remain in game for longer sessions. Social presence will make the rest of the world fade away; your friends will all be here in the game, in the Metaverse. Easier input, longer sessions, more immersive display and audio becomes a virtuous self-reinforcing loop. Gamers game longer.

Let's talk about some potential input mechanisms and how we might use them to let players play better.

MOUSE AND KEYBOARD

For millions of PC gamers, the only truly skilled way to play a game is with a mouse and keyboard. This mindset was so entrenched – particularly for shooters – that for years there was deep skepticism that a competitive shooter would ever be popular on consoles. Rare Software's *Goldeneye* 007 for the Nintendo 64 changed this in 1997, followed by the original *Halo* on Xbox in 2001. It took dozens of tiny but essential features to allow for the level of movement and aiming fidelity required for this particular genre to soar on consoles. And, of course, there are still gamers who fervently believe that the PC is the only true device for shooter fans. Other genres, particularly anything involving lots of text chatting with other players, like MMORPGs, tend to work especially well with a keyboard and mouse. Likewise, real-time strategy games, like Blizzard's Starcraft, and highly nuanced tactical squad games (MOBAs, like *League of Legends*, for example) tend to work very well with the level of precision a mouse gives the player. But largely these are not restrictions, so much as preferences borne from the specifics of user interface design and user familiarity.

It is likely that the keyboard and mouse combination will continue to be popular for a very long time. Typing on a traditional QWERTY is still taught in many schools, and 275 million new PCs were sold in 2020 alone. While this is down from its worldwide peak in 2011,[1] it's a safe bet that all of these featured a keyboard and mouse. This particular input pairing is not likely to go away anytime soon for most types of software, including games.

Are there meaningful advancements in the PC and mouse that we can expect to influence game design?

Keyboards and mice are regularly wireless now, feature fancy lights, and very high DPI optical sensors. Many gaming mice and keyboards both allow for key-customization, which allows hardcore gamers to define what particular buttons or keys do in particular games. Various vendors of gaming PCs and mice proclaim ergonomic improvements every year as well. But this is not to say that keyboards and mice won't be subject to some levels of improvement. You can easily anticipate razor-thin wireless keyboards with months of wireless battery life (indeed, I'm typing this on one now). We should expect the ways keys use lights and simple haptic feedback to improve over the coming decades.

Gaming mice have become more advanced as well, with higher levels of optical sensing and more buttons. Some players even find advantage to using two mice on a PC at the same time now.[2] But for the most part, these innovations have minimal impact on games themselves, and they don't have widespread enough adoption for most game developers to focus much energy on. I don't expect this to change in the next 20 years. Mice will be mice; keyboards will be keyboards.

CONTROLLERS

Dedicated gaming input devices – controllers – first went mainstream on the Famicom, Coleco Vision, Atart 2600, and a few other early home gaming consoles. And it is easy to forget just how far controllers have come from the early days of crude joysticks with a single button to modern PlayStation or Xbox controllers.

Today's PlayStation 5 DualSense controller features haptic "rumble" feedback, a microphone, targeted speakers on the controller itself, adaptive force triggers that offer variable spring-driven resistance the developer can tune, a touchpad, 20 different buttons, lights, and a long lived battery and Bluetooth connectivity for wireless play. In short, these are deeply designed and very sophisticated multi-input and output devices which incorporate a mountain of technology to optimize for gaming. Realistically, a development team needs a dedicated fair senior engineer and designer pairing focused just on maximizing for a controller during much of production in order to truly take advantage of everything the device can do. And they keep improving every few years.

While much of the basic tech which drives improvements in console controllers drafts off of research and applied innovations in mobile phones. And many of the same approaches will work well for dedicated controllers designed for more immersive VR systems, we should expect this area of hardware and software design to continue to receive a lot of focus over the coming decade. Indeed, one of the bigger questions is if

VR style controllers and console style controllers will end up converging. There's nothing about the current dual-stick model that couldn't work well in VR, except that the controller complexity common on consoles right now (so many buttons) is challenging to handle initially without the ability to glance down at the controller.

Will they allow for any truly brand-new innovation for game designers? I'm less sure of this; but allowing players to use their hands, fingers, and ears to precisely control a game will expand the medium on two ends. First, better controllers can be used for ever deeper levels of immersion. Imagine a game whose haptic, audio, and trigger sensitivity allowed players to really feel the precise tumblers of a lock-picking minigame or similar. On the other end of the spectrum, lowered friction from fast wireless connectivity, long battery life, adaptive input to scale with difficulty, and similar can potentially widen the audience of console games, at least for those citizens wealthy enough to afford this kind of dedicated entertainment technology.

GESTURES

But why do you even need to hold an expensive piece of plastic to use your hands and fingers to control games?

With the ubiquity of cameras on laptops, on mobile phones, and in many rooms, and the increasing sophistication of computer vision it seems quite likely that we could easily sort fine motor control and intent by watching a user move their fingers even without touching any physical object in the way that an orchestra interprets fine tuning of their performance just by watching the hand gestures of the conductor.

Indeed, companies like TapWithUs already create wearable devices which perform much of this function, albeit with a wearable hand-harness. This kind of device effectively tracks a user's fine movements as if it were mapped to a keyboard or mouse, then sends the input to a nearby tablet or PC via Bluetooth (Figure 6.1).

But why is there even a need for the finger wearable? With fine enough camera detection and image recognition there probably won't be. And for controllers, is there any reason my 2030 Xbox hardware cameras couldn't just watch my hands for gestures and move a character in a game accordingly? I don't think so. There are sacrifices associated with this approach: Likely this would provide less fine control than dual-stick controllers, and a lack of haptic feedback at an even basic level reduces the effectiveness of some of the feedback loops gamers have become accustomed to. But for

FIGURE 6.1   The TapStrap2 provides a way for a user's gestures to replicate mouse and keyboard input. (*Image Credit:* TapWithUs.com.)

millions, the ability to use gesture controls simply by weaving their wingers in the air anywhere without any expensive dedicated hardware would likely be a huge improvement. And in a world where immersive headset or other tech that impaired a user's real-world vision were common, this would likely be much easier than trying to fumble around for a controller you cannot see.

EYE TRACKING AS INPUT

Thus far, most software hasn't developed the input sophistication to know what a user is looking at or focused on. This will change. There's likely no single better way to improve User Interface design than for us to be able to tell what a user's eyes are focused on currently. As a simple example, imagine how valuable it could be for a tooltip to appear near something on a webpage or game element in a tutorial when a user's gaze hovers on it for some length of time.

User focus group research for games, marketing, and webpage optimization regularly conduct studies where they track where a user's focus is by tracking eye movement in User Research labs.[3] According to Adobe:

> Eye tracking is a technology that measures eye movements and makes it possible to know where a person is looking, what they are looking at, and for how long their gaze is in a particular spot.

FIGURE 6.2   Tobii Pro Glasses 3 tracks the gaze of a player, and provides insights which can improve user interface design to achieve an even better user experience. (*Image Credit:* Tobii AB.)

Companies like Tobii provide sophisticated solutions to help game developers understand how users engage with games on a deeper level. Eye tracking glasses let you see if your designs work as intended by observing user interaction and visual attention from the gamer's perspective. Combined with EEG equipment you can estimate cognitive and emotional states of the player (Figure 6.2).

Right now, these efforts are mostly used during a product's development in order to improve it for an end user. But it is quite easy to imagine real-time software analysis of the same input to control games. (Indeed, Microsoft's Hololens reportedly relies on some advanced eye tracking already.) Could a player indicate where they wanted their character to move based on where they looked on screen? Accept a dialog box with a double blink? Sure. To do this, we need the ability to track iris movement and track it relative to objects in screen space; this takes high-resolution cameras and sophisticated software, but as we can see, this technology exists today and could be easily adapted to consumer grade experiences if the cameras were there. And as we will discuss next, they will be.

Q AND A WITH ANAND SRIVATSA OF TOBII: THE FUTURE OF INPUT MECHANISMS

Anand Srivatsa is the CEO of Tobii AB, global leader in eye tracking and attention computing technologies. Tobii is headquartered in Stockholm, Sweden and operates globally.

TF: Why don't you tell us about who you are and what you do in the games and technology business?

Anand: Sure. My name is Anand Srivatsa. I am the CEO of Tobii. I've been at Tobii a little over two and a half years. And Tobii is in the business of attention computing which is enabling machines to understand human attention. And one of the early areas that we've seen a lot of value in the technology that we bring is to help games become more immersive. That's one aspect where we see a lot of applicability of our technology. But there's a couple of other areas around that, which is not only helping games become more intuitive and easy to use, but also around making games more visually appealing by using some techniques around rendering and things like that.

Also, from a game developer perspective, I think there are opportunities in general to understand how gamers engage with their games. We see multiple aspects of how our technology can be useful in the gaming arena. The one that we are most commonly focused on today is around making the gameplay experience more immersive, and intuitive.

TF: How does your technology help make games more immersive, more intuitive?

Anand: What our technology does is it is able to track people's head poses and where they're looking at on the screen. What we're able to do for example is to interpret natural movements and provide that as an input into games to have the game make choices about gameplay based on natural human movement.

For example, in a simulator game like *Microsoft Flight Simulator* or in a space game like *Star Citizen*, small movement of your head or eyes allow you to move the in-game camera rather than having to go use your keyboard, to go and change the view from the window. And that kind of experience become super immersive for a user who is really wanting to experience that joy of flying or being in a well-crafted space sim. Naturally moving your head and having the world react to you, it gives you that next level of immersion, to feel like "I'm actually flying." So that's one aspect.

The second kind of major utility that we see in games is actually around helping with interaction with objects. So, in games like *Assassin's Creed Valhalla*, where there's a lot of looting of elements in a chest or you're sort of looking through things, what you typically would have to do is you see a chest in your monitor or in your screen, you move your mouse or cursor over it, then the game says, "Okay. Now you want to loot it" and then you hit a button and you loot it.

And what we're able to do is a simple thing where say, you look at what you want to loot. The game understands what you're looking at and can automatically loot it. That reduces a lot of mouse clicks and interface, just going through looting things. And a bunch of that activity is not really the enjoyable part of the game experience. What you really want to do is see what's inside the chest, not spend the time navigating your cursor over it.

There's a couple of those kinds of elements, but we really believe that as game developers get more access to this with our devices having bigger footprints, we really think the magic is going to be from game developers coming up with the best experiences. These couple that we come up with, these aren't things that Tobii invented. These are things that game developers have landed on and we fully expect that as they think through more things in their game there are tons of things that they do, that could be really interesting.

One recent example actually, the *Star Citizen* implemented beyond extended view, is to be able to do target selection with your eyes. So as you're looking over, imagine the kind of world-view we have in sci-fi, which is where you probably have a HUD in your helmet, it's not going to be that, you have to go and put your crosshair on something. Where you're looking the ship should be smart enough to say, "Okay. That's what you're selecting." Then you can do something with it. Like maybe you can go choose to land there. Maybe we want to fire on that object, etc. I think there are these kinds of elements that are starting to come in as well.

Interviewer: How do you think of the technology that is required to track where a user's attention is and the type of hardware that's required in order to do that? Can these things be decoupled or do you expect bespoke, glasses, contacts, or headsets to be required for a while?

Anand: I think that what we see is that there are two sets of things. So one is today, we have been in the business of enabling bespoke hardware in some kinds of use cases, specifically about trackers are attached to a screen. And part of the reason for that is you typically don't have cameras placed in a position that would get a good view of a user's eyes.

You think about a webcam on top of a monitor. The challenge for us is that our eyelids close from top to bottom. If the camera is above you, there's a problem as you're looking down at the bottom of the screen, your camera is going to be occluded by your eyelid closing, when your eyes are half-closed. Our ideal position for cameras is actually on the bottom of the screen so that it actually gets your eyes for most of the periods that you are looking around the screen.

In the beginning, we saw as bespoke hardware, but we used it to go one step further. It wasn't just where it was placed. We did custom sensors. We did custom illuminators, custom compute elements. Those are all things that are part of our solution set. As we see both camera sensors becoming more capable, and compute becoming more accessible. We're actually starting to run on more custom types of components. We may have to actually design a system to go and get your eye-tracking data, but those elements are becoming off the shelf.

An example is we have integrations and the VR headsets like the Pico Neo 3i. It uses off-the-shelf components for everything. It uses off-the-shelf illuminators, off-the-shelf cameras, and the processing is done on the Qualcomm CPU. None of those elements are Tobii-specific. I do believe that over time, if a camera that could get your eye position was there anyway for other reasons or because eye tracking became so important, we believe that over time that the need for custom hardware will go away. But this is part of the chicken and egg that we're trying to drive, which is how can we get the hardware there so that we can deliver the signals that create the value.

TF: At what point do you expect a fairly seamless end consumer blend of eye-tracking technology, as well as immersive heads-up display of the type that would see in VR glasses or even an AR solution? When do you imagine these things merging?

Anand: I think that the first thing that the most likely implementation for the kinds of technologies that I think we drive is going to be around consumer VR. That's because I think consumer VR, you actually don't come in with a bunch of traditional IO methods here. You don't come in with a mouse and keyboard and so there's obviously a lot of innovation around controller types and inside-out tracking and things like that.

Fundamentally, if you have an occluded world space and a virtual world inside it, the fact your eyes can be part of your input modality, I think creates a lot of value in that kind of environment. And I think that's the first area where you can start changing user behavior, where you can start getting them used to the fact that your eyes can be used for intuitive-immersive experiences.

I think there increasingly will be overlap in game title design for VR and either personal computing or console. I think as VR becomes more mainstream, there's going to be variants of this. Which then means that game developers will have done some experimentation of what do you do in VR with eye tracking and hopefully, they'll find some of those methods to also be applicable on the PC side.

I think that actually because of the challenges of AR, I think just from a physical device perspective I expect that by the time we get to AR, some of these eye-tracking modalities will have become more mainstream. I think they are required for AR, but I think the challenge to actually get AR in volume mass market is not an eye tracking challenge. I think it's getting the display low-power enough, good enough, glasses light enough, etc. And I think that's probably six years, seven years out for AR. I think VR is probably starting this year and beyond that I see sort of the smooth move from VR into AR.

TF: Beyond eye tracking and some of the display technologies that we've talked about, what tech or social trends do you think are likely to have the most profound impact on the way humans play games over the next 20 years?

Anand: I think the one major change that we are already starting to see is persistent games. I think gaming really has fundamentally changed over the last 20 years. From titles that had a life cycle to titles that live on their own and morph over time to become more than just the kind of game you expect.

I think *Roblox* is a really good example. You start out with *Roblox*, I think it's one kind of game. But it has all kinds of games as elements inside of it. And I think that as we think about the kind of experience that a user has in that environment, as they're more and more sort of committed to that experience and the variety of choices they have in there, I expect that they will want much deeper personalization of their characters in the game. Because I think what we're starting to see, I believe as a trend would be, it's almost like going back *Dungeons and Dragons*, right? It's not a closed-ended story. It's an open-ended story world. And in that open-ended story world, you're going to want your avatar to represent how you are enjoying or acting in the moment in the game.

And I think up until now that has been either not possible or not relevant. If you were in sort of a close game environment and your character is your character, doesn't matter what you look like. Maybe you can change skin tones and things like that, but there's sort of some built-in kind of framework for how they act and who they are and the story arc that they're progressing through.

I think that is a really interesting potential, which is at the end of this rainbow, is it's going to be 50 big games that billions of people play where it's like 100 million people playing one game, I don't know. That I think is an interesting potential where maybe instead of saying we have a console platform, *Roblox* is the platform and people build many games inside *Roblox*.

CAMERAS

My current phone, a mid-range Samsung, currently boasts six different tiny camera lenses on the back, plus another on the front. My laptop has two. Home security systems like Nest have become extremely common in the developed world. China alone has hundreds of millions of highly-accurate security cameras capable of advanced facial recognition.[4] This will rapidly become the standard for most countries in the world. While privacy advocates may (rightly) express concern about some of the nefarious authoritarian uses to which all of these devices can be put, in the spirit of optimism and positive futurism let us contemplate the ways in which a networks of cameras could be used to facilitate gaming.

The Nintendo Wii, Microsoft Kinect, and Sony PlayStation Camera have all introduced the concept of using cameras into gaming over the past decade. These bits of dedicated hardware and software allow users to be scored on their dance moves, introduced a new level of physicality into some games, were players were asked to jump, duck, mimic sword-swipes with their arms, and so on. We can expect a massive increase in the numbers of networked cameras and AI Computer Vision to hugely expand the ways in which game designers could make use of cameras as an input device.

In a world where your phone knows where you are all the time and what cameras are nearby, could you play a fishing game that let you mime casting with a rod-and-reel, then reel in and lift the rod at the right times? Sure. Could this work based on the camera inputs in your living room? Yes. On a city bus? Certainly, given the right access to that data stream. Could conversational AI in role-playing games receive a player's exasperated hand gestures or an eye roll as input and have a subject-analysis tool that incorporated the unconscious reflexive gestures into building a profile of the player's emotional state, and choosing the right behavioral response? Yes. While sophisticated, this ability to read a player's mood will be essential to NLP driven "virtual dating" type games, and is likely only about 8–12 years away. Establishing an order of magnitude more sophisticated layer of player and user inputs will likely rely heavily on cameras to capture gestures, involuntary responses, eye tracking, even posture. The key to making these kinds of inputs useful to game designers will be to provide libraries of software which abstract the mechanical analysis into higher-order player state descriptions. ("The player is getting bored." Or "The player is angry.") This will allow designers to focus on building gameplay responses rather than getting caught up in lower-level input interpretation. A good game master in tabletop role-playing senses and adjusts game content subtlety and accordingly. Gaming software designers can do the same thing soon.

Of course, there are a few challenges with using camera inputs excessively. The first of these – as designers learned over the last 20 years – is that constant motion for input is fatiguing. A player might hack and slash enemies for hours with a controller in a Dynasty Warriors type game, but very few want to flail their arms around mimicking swordplay for hours in their living room. Different players have different body types, may be unable to stand, may be missing limbs, might lack the motor control of another player, etc. There are accessibility problems. Cultural differences in expressions and gestures make the kind of high-order player mindset interpretation challenging. And of course, there are very real privacy concerns associated with cameras. So while cameras will likely play an increasingly large role in providing input to games, their designers, and the AI directors that assist in running them, this is likely to remain a niche input mechanism until 2030 or later.

DRONES

Fixed-position cameras like we just talked about provide one level of input, but they are inherently limited. Drones can help solve much of this problem, by providing camera, infrared, and other video input from a dynamic perspective. The miniaturization technology, software for steering and navigating, camera technology, and battery technologies for these devices is improving quite rapidly. Because these devices are able to be made quite small, micro-drones are likely to be more popular for consumer use than larger, bulkier models used for commercial grade filming or military action. Indeed, already today the smallest drones are smaller than 1.5 by 1.5 inches and can fly for 45 minutes on a charge while streaming back 4k video. We should expect these to get much smaller.

I expect it is highly likely that most smart-vehicles sold after 2030 or so will feature an embedded drone which can take off from the vehicle, escort and provide information and an eye-in-the-sky camera for the car, then land and charge as necessary even while the car is in transit.

Similarly, one can easily imagine the KinectDrone technology by which a console is sold with a drone that can watch and record players, providing high-quality control input, but also allow for streamers to Twitch-stream themselves with high-quality cinematographic AI helping film while they game.

Of course, a single drone has problems, if only because there is down time while they need to return to a landing station to recharge. So imagine instead that users regularly had a small swarm of drones the size of fruit flies or gnats which could be deployed when they wanted high quality always on camera technology. These could easily be deployed from and recharged by consoles, laptops, or even launched from a bay within a phone. A swarm of drones could easily follow a player around the house, or around the city to catch every gesture, their speech, eye movements, and their expressions. While this may sound a far-fetched use of very complex technology to be used just for entertainment, I believe we likely will start to see and accept drone swarms just as we accept cameras on our laptops today. If we accept that cameras provide valuable input for software, then it is a short walk to accepting that swarms of micro-drones provide better camera coverage, and could be used to augment the same basic need for high-quality input.

FINGER TAPS

Could we allow players to provide input to a game with simple taps and double taps on their fingertips? Yes. Smart watches could likely detect and report the vibrations. Cameras could easily track input at this level, which is much simpler than fine-dexterity controller level inputs.

For a game to exclusively accept this level of input would likely limit us to fairly rudimentary sets of choices, but the value of subtlety and silence could make this a good input mechanism for many types of software. Aided by sophisticated and limited and contextual choices this type of input could be useful for small scale games played primarily on a user's glasses. Alternately, we could imagine group games at a sporting event or movie theater which asked everyone to tap their fingertips together to vote on a particular topic. Imagine interactive fiction, like Netflix *Black Mirror's* groundbreaking Bandersnatch, in which real-time input from millions of viewers determined the twists and turns of a story. IS a simple input mechanic like finger-tapping essential to this vision? Not at all. But we could likely do away with remote controls using some variant in this kind of input theory.

MORE ADVANCED ANATOMICALLY INTEGRATED INPUT

Similarly, could users and players tap teeth together to make a selection or press their tongue against the roof of their mouth to provide input to a game? Yes, though this likely requires a level of biometric sensor hardware integration into the body that isn't common yet. And since there are a host of medical concerns with truly embedded hardware that lives within the flesh of a user for months or years, I suspect we are more than two decades away from this kind of thing being a reality. While it has long been a mainstay of cyberpunk fiction, true implant technology, biometric tattoos, and so forth are likely decades away, and even then probably not something we can count on for mainstream widespread adoption.

More common are simple wearable devices that provide input. Earrings, watches, and rings are likely candidates for these kinds of input devices. I think we should expect these sorts of input devices to become more common over the next decade, but we will likely rely on a user's personal device (phone) to provide a layer of abstraction for games to rely on. Just as a game can "play audio" and leave it up to the device to determine if this is output on the phone's speaker, Bluetooth connected headphones, or similar, we should expect consumer grade hardware and operating systems to translate input from a variety of devices and sources into higher-order concepts for the game software to use. As a game designer, you don't particularly care if a user clicked their heels together or right-clicked on a mouse to accept an NPC's offer to join their adventuring party.

Considering inputs as a higher-level user preference or decision rather than worrying about the specific input mechanics is a valuable way for game designers to think about user input. What, specifically, a user did is not what is really important; what matters is what they want.

THOUGHT CONTROL

But wouldn't it be cool if players could just control the game with their mind?

Cyberpunk writers like William Gibson were comfortable imagining direct brain-to-silicon "biosofts" that would plug into a slot behind a user's ear – something like a USB thumb drive perhaps – and allow direct mental input and feedback. Perhaps this will happen someday, at least for some humans. Perhaps. But how close are we to such direct interfaces to the human brain? How would such a thing work? How could we use it to better entertain the world with our games?

Brain Computer Interfaces (BCI) are a field of study dedicated to answering these questions. A number of companies around the world, including Elon Musk's startup, Neuralink,[5] are attempting to prove out the research and development aspects of this technology before moving on to commercial application. Currently, they are using pigs as a test case, harvesting information on the creatures' neural processes and activity.

The fundamental science behind this technology relies on the notion that neurons in the human brain send and receive electrical signals to other neurons. If we could read, send, and interpret these signals, could we not bypass all of the clumsiness of optic nerves and fingernails and the rest of the meat that stands between a player's senses and their game?

Initial users for this kind of technology have huge implications for people who have been injured by damage to the brain or spine. The kinds of understanding of neurological processes this research will lead to could give us valuable insights into other kinds of memory problems, like dementia or Alzheimer's, which could improve the quality of life for millions of sufferers and their families. Further, it has been posited that this branch of technology could lead to the ability to record a user's thoughts and memories, or even capture their personalities in a digital form. (Dixie Flatline, RIP.)

Another company based out of Brooklyn, New York, has raised funds to focus more specifically on the gaming market. OpenBCI has bootstrapped hardware and software solutions focused on the R&D departments of universities and large corporate clients. They use an open source model, such that code, blueprints, and data are all shared online via GitHub, so they encourage community participation. Currently the hardware kits they provide retail for less than $500 USD, making them affordable to hobbyists and tinkerer inventors the world over. According to the company's literature, their sensors are meant to capture EEG data by fitting sensitive caps to a user's skull. This means that the technology reads gross biometric data from the outside, rather than trying for the far more complex reading to individual neuron clusters (Figure 6.3).

Is it possible that within the next 20 years you personally will be able to control a game with your thoughts? Yes. I think perhaps it is, in a very limited test case. Is it likely that everyone on the planet will be using sophisticated neural monitoring hardware that lives inside their skulls and can be used to control any and all games? No. I think that quite unlikely even within 100 years; there are just too many people and the technology is far

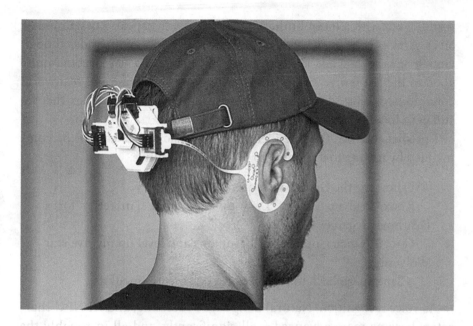

FIGURE 6.3 OpenBCI provides hardware for researchers interested in exploring Brain Computer Interfaces. (*Image Credit:* OpenBCI.)

too complex. It also is not really clear how many advantages this would give us, or that the level of mental discipline and focus required is ideal. Imagine trying to focus your thoughts in such a specific way that you could keep your character edging along a cliff's edge in a *Dark Souls* game. Now imagine that one of your children runs through the room eating pasta with their hands and dropping it all over the floor. Do you have the mental discipline not to notice, not to let this break your concentration? Would you want to? Do most of the people you know?

So while some limited level of reading of data from the surface of a person's brain seems likely in the next 20 years, perhaps to great effect in some fields, I do not expect that BCI will likely become a mainstream interface mechanism for gaming anytime before the year 2100.

SPEECH

By far the most significant advances in gaming input over the next two decades will occur in Natural Language Processing for almost all input. Today, Siri and Google answer questions on mobile phones. Tesla cars will roll down the windows and change the music for you. Amazon's Alexa and the Google Home helper hang out in living rooms throughout the wealthy world… but with a lot of limitations: Alexa doesn't speak Russian today; Siri's Arabic is poor at understanding even basic commands, though Google gets it, but not Hebrew. Voice interpretation has become quite good in the last few years, but the use cases are so diverse and real-world conditions, accents, dialect, and ambient noise often so complex that we still get a lot of mistakes. This will change.

I predict that by 2025 the idea that any basic device cannot be commanded by talking to it is going to seem very primitive.

> TV, show me the Greenbay Packer's game.
> Xbox, load up *Call of Duty* and tell Mike I'm ready for a Deathmatch game.
> Google, Open Contest of Champions and level up my five star Wolverine.
> Claptrap, go back to the base and buy me five medkits.

As voice recognition, Natural Language Processing, and AI NPC characters become more advanced – all significantly, and all in roughly the same decade – we will enter a new phase of interaction between players and their games. It find it highly likely that by 2040 voice and natural dialog communications will be the 95% standard for controlling most games which are not explicitly designed for testing and honing twitch reflex dexterity.

Because this was the ways games were built in the past should not make us believe this is the way they are going; the Atari controller style focus on manual dexterity, and the corresponding generation of games that tested and relied upon this as the primary mechanism of input for player was a function of the input mechanics, not necessarily reflective of the potential of the medium, nor of the desire of most human players. Just because some people like tennis and choose to play it does not mean most people do, or that dexterity-based skill tests are what most people choose. Indeed, these are largely relegated to sports and a few very specialized occupations. Mostly, people don't focus on doing things that force them to master fine motor control for their recreation; there are far more movie watchers than whittlers, for example. The ability for game makers to use speech as the primary input and control mechanism will welcome billions more players to into games.

Imagine playing The Witcher, and in any tavern you can have conversations that feel authentic and natural for hours at a time with characters while you are playing Ghent with them. Not everyone wants this level of immersion in fantasy worlds, but to many people this would be an incredible reprieve from their daily grind.

In tactical games like *League of Legends* how could this work? To start, you could just tell the game what character you wanted, with which spec. "Enter at Silver level, I want Sona or Master Yi with a Kraken Slayer build." You certainly could also provide meta-layer instructions during a match as well. "Tag everyone to rush top lane now!"

Adventure and story games are an obvious fit for this. Could we see a resurgence of the King's Quest series that were entirely verbally controlled? Yes. Would you imagine *Advanced Dungeons & Dragons* or *Zork* style games which were almost exclusively through dialog and text? Certainly. In fact, in *Zork* Dungeon some fans of the original have brought the original text adventure quest to explore the Great Underground Empire to Amazon Alexa, allowing players to attempt to play an entirely voice related adventure (and get eaten by a grue quickly, usually!) using their Amazon Alexa device. This kind of gaming will likely become much more popular as the technology improves.

It is a little harder to see where NLP fits in for games that are more idle or occupy the fingers, (like knitting) by getting players to match or merge icons. Shooters, likewise, aside from in front end menu commands to set up matches or choose loadouts, etc. are a little easier to imagine. ("Set a waypoint west of the enemy base near the exploding barrels!") Fighting games are equally hard to imagine making a full transition to speech controlled. ("Punch, kick! Knee!" Nope.) For many games that specifically delight players through demonstration of dexterity, it is likely that voice commands remain a secondary input mechanism at best.

However, there's a great opportunity for many types of games to drive higher-order interactions by abstracting basic commands (↑↑↓↓←→←→BA Start) to higher-order inputs. So users will likely not give commands like, "Jezeme go north, go north, go east." But: "Jezeme, go check out that mountain. Avoid the lake."

However, sometimes talking aloud is no good. On a crowded bus most people don't want to be shouting out commands to their teammates. For this reason alone, it will be challenging for many games to completely replace other types of input with exclusive voice control.

Games will continue with and without speech and player vocal input. But the majority of games and game capable devices will accept voice inputs most of the time starting fairly soon.

HAPTIC FEEDBACK

Vision is only one of the senses that game makers can use to engage with players. Thus far few games have made use of feedback mechanisms that allow a player's sense of touch or tactile input to give them information or drive immersion. But the level of increased immersion we can achieve by engaging more senses is valuable in driving greater user engagement. Let's look at a few common approaches.

Since the Nintendo 64 controller, game console controllers have included some level of vibration – which qualifies as a very basic level of haptic feedback. Allowing a controller to rumble when going over rough terrain in a racing game like *Mario Kart*, or to vibrate when a user takes a damage from a jab in a fighting game helps reinforce the on-screen animation and gives a player's mind valuable input that helps them understand what is happening in the game. This qualifies as a very basic level of haptic feedback that we have used in gaming for 30 years.

Slightly more advanced variations on these basics have been a part of some gaming mice and keyboards for a decade now. Companies like the gaming peripheral maker, Razer have developed connected ecosystems (like Hypersense[6]) which connect a variety of feedback devices to games. Keyboards, mice, gaming pads, specialized earphones, and chairs can all be connected to a modern gaming PC and provide some level of additional stimulation (though it all pretty much still feels like variations on vibration, at least in 2021[7]) (Figure 6.4).

Still other researchers and companies imagine haptic feedback capabilities embedded into clothing. Some of these, like the Teslasuit[8] (no relation to Mr. Musk's vehicle and battery storage company) purport to offer full-body haptic feedback to advance VR training and gaming both. Wearing a full-body suit which looks like a wetsuit is supposed to allow software designed to support it to ability to apply a feeling of pressure anywhere covered by the suit. These suits also monitor biometrics (roughly similar to what current smart watches can track), which can be ingested by the software to alter the simulation.

While a full-body suit will certainly deliver the most advanced level of haptic feedback and immersion, it is a little difficult to imagine most gamers ever getting suited up in this fashion. To this end, lighter weight integrations into clothing are likely to be a more common use case for most people.

But haptic feedback can get a lot more advanced than making a controller rumble. The human tactile nervous system can be very nuanced in

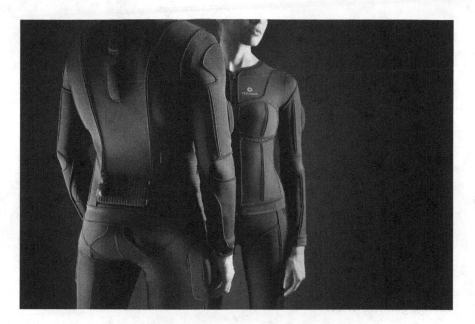

FIGURE 6.4 Haptic feedback enabled clothing like the Teslasuit promise full-body sensation which could be used to enhance immersion in VR gaming. (*Image Credit:* Teslasuit.)

sensing the feeling of different materials, temperature, hardness, moisture, and the like. There's no reason to believe that games could not offer stimulation of these types.

How to deliver these kinds of sensations without forcing users into a bulky suit is one of the challenges which will likely start to require deeper integration of direct neural stimulation through other means. Can we imagine a bracelet or headband which made our mind feel like we were experiencing the chill wind off of Caradhras alongside a virtual Frodo and Gandalf? Sure. At the moment, this kind of technology is likely not ready to be consumer facing until 2035 at the earliest.

DISPLAYS

What are the visual outputs we can expect beyond televisions, monitors, phone screens, and tablets?

More of them all, is the most likely answer. The ubiquity of screens and their decoupling from the specifics of any given device is the best answer. Can players play in their cars? Yes. Can they play on their phone, then keep playing the same game on their TV as soon as they enter their living room or bedroom? Yes. Will windows or bathroom mirrors be able to be turned into screens for displaying games? Yes, they already can in specialized installations; this will become more common (though likely dedicated standalone single-function screens will remain higher quality and far more affordable for most people for a long time).

Already today I can play a game like *Marvel Contest of Champions* on my iPhone, then cast it to my HDTV when I sit down on the couch. As discussed, Cloud Gaming, which will move the heavy lifting of computation off the player's local device will make this even easier.

Giving gamers the chance to play on any screen anywhere regardless of the device(s) used for inputs should be our goal, and we can expect that to become the standard over the coming decade as cross-device interoperability becomes lower friction.

But what kind of new form factors to screens can we expect that might change gaming more?

GLASSES AND VR HEADSETS

> He remembered thin Puerto Ricans under East Side streetlights, dreaming real to the quick beat of a salsa, dreamgirls shuddering and turning, the onlookers clapping in time. But that had needed a van full of gear and a clumsy trode helmet...
>
> – *William Gibson,* Neuromancer, *1981*

Virtual Reality headsets first entered the consumer mainstream with the Nintendo Virtual Boy in the mid-80s, but this device was primitive, with low-resolution display. In the four decades that have come since, VR headsets have become dramatically more sophisticated. Only in the last few years have wireless headsets with high-resolution displays, head tracking, and other advances become commonplace (Figure 6.5).

In 2016, Google and a few other companies approached the problem in a novel way with a device called Google Cardboard. Cardboard was a fairly short-lived experiment in which a headset costing only a few dollars used optic lenses to magnify a pair of images when used in conjunction with a mobile phone. Google build out a higher-end version of the same device called the Google Fabric, which was slightly more comfortable and was covered in a light gray fabric, mimicking the feeling of clothing. On these devices, for which one Google produced mobile device, the Pixel line, were

FIGURE 6.5 Google Daydream VR was a short-lived but innovative look at the future of VR headset displays. (*Image Credit:* Tim Fields.)

particularly optimized, Google deployed an application called Daydream, which acted as a VR hub for a variety of games and applications. Within a few years, Google had moved on from the experiment, dropping support for Daydream and ceasing to sell Cardboard in 2021. While a number of journalists seemed to view this effort as a failure,[9] something akin to the short-lived Google Glass efforts in 2014, I believe this view is too short term. For VR to truly become widespread, the headsets need to be cheap, portable, unplugged. The computing power and display that animates them will need to be highly portable as well. Phones are the perfect answer for this problem, particularly as Cloud Gaming allows more of the processing to be moved off device. Cardboard and Fabric and Daydream pointed to exactly where the VR ecosystem will go: they were just a decade early.

But fully-immersive VR headsets are only part of the solution set gamers need. To become truly mainstream, headset displays need to be less obtrusive, and need to be able to perform both complete vision-blocking immersion like the Google devices or Oculus Rift, but also allow for clear vision when a user wants to walk around the real world without bumping into things. The ability to display atop lenses that a user can otherwise see through is often referred to as Augmented Reality (AR). Using near-field communications, a pair of glasses can transmit data to and from a nearby device, usually a phone in the user's pocket. This level of data transmission, currently common under the Bluetooth standard, is referred to as Near-Field Communication (NFC). This ability to communicate between multiple nearby devices uses short range radio wave technology in the Ultra-High-Frequency range.

In 2021, sunglasses manufacturer Ray-Ban in partnership with Facebook began selling Ran-Ban Stories, some of the first consumer mass-market "Smart Glasses." In practice, these are (currently) little more than a camera and pair of speakers and microphone integrated into an iconic sunglasses frame and paired with an application that runs on Android or iOS. The glasses can record photos or video, be used to conduct phone calls or listen to music. They currently offer no AR display capabilities. However, we should expect the ability to provide overlay images in the glass to become commonplace over the next decade.

Headset displays which look like regular glasses or sunglasses, can provide complete immersion for gaming or AR style overlay displays for real-world vision augmentation (and AR gaming!) are still a few years out, but they will likely become a commonplace display and interface mechanism, allowing 3D gaming experiences on the go.

Will these become the standard use case for games? Yes and no. As mentioned previously, gamers will expect any game they are excited about to be accessible on any screen and interface mechanism they have access to whenever they want it. So we should plan on creating games that offer a way to participate in ways and at a level which are appropriate to the form factor and situation a device lends itself to. When I'm on the bus wearing my Ray-BanXR glasses I may want to check in on my Alliance in a 4X game, seeing their chat constantly scrolling on the bottom of by glasses while I look out the window of the bus. When they need me to send out a defending force to support them I should be able to dial the spectacles up to full immersion, receive a view into the game world in stereoscopic 3D, assign some troops to move out, then switch back to AR mode. When it is time to get off the bus and walk a few blocks to meet friends, I should expect to turn off the AR chat completely if I want to focus on my surroundings. And when I reach the restaurant where my friends are waiting, I will expect to take off the sunglasses, put them in my coat pocket and turn my attention to in-person interaction.

While this vision requires advances on optics hardware (mostly the display on clear lenses tech) and significant levels of miniaturization of the components in VR headsets, it also will require increased amounts of bandwidth for NFC between glasses and a mobile device. Advances in battery technology will also help reduce friction for users, as high-resolution display and rendering as envisioned here will tend to exhaust small batteries quickly.

This level of user controlled hybrid immersion, AR, scaling is likely to be commonplace within ten years, and will likely be a commonplace method for interacting with games by 2035.

CONTACTS AND RETINA PROJECTION

The next layer of visual immersion and reduced friction for display is to project directly on a user's eyeball, or a thin surface attached to it, like a contact lens. This has long been the stuff of science fiction, but the technology to display on a lens is rapidly advancing (Figure 6.6).

Companies like Mojo Vision, recently selected by the Walt Disney Company as party of an accelerator program, have been working on this kind of technology since 2008.[10] Currently, these sophisticated contact lenses can display basic HUD style information for users. While this company and others focused on R&D for lens type projects are, rightly, focused on a lot of use cases to help people with poor vision, to support first responders, and for military use.

> The Mojo lenses, for example, can detect the text on a road sign in the distance and display it clearly. They can magnify objects or project them onto the part of the person's retina that can still see well. The lenses can help people detect objects in front of them by increasing the contrast between the shades or colors of the objects. The lenses can also superimpose graphic lines over the hard-to-see edges of objects within the wearer's view.
>
> *Mark Sullivan, Fast Company*[11]

FIGURE 6.6 The Mojo lens by Mojo Vision promise to transform our ability to receive information overlaid with our traditional vision, and provide data for Augmented Reality experiences. (*Image Credit:* Mojo Vision.)

The application for VR and AR gaming technology is obvious. Eye-mounted LED displays can work. The displays themselves are about the size of a grain of sand, but can display 70,000 pixels in this tiny surface. In 2020. Parts of the retina are great at observing extremely close image detail. There are challenges with refresh rates, providing power, and above all with safety concerns. But by 2040 we should expect these devices to be in millions of eyeballs around the globe.

I believe we should expect consumer grade contact lenses which can display high-resolution images that can serve particularly well for AR style games to become commonplace over the next 20 years. Will they be a primary mechanism for gaming for billions of people? Probably not. Only around 125 million people use corrective contact lenses on Earth today.[12] And glasses are still much easier to build, distribute, wear, and maintain.

These will remain a high end elite item by most of the next 20 years, but will start being used medically to augment human vision regularly within that time. Then, gaming.

WRAP UP ON DEVICES AND INPUTS

When thinking about the huge variety of input and display types which are possible today, or plausible for the near future I am reminded once again of science-fiction writer William Gibson's famous quote:

The future is already here; it just isn't very evenly distributed.

As game makers, how do we entertain a world where a user in a Moscow penthouse is playing our games on million-dollar-a-pair contact lenses, providing input with tooth-taps and having their expressions analyzed by swarms of micro-drones, while playing alongside a player using touches and swipes on the cracked-screen of a hand-me-down Xiaomi phone in a Dhaka slum?

There are a few ways of thinking about this problem, few of them fully satisfying:

- We've been dealing with hardware & bandwidth inequality for a long time.

- We've been dealing with spend inequality for a long time, bracketing by spend group or level is the best answer.

- Building "Gifting" features into our games allows players of different monetization levels to play together more easily.

- Games which rely less on frame-specific dexterity skill testing can help.

- Gamers will understand and adapt; they will have to, some level of hardware, software, connectivity, time, money, dexterity, and a thousand other factors will give some players advantages. Just as a well-funded sports program will – in the long run – have advantages over lesser funded teams. Some contests will inherently be unequal. Our role as game makers and players is to find ways to find the fun in games (and sports) despite their inequalities and flaws.

- But more awareness, lower friction input and responsiveness will give an advantage, and that's just the way it is going to be... As with most other fields of human endeavor.

- And there are room for lots of different games. Very few can appeal to everyone, so knowing the market you are targeting is essential.

Our job is to provide a great experience to as many people as possible. It is not to try to make every person's experience equal; that road leads to Harrison Bergeron.

NOTES

1 https://www.statista.com/statistics/273495/global-shipments-of-personal-computers-since-2006/.
2 https://www.pcgamer.com/im-a-two-mouse-man.
3 https://xd.adobe.com/ideas/process/user-research/eye-tracking-and-usability/.
4 https://fortune.com/2020/11/03/china-surveillance-system-backlash-worlds-largest/.
5 https://www.zdnet.com/article/elon-musks-brain-computer-startup-is-getting-ready-to-blow-your-mind/.
6 https://www2.razer.com/au-en/concepts/project-hypersense.
7 https://www.pcgamer.com/razers-haptic-ecosystem-for-pc-works-but-it-overloaded-my-senses/.
8 https://teslasuit.io/.
9 https://screenrant.com/google-glass-smart-glasses-what-happened-explained/.
10 https://www.fastcompany.com/90441928/the-making-of-mojo-ar-contact-lenses-that-give-your-eyes-superpowers.
11 fastcompany.com/90441928/the-making-of-mojo-ar-contact-lenses-that-give-your-eyes-superpowers.
12 https://www.sciencedaily.com/terms/contact_lens.htm.

CHAPTER 7

Business Models

Do these smiles seem fake? It doesn't matter where they come from. The joy is real.

– P.T. Barnum, The Greatest Show

Game development and publishing is a massive business. You know this.

In 2000, the industry generated a gross revenue of $7.9 billion[1] (including a small fortune in arcades in Japan). By 2020, this number exceeded $180 billion,[2] If this were to continue apace, we would see more than $4 trillion in revenue by 2040. This will not happen, because the population of gamers cannot continue to grow at the rate it has been; 20 years ago most people alive did not play games. Today, most people alive do. Still, we can expect the global video games business to approach a half-trillion-dollar-a-year industry by 2040 as gaming continues to supplant other forms of entertainment.

While there have been a lot of innovations in economic models for games, they've all followed a few major threads, at least until recently. Let's look at the common ways people and businesses make money off of the games they create and publish. Along the way, we will explore the ways they may evolve and discuss a few new potential models.

RETAIL DISTRIBUTION OF GAMES

In the beginning, commercially successful games were packaged goods, sold in specialty retailers like Babbage's for personal computer games, or

DOI: 10.1201/9781003291800-8

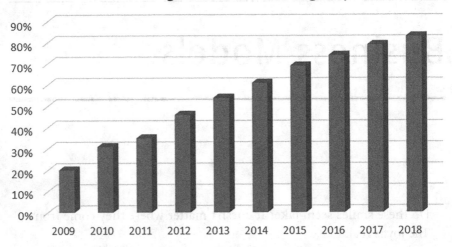

Percentage of Games Sold Digitally

FIGURE 7.1 The move from physical to digital goods has been steady over the last decade. It will continue. (*Image credit*: Tim Fields, Data from Statista.)

on cartridges for Atari or Nintendo games, usually in mass-market retailers. The retail model has had a long and profitable run. For 40 years game developers partnered with game publishers who did deals with retail giants in various countries to distribute boxed products containing floppy disks, cartridges, CD-Roms, DVDs, or Blu-Ray discs. Retailers bought the products in bulk, end users bought these items individually at some markup. The supply chain involved a lot of fulfillment agencies, shippers, and such. Margins were thin for each link in the chain and this model reflected a lot of needless waste in gasoline for trucks, packaging for game boxes, and so on. It was clearly 20 years ago that as bandwidth increased retail would go into decline for digital good, and indeed, it did. By 2018, less than 20% of the games sold were sold in physical form.[3] Digital distribution of software effectively took over and all, but killed retail in most markets over a ten-year period. It seems very unlikely that this trend will slow. It's hard to imagine that this would be a surprising or controversial statement at this point (Figure 7.1).

DIGITAL DISTRIBUTION OF GAMES

Once high-speed internet with sufficient bandwidth became a standard across most of the world, delivering software directly to devices became inevitable. Game makers and publishers were more than happy to cut out the complexity, cost, and logistics of building physical goods and trucking them around the world. The supply chains were simplified, and the revenue from game sales was distributed to a smaller group of players. Various digital platforms took hold, most notably Steam on the PC, Apple, and Google app stores in most of the world, and a host of different online (mostly mobile and web-based) distribution channels in China. Of course, there's nothing to stop PC or Android-focused developers from building a piece of software and distributing directly from their own webstores; many do. And there are hundreds of smaller distribution storefronts, from regional giants like Kakao in South Korea to specialty digital retailers like GoodOldGames in the West. On the console, Sony, Microsoft, and Nintendo all manage curated storefronts accessible from the gaming console which allow users to buy the latest releases and download them directly to the hard drive on the console.

Digital distribution will likely remain the predominant distribution mechanism for the next 20 years or longer. Millions of games are sold each day using a digital-retail model, in which users pay the storefront prior to download, which then remits payment minus a percentage to the developer or publisher. Fundamentally, this is little different from the retail model, except that there are fewer entities in the value chain, and creators tend to get to keep a higher percentage of the final sales price.

But increasingly, "premium products" in which users are asked to pay before playing the game comprise a smaller portion of the total downloads worldwide. Unsurprisingly, "free" entertainment is popular. But not getting paid for your work rarely is. This has led to a few different ways for developers and publishers to monetize their products.

FREE TO PLAY

"Free-to-Play" games now exist on mobile phones, consoles, the PC, and the web. Typically, users get to download and play these games at no cost – usually for as long as they wish. But various pieces of content or power levels are largely inaccessible without either playing for a very long time ("grinding" in gamer parlance) or earning some in-game currency. In-game currencies are usually sold directly from within the software, making use of the distributor's storefront sales and financial reporting mechanisms. This is called In App Purchasing (IAP). Alternately, gamers can (or are forced to) watch short-form advertisements which grant them currencies. This is called In App Advertising (IAA). Both of these techniques for monetizing the otherwise free-to-play game are widely in use on most applications on mobile devices. Collectively these techniques generate billions of dollars a year in revenue, comprising the majority of the income in the gaming industry in 2021.

I believe that IAP and IAA will continue to be the predominant way to make money from the development, publishing, and distribution of games for the next two decades. The sheer volume of users who will try out a game when it is free to engage with (at least initially) simply dwarfs the number who will shell out $50 or more for a "premium product."

In App Purchases range from very straightforward "spend $0.25 to buy more energy to keep playing", which harken back to arcade models designed to keep players plugging quarters into a machine, to very complicated monthly payment cards or subscription models in which users sign up for recurring payments which grant them time-released in-game benefits. The magic to making these types of systems compelling comprises the arcana of an entire school of game and systems design philosophy and technique. The lexicon of this depth of design detail, from "step-up gatcha" to "nested limited time offer" techniques is nuanced, rapidly evolving, and increasingly aided by machine learning which can deliver the right offer to a particular player at the right moment. Indeed, this topic could cover a book unto itself and still would be likely to miss as many techniques as it managed to cover. Suffice to say that a lot of very bright game makers spend a lot of time thinking about how to get players who love their games to give them money.

For this reason, there has been a certain stigma attached to "free-to-play" games for the last decade, particularly in the West. I tend to view this mindset as misguided, perhaps something similar to social philosophies which regard moneylending at profit in a negative light. While usury certainly has negative effects on some people, the overall social good that came from enabling deployment of capital which mandates certain levels of return to generate profit has enabled the modern world. Similarly, allowing people around the world to play games for free until the moment they choose to pay for something has proven integral to the massive expansion of gaming as a pastime for the human race. As a creator, there is something quite affirming when someone who doesn't have to give you a penny to keep playing your game elects of their own free will to give you money. And, while for most free-to-play games only a small percentage of players ever deposit money, some of those who do end up spending quite a lot. This "whale" driven economy describes how much of the gaming industry generates revenue today.

IN APP ADVERTISING

For the billions of players who do not choose to spend what disposable income they have access to on games, there are In App Advertisements. This is the majority of gamers in the world. Let this notion sink in for a moment, and consider the implications. What this means is that games are – primarily – a channel for advertisers to sell products, and that's driving more than a hundred billion dollar a year business already. On some level, this is a strange way of thinking about the medium, but since it puts games in the same category as magazines, newspapers, and (most) television, perhaps it should not feel so strange. Symbiotic relationships between commercial interests and works of entertainment, art, and enlightenment have a long history.

In many ways, highly tailored In App Advertisements are one of the monetization techniques I expect to continue to evolve the most. Over the last five years, mobile (and some PC gaming) have started to drive a healthy advertising ecosystem and driven the creation of a number of high-quality integrated solutions for allowing game makers to tailor the places advertisements (particularly "rewarded video" ads) appear in the flow of games. Creators can now select users based on their profile to determine when, how many, and what kind of ads they should receive. For example, a developer might choose to show no ads to a player for their first two days of play, then only show some ads to those users whose behavior (or spending habits in other games) indicated they were unlikely to ever make an In App Purchase. Of course, different users have different values to advertisers, so most ad networks now tailor targeted ads to different users. (For example, a non-spender who is known to be a teenager in the Philippines is a better target for a Jollibee fast-food chain, whereas a Knightsbridge middle-aged man who has spent 10,000 dollars in games might be more likely to be shown an ad for a Patek Phillipe watch.)

Generally speaking, everyone wins in this arrangement: The gamer gets free currency in a game for watching a short ad, which is increasingly likely to be relevant to them. The game maker gets a small amount of revenue from a user who might not have every game monetized. The advertiser gets to advertise their product to a potential customer (and gets lots of information about click-through rates on the ad, etc.) And the ad network does a brisk business and gathers valuable data to improve their business.

Of course, there are privacy and consumer protection concerns about the use of targeted data, storing Personally Identifiable Information (PII) about users. Some have also raised interesting legal and philosophical questions about who should own data generated by a user, who should profit from it, and so on. But almost none of these questions are particularly unique to the games business or to gamers. Advertising allows millions of gamers to play high-quality games for free, which I judge to be a net positive for the world.

As the daily population of gamers increases and the ability of the AI that run ad networks improves based on increasing speed and access to data about users we should expect these kinds of ad targeting systems to get better and better. We should expect micro-targeting for advertisements to become ever more sophisticated, both in their targeting and in the interactivity of their execution. There's no reason a particular ad network cannot know that you were looking at purchasing a tropical vacation and offer to give you in-game currency for spending five minutes walking through the virtual lobby of a resort hotel.

We should expect paid sponsorship networks to partner more deeply with particular game publishers. It's very easy to imagine a sports clothing company like Under Armor doing an exclusive deal with EA Sports titles in which in-situ ads appear in arenas (various incarnations of this have been happening for years already), but also popup targeted ads congratulating a player for a victory, and offering them 15% off something if they click through a video ad, or another 5% of if they win another five games in the next 24 hours. The ability to micro-target more effectively, and an increase in inventory from ad provider networks can ensure that (at least for some games) the product advertisement can potentially add to, rather than subtract from, the sense of immersion in the game.

Depending on the data that ad networks are allowed to access, these ads could become extremely sophisticated. To hearken back to the idea of drawing upon a user's biometric data provided by a smartwatch, crossed with information from their visual feed or machine learning that understood their social media interactions well, could you imagine an ad that popped up and said:

> I cannot help but notice that that new person in your math class whose posts you keep liking and whose photos you keep looking at for longer than average just started playing *Genshin XV*. Would you like to install the game and get a free gift to send them?

While something like this would force close analysis of a few different data streams, there is little about it that is technically difficult, privacy concerns and regulations notwithstanding.

But how can we move rewarded advertising into better integration in-game worlds? For some types of games, that is easy to imagine: billboards on sports arenas can hyper-target ads to particular players, billboards in *Grand Theft Auto 9* can show ads for Ben & Jerry's ice cream on a hot day where a particular user lives, ads for Burlington coats to users where it is cold that day. When analog to real-world ad display spots and the fictional context of a game world aligned with the real world, this is pretty easy. It's harder in a game like *The Legend of Zelda: Breath of the Wild.*

Proximity to real-world locations is another area in which this kind of ad integration becomes pretty easy. "Buy a Starbucks latte in the next 15 minutes to get another crystal to open for free!" is a pretty easy geolocation ad integration to imagine.

Could smart contracts that drive in-game economies offer new or more complex monetization systems, either using in-game advertising, or using other real-world services? Could every Uber ride a passenger takes grant them UberCoin which gave them an additional tiny fraction of ownership in the company, or in dividends from the company's stock? Sure. So how could we apply this to games? What about cascading ownership rights that carry permanent benefits to one-time owners of a thing? Smart Contracts certainly allow for this. How could such advanced structures be used to monetize games?

CARRIER BILLING AND REGIONAL PAYMENT SYSTEMS

One challenge for many free-to-play games is that players in many developing countries don't have access to credit cards. Sophisticated, complex regional payment systems have arisen in every country, which allow for the network provider (the "carrier") to accept transactions within the game and remit payments on behalf of the player to the game publisher. The mechanics and specifics of these approaches differ by region, but in the last five years or so aggregators who provide game makers dedicated SDKs that allow for a bundle of third-party payment providers to integrate easily into a game have made millions more people around the world be able to conduct IAP and microtransactions in mobile games.

Over the next 20 years, we should expect many of these frictions to all but disappear. The global mobile transaction infrastructure is still in awkward adolescence in 2021, but with millions more getting connected daily, protocols for providing digital services and billing of many flavors are rapidly improving. The widespread rollout of 5G networks offering significantly higher bandwidth and supporting far more end-device connections will further drive adoption of standard payment systems. Going forward, we should expect almost any user almost anywhere in the globe to be able to transact with a game on a mobile device or their PC with relative ease, provided they have the money to spend.

REGIONAL AND SACHET PRICING

As gaming has spread across the world and proliferated through free-to-play models, game makers need to account for extremely variable amounts of disposable income from different players. This uneven distribution of wealth available to indulge in leisure activities has always been a factor in societies, but globalism and the ability to use the internet to distribute the same game to the whole world has brought it into sharper focus. Simply put, different countries and populations earn dramatically different amounts of money. Different places also have very different cost structures and economies, so economists have determined ways to normalize a number of these factors to allow for quick comparisons between the purchasing power of consumers in different places. One of these measures, "Purchasing Power Parity" (PPP) helps provide a good way of thinking about income disparity and the amount of disposable income available to average citizens in different countries. In 2019, in the top countries in the world (Iceland, Switzerland, and the United States), the average person earned an annual wage of about $65,000 USD. Even modernized countries like Mexico, Hungary, or Portugal came in at a fraction of this, averaging around $20,000 USD per citizen. Other countries where people game come in far lower still; in places like Indonesia, South Africa, or Belarus average yearly income can settle closer to $5,000. For some gamers, $10 isn't much money; for others, it is a week's wage.

So how can we create games to entertain the whole world, still generate profit from them, while allowing people with wildly differing amounts of disposable income to enjoy? There are two broad approaches to this problem.

First, for games which people do not play together, we can simply sell them at different prices. You could price a game (or an in-game asset) for sale in the US at $50, while just charging $1 for the same software or digital item someplace else. This has a few problems. First, determining the amount to charge, how often to update the price, etc. can be quite time-consuming. Second, given how easy it is for people to fake their location using VPN or similar software, it becomes very easy for gamers to buy the game at the lowest price on offer regardless of where they live. This kind of fraud is widespread, and can easily break a game economy. Finally, this approach tends to generate significant backlash from gamers. ("Why are you charging me $50 for what someone else can get for $1???!")

Another approach, which works better for games where people around the world can play together is to create different in-game offers in which different amounts or qualities of similar goods can be sold at different price points. This is often referred to as sachet pricing. For example, while a 64 oz box of laundry detergent might sell for $10 in the West, a vendor might choose to sell an ounce at a time for 15 cents in places where consumers could afford less. Sachet-pricing models like this, which are common in many industries, can be very useful when considering how to keep game economies fair. Sell smaller amounts or small value in-game goods to players who can afford less; in this way, they can still show their enthusiasm for the game and use money to save themselves time without breaking the game economy for your top spenders.

As wealth disparity is highly likely to increase globally in the coming decades and game developers will increasingly want to allow people around the world to play together, I expect regionally targeted sachet-pricing models to become increasingly common. Assessing, tuning, and setting these prices (and the offers which expose them) is a great job for machine learning algorithms as well, who can micro-tune the amounts to drive (and extract) maximum per user value on a near-individual basis.

eSPORTS

People love watching games. And some types of games lend themselves particularly well to the team versus team competition. Games like Riot's *League of Legends* and Blizzard's *Overwatch* have done incredibly well by promoting themselves not as mere video games, but as eSports.

According to a popular legend, the first gaming competition took place on the campus of Stanford University in 1972, in which the game Spacewar! was played. The winner took home a case of beer and a subscription to the *Rolling Stone* magazine. Since then, gamers have gathered to watch one another compete in games from Doom to Warcraft. While spectating or wagering on competitive video-gaming is not new, it has taken on huge new popularity over the next five years.

According to Riot Games, who have done more to advance eSports than perhaps any other company in the world:

The 2021 *League of Legends* World Championship set an all-time high in terms of viewership numbers, with more fans watching the final match of the prestigious tournament than ever before. The grand final series... accrued an audience of over 73 million peak viewers.[4]

Riot, Blizzard, Valve, and many other publishers continue to aggressively promote the eSports market. Many set out large sums of prize money each year to entice players. (Epic claims to have spent over $100M as prize money to promote *Fortnite* as an eSport in 2018.[5])

By 2020, eSports was expected to bring in over $1B in annual revenue,[6] and many forecasts expect this to grow considerably over the coming years. Can we expect a billion humans to watch an online team vs. team game by 2040? Yes, I expect that we can.

Of course, at $1B in annual revenue, eSports still represents less than 1% of the global game industry revenue. And yet, because of how massive popular esports is among fans and players, and because much of the effort that goes into this portion of the games business serves primarily as a marketing effort to drive more players into games, its importance to the future of gaming is outsized in proportion to its revenue.

Still, it is worth looking at how eSports generates revenue and why companies are excited about pursuing it. First, esports events sell tickets to fans who attend the events in stadiums, usually physical, sometimes digital. (Though digital viewership is usually free, a notion that broadcasters who sell subscriptions to traditional sporting events through PayPerView and similar would be wise to contemplate.) Second, the stadiums themselves usually make money through the sale of concessions to attendees. Third, the teams and publishers often generate revenue by selling physical merchandise to attendees, just like at conventions of other sorts. But most important, eSports events generate most of their money from sponsorships. Companies like Intel, BMW, and a hundred different gaming peripheral companies advertise and give money directly to the companies they sponsor. Finally, many local governments encourage eSports with funding because of the lucrative construction efforts building esports stadiums can generate. eSports is a business that many want to succeed, sufficiently such that governments and companies around the world are pouring money into promoting eSports.

If this sounds cynical, it should not. Players love to play, but it is quite likely that the number of people who enjoy watching others play games is far greater. A person could do worse than to ask: By 2040 will gaming be primarily a spectator sport?

Many designers have done interesting work thinking about the spectator experience, from Twitch viewers to in person attendees. Perhaps the most interesting design question is the degree to which allowing spectators to influence the outcome of events improves or harms the games themselves, their profitability, and the enjoyment of everyone involved. Game design purists would suggest that games should be played within a metaphorical bottle, unaffected by those who may observe. On the other hand, just as throngs of shouting fans add pressure and motivation for athletes, an inherent part of playing games or sports can be performative.

Should attendees or viewers be able to directly influence a game? Should they be able to vote collectively to give some small boon to a competitor who pleases them? What if fans on each side of an event could drop boosts to help their favorite team by donating small amounts of currency while observing? Could you build a game-within-a-game that viewers could play during a halftime break, with the winning side conveying a perk to the team to whom they have sworn allegiance? Are there meta-level games that could exist around the main event?

Beyond game design features to alter the spectator experience, the nature of games themselves are unlocking new opportunities for eSports. In particular, the rise of widely popular competitive mobile games, particularly in emerging markets, is making the dream of being a top competitor (as important for fueling interest in eSports as community basketball hoops are for driving interest in the NBA) real for millions in India, Indonesia, and China. Games like Riot's *League of Legends: Wild Rift,* which offers streamlined Multiplayer Online Battle Area (MOBA) experiences for anyone with a phone, as well as massively popular games like Tencent's *Honor of Kings,* allowed almost a billion people to play competitive eSports games together in 2021. Consider this: More people probably played MOBAs in 2020 on mobile phones than on any other device. eSports is primarily mobile already; by 2040, it will be overwhelmingly so.

The obvious implications are that mobile devices unlocking emerging markets as gaming customers. And because free to play is the dominant business model in mobile gaming, and particularly well suited to markets with lower average disposable income, mobile free-to-play gaming will increasingly dominate the world gaming market in coming years. The movement of traditional PC games (like competitive shooters, battle royale games, MMORPGs, and MOBAs) onto mobile devices will continue accordingly. A lot more people will play *Call of Duty* Mobile in 2024 than *Call of Duty* on any other platform. (Though, as discussed, we should expect cross-platform play for those wealthy enough to possess multiple types of devices.)

Finally, we might ask what to expect from the intersection of eSports and Play2Earn or NFT driven game elements? Could algorithmic cameras capture a Matrix bullet-time style shot of the decisive moment in a world championship match, then sell it to the highest bidder, or give it out in a random prize draw to every viewer who purchased a premium ticket? Certainly. Are there moments in gamer lore that fans might want to own the digital rights to? Sure. Certainly we can imagine that Blizzard could sell an NFT right to a capture of Leroy Jenkins' famous last stand. The addition of team versus team based competition and league allegiances will make this even more popular.

REAL MONEY GAMBLING

One of the likely results of these type of competitive online games playing a big role in emerging markets on mobile devices is a shift toward formalized support of wagering on the outcome of these games. Participants and spectators alike will likely be able to wager in-game currency, real money, or crypto-currencies on the outcome of games. Indeed, in a number of markets this is already beginning to be an interesting trend. A number of sites[7] already exist where users can place bets on Player Unknown Battle Grounds Mobile (PubG) and other mobile games of skill. At the moment, these are (mostly) more akin to illegal bookies taking bets on sporting events. But we should not expect this to remain the case; while wagering on games of skill has a negative stigma in some cultures, in many it does not. And, of course, people have gambled (legally and illegally) on sporting events since the Greeks started competing in the Olympics. Game developers, publishers, and license holders should likely all contemplate how to structure their businesses to benefit from this trend (and get right with authorities in various jurisdictions).

I believe we should expect games to evolve to suit this sort of market. One area ripe for eSports and gambling is skill-based games based on actual real-world sports themselves. Will people turn out to watch and bet on the top Maddin players in the world take the digital equivalent of the real-world American football teams who will compete in next week's Superbowl head to head? Definitely. Could users gather virtually and bet on social competitive betrayal-based games like Among Us? Absolutely. Any game which adds skill, teamwork, and human drama could potentially be well suited for spectating and real-money gambling. Moreover, beyond profiting on the wager transactions, gaming companies can sell physical or digital goods celebrating the contestant. Imagine team skins for the game being popular, in just the way that real-life sports fans regularly parade around in jerseys representing their favorite teams or players.

PAID TO PLAY

We've talked about ways in which players might pay one another for gaming. We've talked about ways in which players or spectators might gamble on games to earn money. But are there ways in which game companies might pay users for playing their games?

In App Advertising is one way that the economics of such a model could work. In practice, if a player is valuable enough as a target for advertisers, we could imagine a game company paying the player with currency for the time they spent playing... So long as the value advertisers were willing to give for advertising to that user exceeded what the user needed to be paid.

Alternately, if a user's computing power could be used by the game software, for providing computing power that could offset "gas fees" from cryptocurrency or distributed ledger transactions, perhaps. If the actions a user were performing in game helped solve a complex simulation, mathematics, or modeling problem, it is possible that their time would be worth money in the game. And, just as night clubs sometimes pay beautiful or famous people to appear in their club to attract punters, we could imagine certain games playing influencers to appear publicly. Indeed, this already regularly occurs for influential Twitch streamers as a form of Influencer marketing.

If in-game currencies are tied to in-game trading mechanics and pegged to crypto-currencies or governmental fiat currencies, could a game publisher make money on exchange rate fluxuations in the way that currency exchange companies have historically? Perhaps.

Are there other economies you could imagine in which publishers might pay some or many users to play their games? While this sounds counterintuitive, if the real profit center for a game is the advertising revenue it can pull in, or the seats it can pack in a (real or virtual) stadium, why should we not expect this to more closely mirror the economies of real-world sports?

PLAY2EARN

But when people talk about "Play2Earn" (P2E) today, mostly what they refer to is the kind of economies in which people play, earn assets, and sell them to other players. This notion is strongly associated with NFT and crypto-currency-based gaming, but there is no particular reason it needs to be. So long as a game economy allows users to receive currency that they can then take out of the game's ecosystem, P2E gaming can work. The association with digital cryptocurrency "wallets" like MetaMask just makes this a little easier, and crypto-currencies currently evade most of the regulation that would impact a publisher's distribution of governmental fiat currencies. But there is really no reason we should expect this to remain the case. Just as gamblers are expected to declare their Vegas casino winnings, and casinos are expected to report winnings to authorities, so should we expect Play2Earn gaming with cryptocurrency payouts to be eventually subject to taxation.

Fundamentally, any game that allows players to buy and sell and trade goods to one another can be a P2E game. (Think back to the early 2000s example of gold farmers in MMORPGs like *World of Warcraft*, just if Blizzard had allowed the payments to occur in game instead of through third-party broker sites.)

THE VALUE OF PLAYER DATA

Player data is valuable.

Anonymized data about how players interact, their demographics, how they respond to in-game events, when they play and on which devices, and so on are all pieces information that have a lot of value. Consumer insights companies, manufacturers and vendors of hardware, other game companies, and assorted other groups are willing to pay a lot for such information. And as our ability to parse large volumes of data increases, such that AI can even consume and turn thriving chat channels into actionable information this value will increase significantly. And, of course, if the data contained Personally Identifiable Information that would allow even more directed insights and advertising that value increases.

Of course, selling player data is considered a serious ethical breach of the relationship between a player and a game publisher. It is also illegal in many places, or at least subject to significant regulation. However, this area of law and ethics are both evolving quite rapidly; it is not hyperbolic to suggest that we are currently living with twentieth-century regulations and thinking governing a field of human experience and interaction which will change so profoundly in the coming decades as to demand entirely new sets of laws and codes of ethical behavior. Some scholars, like Louis Rosenberg, have raised a number of great questions about the kinds of data that should be allowed to be harvested and acted upon in coming "Metaverse" levels of immersive software, pointing out that when we add AI agents who are algorithmically attuned to assess and manipulate a player's emotional state to maximize profit, we potentially run into fairly dystopic scenarios.[8]

As AI increases in power and sophistication, every bit of data a player generates becomes more valuable. We should expect new businesses and new rules to emerge to define who captures this value.

THE BUSINESS OF CREATION

We've discussed the soaring costs of development and marketing many game projects, and we will talk more about how this will evolve in a later chapter. But how should we expect the process for determining where publishers and game companies will invest to evolve?

First, let's talk about how teams have decided on what bets to take historically. Before gaming was a real business, a single creator or an enthusiastic trio likely got excited about what was possible, made it, and released it in local retail stores or on early Bulletin Board Systems (BBSs) that predated the modern web.

By 2000, a game team focused on PC or console gaming would put together a short game pitch, a proposed schedule and budget, often along with a playable prototype or some "visual target" materials and approach a publisher or a greenlight group within their publisher (if the team was internal). Based on the estimations and forecasts or some combination of marketing department and the finance team a forecast would be built. These models were usually the product of a few bright quantitative minds within a Business Intelligence or Financial Planning department. The forecast would use an Excel model to estimate sell-through numbers, sales price over time, development costs, marketing costs, the price of customer service, remittance to license holders where applicable, distribution channel costs, and so forth. The models were regularly updated to account for lessons learned from other products released and changes in the market. Based on how confident the group greenlighting a project was in the chance of a positive financial outcome of the project, the game team would be given the go ahead and funding to proceed with development.

At various points in development, progress from the game team would be checked by the funding group sometimes with updates to a financial model based on new market insights or the subjective assessment of a publishing group, usually with some focus group input considered. While the particular checkpoints, criteria, and process for determining to continue or kill a project different from place to place, and has evolved some over the last 20 years, this is still largely the way most game development projects are greenlight in 2021.

We should expect one very important changes to this basic model over the coming years. The role of the Business Intelligence team will likely be hugely aided, abetted, and largely replaced by Artificial Intelligence- and ML-driven insights over the coming years. This kind of quantitative prediction is exactly in the sweet spot of what AI is great at. Moreover, the market complexities driven by globalization and the importance of ad revenue (as opposed to straightforward sales targets) is much better suited to machines who take easily manage exceedingly complex models with a huge number of data inputs.

As Gareth Wilson, Creative Director at Traveller's Tales, speculates:

> When it comes to greenlighting projects and expanding games post launch, we'll see analytics and AI increasingly being used to help make decisions on which games and new content get made. We're already seeing this in movies and TV, which could mean people get more of the games they want and we get less flops, but equally could mean games get more formulaic to serve established audiences.[9]

It will likely be a long time before AI replaces the notion of a studio or publisher's greenlight group, because – for games designed for humans – some level of subjective assessment of the product appeal and quality based on experience is valuable. However, between focus testing and predictive modeling driven by AI, we should expect big publishers to begin to rely more heavily on algorithmic prediction to determine where they will place these increasingly large bets.

THE EVOLUTION OF GAMING LEGAL MATTERS

Generally speaking, most of the legal action in the gaming business is commercial. Contract drafting, details of Non-Disclosure Agreements to preserve confidentiality of trade secrets (NDAs), licensing deals, breach of contract litigation and resolution, battle over control of intellectual property rights or process patent disagreements, and so on. These types of commercial agreements and their dispute and resolution define the bulk of most of the legal work in the gaming business. High-profile cases like the recent public spat between Apple and Epic Games may have far-reaching ramifications for the value chain in the online distribution and payments part of the business. Sometimes these may even impact the efficiency of various business models, but few of them are likely to fundamentally change the nature of the business.

Labor matters will continue to consume lots of energy as well; indeed, we should expect this to increase slightly in coming years. Are non-compete clauses really enforceable? Does an employee own a great idea or invention?

When they take it to a competitor and two companies profit from the idea and end up in litigation, is the employee who violated an employment agreement liable for the legal fees of the loser? How should employees, employers, or the courts think about overtime? In a world of increasingly remote work, what jurisdiction should the fruits of employees' labor be taxed in? How far does an employer's obligation to provide safe working conditions go in a time of rapidly evolving pandemics? Is emotional safety and freedom from feeling harassed or stressed a right? How about in cross-cultural, cross-border team environments? How does the right to unionize intersect across these rights, obligations, and commercial agreements? Each of these questions will be debated, litigated hundreds of times across most jurisdictions in the coming decades. As development teams get bigger, as the revenue and profits from hits continue to rise we should expect the litigious relationship between employers and employees to continue to calcify. The result here will be the need for ever larger human resources, internal legal, and accounting teams; this G&A increase will continue to add friction to the development process, but it an almost inevitable result of an industry reliant upon increasingly large labor pools maturing.

INTERVIEW WITH KIMBERLY CORBETT: PUBLISHING FOR THE FUTURE

Kimberly Pointer Corbett is the Senior Vice President of Digital Publishing at Warner Bros. Games

Publishing for the Future

TF: Hello! Tell us who you are and about your role in the games business.

Kim: I'm Kimberly Corbett and I've been in the gaming business for over a decade now. The way I describe my job to my family and friends who don't know the industry, is that you have all the cool people who make the games, and there's me. Kidding aside, I manage publishing, which is everything from marketing, user acquisitions, analytics, customer service, QA, community, ad monetization, market intelligence, and first-party relations. It's super fun because we to take awesome games being made and let the world hear about them. We want you to see them, download them, buy them, and play them.

TF: And so, you work on games that are mobile, console, PC, and all of the above?

Kim: Yup.

TF: That's pretty awesome. The business looks like it's going through a huge change right now. I'm really interested in thinking about what the next 20 years have in store for the games business. I'm curious, how do you see the mix of gamers around the world and where they like to play their games changing?

Kim: Well, in 20 years you and I will be in the Metaverse, right? Cyborgs in the Metaverse. [Laughs.] I mean, I don't see that current players are changing a lot, but our kids are growing up gamers. This is where they're interacting socially instead of social media – games are serving that purpose digitally now.

Games are where we congregate digitally for hours a day, and I think that comes with a lot of responsibility. This is something we've been talking a lot about lately as we have these Metaverse conversations. What's healthy? What's good for gamers?

I think one difference is generational. With our generation, we played games as we grew up, but it wasn't the main place where we connected, congregated and socialized. Games are fundamentally where kids gather now. So that's the greatest difference to me. Games have moved beyond maybe a short thing that you could do on your phone on your commute – or maybe you play a console game in the evening. With our younger generation, it's the place where they're spending hours together.

TF: As a publisher, when you think about which games to promote in which markets, how much do you think about the way that the games create a social environment for players to hang out in? How do different territories influence your thinking on that?

Kim: You're very familiar with the Chinese market, which is even more gamer-centric and part of their social fabric than Western markets. This means the way they publish games is different because it's part of the culture in a way that hasn't been the case in the West yet. To be specific, they rely less heavily on paid user acquisition and more heavily on their own owned platforms and what we would consider brand marketing. You can do more brand marketing and have a good return on investment, when something is as ubiquitous as gaming is their culture. This also works well with their very fragmented Android device and store structure. Owned users make a huge difference too. If you're Tencent and you launch a game, you can broadcast it all day on WeChat.

In Western markets, gaming is certainly becoming more predominant as a form of entertainment, and in publishing – we're trying to be present in the places gamers are showing up. That includes social media, platforms, streaming. The biggest shift over the last five or so years in terms of where gamers are congregating has been the importance of streaming platforms like Twitch. But ultimately because gaming companies are not also the platform and gaming is less ubiquitous here, this leads to more performance marketing style of publishing than in China.

So that's China and Western publishing – which are both totally different than emerging markets, where devices are different, and gamers monetize different. You need to have a different plan for an Android heavy market, like South America or India for example, than you would in the West or in a highly monetizing Eastern market like China. In these markets, the cost to acquire a user is much cheaper but so are the ltv's. If you are working with a super high fidelity mobile title that requires a lot of a device, it might not scale well in emerging markets.

TF: How do you think over the next five to ten years the notion of communities for games are going to change, and how should we think about using the community as the basis for getting the word out there about these games that we build?

Kim: You have these games that are operating for a decade plus. And so, community means something different than it did when you didn't expect games to last that long. These are deep connections and relationships. These people are experiencing entertainment by playing together, laughing together, and challenging each other for five, six, seven, eight years at that time. So, the notion of community, I think, is a much deeper word than it was several years ago. In terms of getting the word out, we have these trusted connections and bonds with other players. If they recommend a game, you're going to have a very valued install because they trust that person. How you engage with these communities is a different distribution model. This isn't something that we had when we distributed mobile games ten years ago.

TF: When you think about engaging communities in different parts of the world, to what degree do you think it's necessary to use local boots on the ground publishing in different regions like in Latin America or in India?

Kim: Sometimes, the government requires us to, like in China. I think this part is really necessary when you have platform differences. So, if you go back a few years to Facebook; at a point they had captured market share in every market except Russia. Facebook never took off there, Mail.ru was the dominant way of marketing there, so Russia never scaled for them. What this means is you can't rely on one platform to find players everywhere. Boots on the ground becomes necessary when those platform, culture and language difference are so different you can't successfully launch a game unless you're there. This is primarily in Asia.

TF: That's a good insight about how the different platforms are.

Kim: When you don't have big Western communities you can even leverage in these markets, you have to go direct, and this can be kind of hard because there is a lot of fraud in advertising channels in different regions. As you are scaling, you can get false signals on success in a territory. And that tends to happen in markets where you don't have platform dominance, so there are a lot of areas you don't have the analytics and control over.

TF: Speaking of the evolution of analytics and growth marketing, we both lived through the rise of basic machine learning in driving user acquisition and so forth. We are right on the cusp of the ascendancy of real AI, I think, over the next ten years. How do you expect AI to change the way we tell people about our games?

Kim: This is all directly up against privacy laws. If the advertising industry was left unfettered with privacy laws, it would be much more efficient than it is today to find users via the methods you mention – but that isn't necessarily what's best for the consumer. The platforms of the world can easily direct you to users; we saw how sophisticated we were getting before IDFA's were deprecated. So, on the one hand, there was a time where our ability to predict who is likely to play and spend in a game is very sophisticated. But on the other, we need to be cognizant of prvacy.

The companies that win in this privacy-centric future will be the ones with big walled data gardens. Your ability to search for players in a super sophisticated way will be restricted within your own ecosystem, your own MAU and DAU across your portfolio of games – who is likely to play another one of your games or churn out. I think companies that don't have the ability to do that within their own portfolio are going to really struggle. You're already seeing this in the market with recent game launches falling flat in terms of installs and revenue compared to prior years.

TF: Do you expect that this lead to further consolidation in the industry?

Kim: Absolutely. You're seeing it across the industry now. Not only as an advertiser, suddenly you need gamer data. But you don't just need gamer data, you need gamer payment data. And this gives more power to companies that have large walled garden of different games and even more so to ones who may also have front of the funnel advertising data as well.

TF: It's a good insight. Thank you. I'm curious as a gamer and as a parent of a gamer, what are the things that get you most excited about the way games are going to evolve over the next ten years?

Kim: That's a very interesting question. I like that we can sit down as a family and play games that are fun for the whole family like *Lego Star Wars* or *Mario Kart*. We're all having fun together.

With that said, gaming is replacing other forms of entertainment for families. And with games, you're doing something that I view as more fun and intellectually active and stimulating and challenging – plus interactive. And when we do consider things like the Metaverse, how could we maybe be able to do that with family members in another location? I think that it's exciting.

But with great power comes responsibility. Leaders in the gaming industry have to be very careful and thoughtful about the future that's being created so that it is an interactive and healthy one. How do we build these experiences in a way that allow for the best version of society possible? I don't think the answer to that is in being cyborgs in the Metaverse.

REGULATIONS AND WRAP UP

The Effect of Regulations on Business Models

How much should we expect governmental regulations to impact gaming business models in the future?

Tech writer Benedict Evans addresses the question this way in early 2022: *"If you haven't already presumed that there will be a US FTC investigation into every significant part of every big tech company, you're not paying attention. The only gate is time and resource."*

The Federal Trade Commission has already set its sights on the large data storage and cloud service providers which provide the backend technology for most games.[10]

This will likely include games publishing companies. And as the borderline between games and "Metaverse" further blurs, regulatory oversight into many activities, platforms, and technologies we are concerned with will increase.

There's an interplay between governmental regulations and game design whose influences on game business models has been relatively subtle to date. While in the casino business high levels of regulation have been a standard for a very long time, this has been less true for interactive entertainment. We should expect this to change. Let's look at how.

Starting about 20 years ago concerned parents groups and regulators began to take notice of the popularity of games. Violent or sexually explicit content was their primary concern at the time. In an effort to avoid governmental regulation a group called the Entertainment Software Ratings Board was formed in North America. This group was joined by many major publishers and began to apply ratings to retail games similar to those applied in the movie industry. This practice spread around the world, and while a few governments got in on the act, the industry remained largely self-regulating (with the participation of retailers) when it came to content.

But this did little to change the business models in play; it just added a few extra steps to ensure compliance, and encouraged some game makers to tone down content for some regions. (German games were famously disallowed to show red blood for a while, for example.)

The rise of online gaming and concerns about predation on children by other gamers led to laws and regulation in an attempt to ensure their safety. The Children's Online Privacy Protection Act of 1998 in the United States of America is one such example. This law imposed requirements on a variety of online service providers or operators to ensure that users under 13 years were unable to give out personal information (like an address or phone number) to the provider or to other users. In practice this also limited the ways publishers could target advertisers. Similar laws appeared in other regions, and the net effect is that users under 13 are often "prevented" by the end-user licensing agreement (EULA) for many games. By playing the game, users were agreeing that they were older than 13.

Around 2015 we saw a rise in concerns about the addictiveness of certain types of in game design systems, notably "loot-box" or "gatcha" mechanics in which users interact with stylized random-number-generators to attempt to win a prize. In practice, these sorts of systems use many of the techniques perfected in slot-machines to make the act of opening the prize box exciting. A number of countries, from Japan to Belgium[11] enacted various laws which fined game operators who did not adhere to certain rules. Commonly, these kinds of laws forced developers to publicize the odds of getting certain prizes (similarly to what is required on lottery tickets in many jurisdictions). Many laws associated with traditional gambling morphed to encompass these types of in game systems, and many games changed their mechanics or displays for particular countries.

As Real Money Gaming and wagering on eSports become increasingly mainstream and legitimized, we should expect considerably increased regulations across many jurisdictions. "Gambling" is viewed quite differently in different cultures; just as unregulated boxing matches have long been held in places with more lenient rules on certain types of interactions, we should expect to see eSports events to begin to select their locations based on accessibility for tourism, stance toward wagering, and potentially even tax implications. And then there are significant concerns of unregulated fraud in the contests themselves. If a team is found to have received payment from bookies to throw a *League of Legends* match, are they civilly liable to their sponsors or supporters? What about teams who engage in hacking or bots to cement victories?

In 2021, as online gaming continued to increase in popularity we saw the first significant crackdown on the popularity of online gaming in the People's Republic of China.[12] By 2020, China was the biggest gaming market in the world by population and by total annual revenue. In the summer of 2021, China's leader, President Xi Jinping, who has been an outspoken critic of video games, asked the Party to enact several laws targeting the entertainment sector in general, and some targeting gaming in particular. The most notable of these severely reduced the amount of time anyone under 18 is allowed to spend playing games. Using sophisticated facial identification software, game publishers are forced to ensure that players game for a total of fewer than three hours per weekend, and disallow gaming at all on weekdays. These laws have already had significant impact on major Chinese and Western publishers alike.

And yet few of these have begun to address the most interesting questions of regulation we are likely to see emerge in the coming decade: As Artificial Intelligence agents, celebrities, counselors, friends begin to play an ever larger role in the social gaming space, we should expect a far-ranging constellation of complex issues that governments around the world will need to wrestle with. At what point does an AI *persona* gain citizenship in some country? This likely will happen before 2040. Already, some governments are beginning to evaluate requirements for machine learning decision-making algorithms that lead to AI personas online to be clearly labeled as such.[13] Right now, faceless algorithms shape public policy, university admissions, insurance rates. And their impact on the lives of people in online gaming spaces are still trivial. But as we see in this book, this will not remain the case. When a malignant AI driven authored by hackers befriends a child and convinces them to commit suicide, can the parents sue the company whose game this happened in? Definitely. To consider a slightly less macabre example, what happens when AI convinces someone to move across the world for a marriage that will never happen? Or, more intriguingly, is there a world in which such a legal union could occur? Probably. Can we imagine game companies to be required to identify which characters in an MMORPG are AI driven and which are played real humans? Almost assuredly.

And these topics don't yet even deal with the question of data ownership, responsibility for protecting the user data, and so on. Already the rise of AI-driven "Therapy Bots" which are proving to be a good precursor for in-game AI companions has led to a host of issues around regulation and privacy.[14] In 2021, the American Psychological Association estimates there are more than 10,000 different Therapy chat bots in the wild. In October 2020, hackers infiltrated the servers of Finnish startup Vastaamo and stole files from more than 30,000 patients, then set about blackmailing them, demanding ransoms paid in cryptocurrency lest they start releasing personal and intimate details. As humans in and out of games begin sharing more of themselves with increasingly convincing bots who act as friends, therapists, confidants, and simple NPCs in games, this will escalate.

There are hundreds of interesting questions surrounding the acceptable use of digital personas. If I create a bot that looks just like you and give it your name, then go on a rampage in a game, or say a bunch of inflammatory things in a chat channel, can you sue me? What if your likeness is used for even more sinister purposes by Latvian hackers? What legal recourse becomes available for citizens in different countries? Most current legal concepts of self, identity, and personhood were born in an age of print journalism, adopted for a century of broadcast television, limped into the world of digital identities, and are wholly unprepared for virtual worlds of agents who are indistinguishable from real people.

These are just a few of the thorny issues awaiting efforts at regulation by various governing bodies around the world. Likely, there is a strong need for international agencies which do not exist today who are able to study, regulate, and provide enforcement and recompense mechanisms for online cross-border gaming.

I believe we should expect other countries' regulators to pay increasing amounts of attention to the gaming market in the coming years. As mentioned elsewhere in this book, we should expect widespread online identity verification similar to India's pioneering Aadhaar system, or the way WeChat[15] is widely used as government-approved ID in China. As hard-to-track crypto-currencies begin to play a bigger role in game economies, and as users begin to earn money from gaming in the ways we've discussed, the need to track and tax this money will drive additional scrutiny. As players spend more time in games, crimes committed in the social spaces provided by games will become more common; this will lead to an increased desire to record, track, and analyze in-game communications.

Gaming is a big business, and it will keep getting bigger. The games industry has existed in a space that has been only lightly regulated thus far (though many in-house counsels for major publishers may disagree!). This will change significantly in the next two decades.

NOTES

1 https://www.supermarketnews.com/archive/game-sales-hit-74-billion-1999-playstation-tops.

2 https://www.gamesindustry.biz/articles/2021-12-21-gamesindustry-biz-presents-the-year-in-numbers-2021.

3 https://www.statista.com/statistics/190225/digital-and-physical-game-sales-in-the-us-since-2009/.

4 https://dotesports.com/league-of-legends/news/worlds-2021-viewership-increases-60-percent-from-2020-breaks-all-time-record.

5 https://www.epicgames.com/fortnite/en-US/news/epic-games-will-provide-100-000-000-for-fortnite-esports-tournament.

6 https://venturebeat.com/2020/02/25/newzoo-global-esports-will-top-1-billion-in-2020-with-china-as-the-top-market/.

7 https://sickodds.com/pubg.

8 https://venturebeat.com/2021/12/04/the-metaverse-needs-aggressive-regulation/.

9 https://www.ign.com/articles/the-games-industry-on-what-gaming-might-be-like-in-2030

10 https://www.bloomberg.com/news/articles/2021-12-22/amazon-cloud-unit-draws-fresh-antitrust-scrutiny-from-khan-s-ftc.

11 https://thelawreviews.co.uk/title/the-gambling-law-review/belgium.

12 https://win.gg/news/new-chinese-gaming-law-launches-whistleblower-website/.

13 https://venturebeat.com/2021/12/08/the-u-k-s-new-ai-transparency-standard-is-a-step-closer-to-accountable-ai/.

14 https://www.economist.com/business/2021/12/11/dramatic-growth-in-mental-health-apps-has-created-a-risky-industry.

15 https://www.thefuturescentre.org/signal/wechat-to-be-the-official-online-id-card-in-china/.

CHAPTER 8

Data and Analytics

Confusion and clutter are failures of design, not attributes of information.

– Edward Tufte

At first, humans communicated information through an oral tradition. Cuneform writing, which is the oldest known mechanism of recording information, is believed to have started around 3400 BC in Mesopotamia, near the present-day Baghdad. The printing press, invented by Johannes Gutenberg in 1436 AD, allowed for mass distribution of printed material and is widely regarded as another significant milestone in human-kind's engagement with information. In 1974 the use of the transistor allowed us to begin storing binary information, followed by integrated microchips in 1956. Sometime in the mid-1990s, digital storage of information began to take over from paper. By 2020, the total amount of digital data in the world was estimated at 59 ZB, which is to say, 59 trillion GB. This amount is increasing quite rapidly, expecting to exceed 175 ZB by 2025.[1] We can all be forgiven for having a hard time even contemplating how much information this is. I'll spare you some factoid explaining how if you stacked this up on sheets of paper it would reach the rings of Saturn or something. This data is stored in many places, but the majority of it in large data centers, mostly in the United States, China, Japan, the UK, Germany, and Australia.

Data centers are warehouse style buildings containing vast racks of servers, computing power, security equipment, and a lot of power and

DOI: 10.1201/9781003291800-9

cooling equipment. If you'd like to imagine these physical spaces as mostly underground with vast rows of machine with blinking lights, the hum of thousands of fans, and very few people, you're about right. Their maintenance needs exist at the intersection of sophisticated mechanical engineering and highly advanced Information Technology. These data centers are connected with huge amounts of sophisticated fiber-optic cable and switching equipment, which connect out to the rest of the world. Collectively, they form the bulk of the information on the internet today. Google alone has 21 major data centers around the world,[2] which they have invested more than 20 billion dollars into building. Microsoft, Amazon, Oracle, Tencent, and a few other companies have comparable numbers. These all exist to provide fast access and redundancy to this massive amount of information; and already it is not enough.

From here, data storage and access gets pretty complex quickly. Data lakes like Amazon S3 store massive amounts of information, much of it lacking common schemas or format that make it easily searchable. Determining which systems, individuals, AI algorithms have what kinds of access to this vast store of data is a complex, rapidly evolving, and ill-regulated mess of interesting challenges. Making the right data visible, moveable, and able to transition between various types of data storage is an architectural school unto itself. As users start generating massive amounts of data early in life and carry it with them for decades, the perseverance of data – along with thorny ethical and practical questions about its ownership and the right to choose to have it destroyed – pose new challenges which were simply not much contemplated until recently. This rate of data increase will not slow, though there are practical limits associated with total amount of energy consumption required and limits of current storage and addressing mechanisms. We currently lack the tools, techniques, and legal framework to deal with what is coming. (Though some great minds are working on all of these questions!)

The rise of big data – a phrase which is already starting to seem quaint in light of the sheer volume of information coming soon – has already profoundly changed the way games are made, analyzed, distributed, and the way we make money from them. And we are just beginning this journey; it is through the widespread availability of truly massive amounts of information and the ability to store, sort, analyze, learn from, and act upon this data that the games industry will most change in the coming decades.

DATA GATHERING

How do games generate data? How do we collect it? Where is it stored? How is it analyzed?

Data instrumentation is the practice of intentionally putting moments into game software which records and reports back some bit of information to a server for later reference. For example, an action platformer like Nintendo's original *Super Mario Bros.* might record a timestamp and the x, y location of Mario every time a player presses a button to jump. Once this data has been uploaded to the server, data analysis and game design teams can map this data to determine where players jump. If other player events, like each time a player falls to their death, for example, is similarly recorded, level designers can build a map of places players are most likely to fall to their death inadvertently by missing a jump. Cross referencing this against where a particular level appears in a game's flow might help designers assess and tune difficulty, for example. This example is fairly simplistic, but it gives a good sense for the way game makers can use data instrumentation to tune a game based on objective and quantifiable input from a player population.

Games generate data every frame, often thousands of datapoints. It is impractical due to bandwidth constraints to upload all of this information to a server usually. Bandwidth usage for games can cost users money depending on their connection to the internet. Transmitting data also costs game publishers, who pay data storage companies by usage. So, determining precisely what types of information to track and upload, store, and assess is a complex and very important part of many modern games. And this too is about to get more complex.

As the ecosystems for input and display increase, the number of data sources and the complexity of harvesting, properly referencing, and drawing conclusions from these sources will increase considerably. Determining which pieces of information to harvest, how timely its delivery needs to be, and how to collate the information with other sources will be a fundamental component of Information Architecture for big game data teams in the coming years.

As an example, let's take a game more sophisticated than *Super Mario Bros.*, something like a large-scale MMORPG, for example, with hundreds of players and AI avatars interacting in the virtual equivalent of a town square, real-time translation software translating out each player's comments to others, each in their own language. Now imagine that some of these players are on mobile phones, some on VR headsets, some wearing technology which monitors their heartrate and other biometric data and communicates some of this information back to the game servers. For each device what are the most important pieces of data we would need to harvest? When? Is the server providing real-time performance tuning instructions to the low-end phones so that they run as well as possible even in complex scenes? Are the AI agents making real-time decisions and tailoring their behavior based on their assessment of players' moods in order to maximize enjoyment? Are trust and safety algorithms (or government censorship filters) checking each player and NPC's speech before it is allowed in the conversation? For a scene with a hundred players, spanning 250 total devices, across ten countries, how many total datapoints could you imagine needing to be processed per frame? Given that each of these devices may have different connection speeds, such that data is not all arriving at the same time, how do we coordinate the logic for knowing which pieces of information to weight and when?

Data is not free to store on servers. Depending on the speed with which it needs to be accessed, the criticality of its availability at any moment, specifics of how it is backed up, and how secure it is the cost of data storage and transfer can vary hugely. For this reason, many game teams have determined elaborate systems for migrating older data to different places over time. And how long should data be stored? When a player hasn't logged into a game for a week, do we still need to preserve their information? What if it has been a year? Might we decide we should keep their character data but purge last year's biometric analysis data? Are there rules around how long we can keep different types of data? Which parts have to be anonymized to remove and which explicitly need to be able to be accessed by customer service bots on a per account basis?

Determining when to clean up and do away with data remains a challenge for many teams as well; assessing what is still needed and what can be done away with is technically complex work, time consuming, and usually relies on people who have plenty of other things to do. To properly think through some of these complexities requires data analytics experts as well as experienced backend software engineers, plus all of the legal and corporate compliance work it generates. I think it almost a guarantee that game studios around the world waste hundreds of millions of dollars per year in unnecessary storage and transfer costs because assessing and acting on all of this is so complex.

DATA PROCESSING

Once data has been uploaded to a server somewhere it needs to be processed so we can use it. Usually information is transmitted compressed, stripped from all duplicative elements, and not particularly readable. But once received on the server, we can run software to process and cross reference the information against other known datum. From there, we can start to transform and transmit the information to the other processes which can make use of it. For example, transaction data on each purchase a user makes can be cross-referenced from the game client software against the payment provider (Apple Store, for example) in order to build reliable and auditable transaction records. There are typically a dozen or so end consumers of the data games generate, (finance, designers, live operations teams, performance optimization teams, etc.) getting each of them the information they need at the right time, in the right format is no small feat.

Ten years ago, only a small fraction of this work needed to be done for most games. Twenty years ago no one but MMORPGs dealt with almost any of what we've just talked about. Over the next few decades these matters will concern almost all games.

The amount of human capital and investment in processing increasingly large amounts of data from always-live products will come to comprise an increasing portion of most game teams over the coming decades. 5G and other high-capacity networks, Metaverse-style massively social gaming experiences, iOT-style ecosystems, and enabling deep machine learning systems, AI companions, and most everything else we've discussed in this book will require a significant increase in the amount of data games process.

DATA ANALYSIS IN REAL TIME

Machine learning driven by large data models take sophisticated, powerful CPU and GPU hardware, and loads of storage to keep all the data. So this work is usually done in the Cloud, in data centers, far from the user and their device; we process data far from the game. This distance introduces further delays. This introduces a delay which – over the last few years – has mostly meant that the kinds of ML questions game makers can ask cannot be very timely. This has drawbacks. Let's look at an example:

If a player is likely frustrated enough to stop playing a game, can we give them something in the game that will renew their excitement? Definitely.

Imagine that we know that players who are in a social group like an alliance are much less likely to stop playing. If we can analyze player data each day, then give a gift and a recommendation for a new alliance to a player when they next log in, will this help improve the game experience for some players? Again, definitely.

But if the most recent player data we can analyze using ML is eight hours old, then we cannot necessarily serve them when it most matters, which is at the moment they start to demonstrate a pattern that indicates frustration and likelihood to churn. We need to be able to be much faster. How much better if two minutes after they got kicked from their Alliance and started down a path that was likely to lead to loneliness and churn we could recommend them a great new Alliance?

One solution to this is moving some level of ML calculation and processing onto the device itself. Of course, this is easier on hardware that has more storage space and RAM to keep datasets, more powerful processing in which power consumption is not as big a consideration.

As hardware and software companies develop dedicated chips and integrated hardware, which specializes in the kinds of processing required for Machine Learning the ability to transform volumes of data quickly increases. Nvidia and Google lead the charge on this kind of technology in North America. Google's Tensor Flow Processing Unit family of chips are now being widely distributed to different manufacturers, including on Google's own Pixel brand smartphone. By having dedicated chips on devices that end users can keep with them, games can begin to do more of the logic that drives advances in AI locally.

Broadly speaking, this philosophical approach is called "Edge Computing." By distributing processing and data storage capabilities closer to end users we can reduce bandwidth and increase response times considerably. This allows us to create ML and AI agents, which are able to make predictive decisions based on local data in seconds or milliseconds rather than minutes or hours.

The more rapidly we can do near-real-time data analysis, the more immediate impact this kind of thinking can have on how we design games. Dynamic difficulty can track how a player is performing in a game or in a particular mode and adjust the difficulty of puzzles or opponents to maximize their challenge while still delivering victories and rewards at an optimal cadence for that user. Scenarios can be authored seconds before a group of players encounter them based on analysis of their playstyles, the effectiveness of their teamwork, or even their conversation leading up to the event. Is one player expressing excessive negativity toward others in chat? Perhaps we can tweak their experience to push them into a more positive frame of mind toward their teammates by setting up a scenario where other players are able to rescue or assist them. Real-time analysis of the audience of an eSports event or users watching a Twitch streamer can start to blur the lines between spectating and play in a way that is beneficial to both. Could AI driven choices about camera cuts and perspective in a sports game be used to devote more time to today's fan favorite contestant just as real-world camera operators and editors have for years? Certainly.

The more rapidly we can analyze data the better we can change the game experience to improve players' experiences.

DATA —> AI BEHAVIORS AND RESPONSES

We will talk more later in this book about the coming era of AI and the way they will be able to create characters who interact with players. On some level, this may not seem meaningfully different from NPCs in games like *Skyrim* from decades past. But the hidden underground sea of data that drives their behavior allows them to interact in ways that will feel fundamentally new. Natural Language Processing and easy speech will be the tip of this iceberg, which over the next five years will make the whole world take notice of AI characters in games. But it is the ability to create bespoke responses based on knowing players better than the players may know themselves that will truly make this technology transformative.

To be able to pass convincingly as a human is one thing. Any stranger in a bar can do that. To be able to convincingly act like a human who knows everything about what YOU want is quite a bit different. Strangers in a bar cannot do that. For most people, there are very few other humans who ever will know them so well. This is likely to fundamentally alter the depth and frequency with which players – humans in general – interact with AI characters. We will explore this in much greater depth in coming chapters; the point for now is just that this is made possible by the collection, storage, and effective use of massive amounts of data.

DATA VISUALIZATION

Humans can only interpret data effectively if it is well presented. The recognition of the relationship between data visualization and people's ability to draw valuable conclusions from it is one of the great unsung advances in human thought over the last two centuries. The advent of modern data

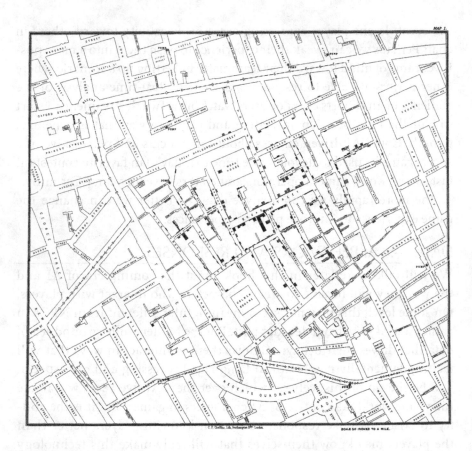

FIGURE 8.1   Dr. John Snow's 1854 map of incidents of cholera in a London sub-urb helped track down the source of the outbreak to a particular contaminated well; this example of correlating two pieces of data leading to an actionable insight is now canon among devotees of data visualization. (*Image Credit:* Wikimedia Commons freely licensed.)

visualization is beautifully covered by Yale Professor Emeritus of Political Science and Statistics, Dr. Edward Tufte in books like *The Visual Display of Quantitative Information*,[3] and it is critical to understanding how humans can think about data (Figure 8.1).

Gathering data from modern games is valuable when funneled into Machine Learning, as has been the subject of much of this chapter. But we also cannot discount the value of human data analysts, and present-ing data effectively to game designers, product managers, and engineers. Tools like Tableau, from California company Salesforce, effectively allow creators to visualize data, share different views with their teams, and

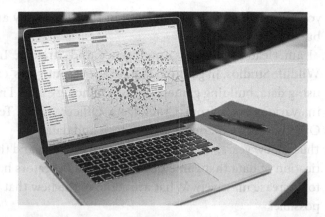

FIGURE 8.2 Data visualization tools like Tableau can allow game analysts, designers, and product managers to effectively make sense of a large volume of information about players. (*Image Credit*: Salesforce.)

subscribe to regular updates as new data comes in from the game software. Training teams to effectively slice data by user characteristics, platforms, regions, and so on is a critical component of effectively optimizing games as a service (Figure 8.2).

INTERVIEW WITH ROB FINK: THE FUTURE OF DATA

Rob Fink has 25 years of experience running engineering and data science teams. He currently is the Head of Publishing, Analytics & Insights for Wildlife Studios.

TF: Will you tell us about your experience in the technology and games business?

Rob Fink: I am Head of Business Intelligence and Strategic Insights at Wildlife Studios. In gaming, I've got about four years' experience using data, building games. In the technology field, I'm 25 years in, various roles from Chief Data Officer, Chief Technology Officer, lots of experience within tech and data.

TF: Over the last few years, we've seen the amount of data and the sophistication of data that game developers and operators have access to, increase massively. What are some of the new that has made possible?

Rob: Really understanding how players interact with our toy. Certainly, if you compare and contrast what you have access to in the console arena as compared to mobile gaming, it's vastly different. As a console developer, you're building a game, you're guessing what your audience may like, you may have done some research in advance, but you build it and release it. You really don't have that feedback loop and you don't have the opportunity to customize the content, for your target audience until the next version, as opposed to mobile gaming which is where I think the future's going.

Now, you have a world that can be completely customized based upon how I want to interact and play within this world. You can truly tailor that experience using the data. There are a lot of techniques from the data science world or even just basic algorithms that allow you to do that. Because you can release content so quickly based on data, and that just makes it even more powerful. I think as an industry, gaming will surpass the top three entertainment industries. If it hasn't already.

TF: When you think about the challenge of how much data games can generate, how should game teams think about determining what data they should pay attention to?

Rob: It depends on what they want to optimize for because it really is an optimization problem at the end of the day. If I look at it from a business perspective, I want to optimize for a couple things usually. One, I want to keep my players happy, so I have a retention strategy. This is figuring out where people might be struggling as I move them through the experience. And then on the monetization side. I have to combine enjoyment with the opportunity to spend because some people like to spend to progress faster or further in games.

If I am launching a new game, I'm looking for key indicators. You're looking at your retention curves, you're looking at the percentage of users who convert, because I have to keep the lights on. Those are the big areas that I look at first.

TF: Over the coming decade, we can expect to see huge transformations in the way we collect data, the way we transform data, the way we store data, and the way we're able to visualize data. What are some of the things that you believe would really help game developers make better use of the data they can get from their players?

Rob: It's the instrumentation. Having access to data in near real time. Imagine a world where I'm hosting a massive tournament and I'm worried about having enough critical mass there so I can field the teams and I want to make sure that my technology is scaling appropriately. It's those dashboards, and so I'm looking at my matchmaking capabilities. I'm looking at where people are in the world. I think the instrumentation has come a long way, the underlying technologies facilitating near real-time data and so I can grab massive amounts of data in a reasonable amount of time and actually put it on the screen for the micro tweaks if I need to.

That's a huge opportunity there. Not only can I have the technology make decisions for me, but I, as a game maker, I can almost curate the world. I look at it that way. You go back to the days of the early D&D and your dungeon master where you can almost do this in real time for players. When you put VR on top of that, things go crazy. There are just some really interesting twists there. In 20 years, I won't be surprised if we have an all-encompassing eSports league that is leveraging VR within a curated world. This is going to be huge. Just think of the advertising opportunities alone!

TF: How do you see the rise of virtual reality, augmented reality, the Metaverse, and decentralized or cryptogaming changing the way we consume data and use data?

Rob: I think it's going to materially change the way that we use data and think about gaming, in general. There's a big push with NFT, in gaming where it's backed by blockchain, and I can actually own something. I'm playing like a *Minecraft* type of game, I can own a plot of land and I can charge rents if you want to go and do something on my land. It opens up the door for what YouTubers are now making side money doing. I can actually make a living by playing in this space and buying and selling. This is just another virtual economy.

With VR, it's all encompassing. Now, I can go and have true immersion in a game. Instead of just seeing it on my screen. *Ready Player One* comes to mind. I won't be surprised if we get to that point pretty soon.

TF: Does the way that we need to think about ingesting and analyzing data change when games or big chunks of game information lives on chains?

Rob: I think for the game makers, not as much. In terms of the creation things like that, I think, from an economy design perspective, it will change.

For example, if I think of a Marvel asset, some of the contracts will likely have to change. Who truly owns it if users are trading these assets as NFTs? I think the legal aspects may change the way contracts are written and how some of these assets come into play.

The blurry lines between gatcha and NFT becomes interesting, as well. I want to think about the data and the technology. How quickly can I create these unique assets? Because the value proposition for NFT assets in games is unique. If I have a car game as an example, one of the players can actually own a car, and the individual parts inside the car are NFT items, as well. There're a ton of data there, I think, that you don't necessarily care too much about right now, but you would in that world. We would have to worry about inventory management, SKU tagging for each component of the car, and all that stuff, and then also fraudulent activities. There might be additional vectors that we would have to consider that we don't today. Blockchain will eventually completely change how we track, monitor, and transact on our SKUs within games today.

TF: You mentioned regulation. One of the things that we've seen change over the last few years is regulation that is concerned with consumer privacy for their data, GDPR and so forth. How do you expect consumer data privacy regulations to evolve over the next decade?

Rob: It would be good and it would make our lives easier if they converged on an international standard. Right now, California keeps trying to one-up GPR, and there's a ton of new privacy regulations, which may be great for the consumer. It's a little bit more difficult for the game maker. Taking NFTs for example, how does that come into play? If it is a global space, I think it is ill-defined, and so I would go cautiously. I think you'd almost want to have a team specifically keeping up with that. I think most of the bigger game companies will, probably already have legal teams tracking all of this. From my data standpoint, I'd almost want to lean into a solution where everything is anonymous. Some game companies are already doing a good job of this. But there will be additional things that we have to think about in the future, things that we probably aren't really thinking about today. It will get more complex. The first company that truly figures out how to leverage NFTs effectively within a sticky game will basically be printing money.

TF: In the early 90s, we were introduced to the idea of data havens. They were offshore, built on oil derricks and things like this. Do you expect that as data privacy regulations increase, that we will see a move from game companies and other technology companies to move their headquarters or move their data to locales that are less regulatory?

Rob: Like Cayman Islands for taxes, but for data?

TF: Yeah.

Rob: I won't be surprised. Some companies will, I think. I think if push comes to shove, I won't be surprised if we see that happen, how pervasive will that be, I think will depend on the regulations themselves. For example, if there was a regulation that would basically shut down your company, you'll probably look for creative solutions to move it around the world. Hopefully, it doesn't come to that. In the world where everyone is working remotely, anyway, it just comes down to where you're registered, to be honest. We could start a company tomorrow, register in Cayman Islands, we could work subject to that, sure, but we can work anywhere.

TF: Often the idea of very large datasets is described as fuel for Artificial Intelligence. How do you see our capabilities to gather and understand large amounts of data and then to train up machine learning algorithms evolving over the next 20 years?

Rob: It's a technology problem at the end of the day. How fast, how much hardware and processing power can I throw at it? If I compare what we have access to in Amazon today versus back in 2006 when I'm sitting in Azure beta training, it's vastly different. Just the sheer accessibility to that kind of power just allows us to do so much more with the data. The ability to capture in real-time and stream data from millions of endpoints, it's astounding. I think a factor of ten or more will be so much better. Also, one of the things I think we'll see more of 10, 20 years from now is embedded models on your device. Not only will we have the ability to do stuff like we do in the Cloud now, but you'll be able to do a lot of stuff that we can't even do today on your own device. That opens up a ton of possibilities. I can fragment that out almost like a parallel computing space in all those devices, too. It's going to be interesting. The customization is pretty incredible.

TF: What advice would you give a young person who is interested in moving into the intersection between data, Artificial Intelligence, and game development?

Rob: One, have a passion for games. I think that helps. Be curious, be willing to ask lots of questions, and know that you're going to fail a ton at the onset, but that's part of the journey and the fun. Pay attention to your stats class, that's going to pay big dividends. Jump in, don't be afraid. You don't have to have an advanced degree to do it. What I think of when I did my undergrad, the amount of information I had then as compared to now, and in fact when I mentor young people who are trying to get into the space, it's actually I think those that come from a political science background or some of the social sciences with a bit of econ, because of the questioning and the methods that they have, that helps. It's a fun space to play in. Jump in.

DATA OWNERSHIP

Data Ownership: People, Corporations, Governments, DAOs

Who owns data?

This question languished in relative obscurity for most of human history. But this is now among the most complex questions of the modern economy. Google, Facebook (Meta) and hundreds of other companies derive most of their market value from their vast stores of data. This data is generated by billions of users, largely unwittingly. Gamers do the same with every interaction with social online games. This data is valuable to the game makers for reasons we've now discussed, but it also has value to third party advertisers, to other companies, and to regional governments.

Recent Apple changes to Advertising Identifier Declarations (IDFA) in early 2021 were couched as striking a blow for consumer data privacy, but in fact served to largely shift the economics of data ownership in the value chain for online applications away from Facebook in favor of Apple. A number of tradewar skirmishes between the United States and the People's Republic of China over the last few years have – at their heart – been about securing and controlling end-user data. The EU has passed a host of laws starting in 2018, collectively referred to as the General Data Protection Regulation (GDPR), attempting to provide some level of consumer protection.

As more sophisticated ways of gathering data take hold, as collation of biometric data, and other insights from an ecosystem of connected devices allow us to deduce unprecedented depths of information from players, this data becomes more valuable still. And as even more advanced AI Machine Learning systems become commonplace, both for gathering but also for acting upon information data ownership will rapidly become as contentious as access to sources of petroleum was in the twentieth century. Whoever controls the data controls the users.

So who should own the data players generate from games?

These questions will not quiet in the next two decades.

Using Big Datasets to Create Content

Another exciting area of game development that has only recently received much focus is the ability to create content based on external datasets. The way Ninantic, the parent company behind the smash hit *Pokémon Go*, accomplished this was to tap into existing stores of Google Maps data in order to allow players to use "the real world" as their playspace. A number of game companies since then have made use of Google Earth and other real-world map databases. United States Geological Survey Data provides topographic information that could be used for RTS games, Navitronics provides huge amounts of real-time marine data on tides, wind, depth, and the like which could influence games about piracy or naval battles set on the high seas. Live data from mass-transit systems could be used to create and inform crowd simulations. Traffic information could easily be used to populate vehicle traffic in large-scale simulation games like Grand Theft Auto. And so on.

FIGURE 8.3   Exhibition view from Refik Anadol's "Machine Memoirs: Space" at Pilevneli Gallery in Istanbul, Turkey. (*Image Credit:* Refik Anadol.)

In one interesting example, Turkish artist Refik Anadol[4] drove a project in which humans and AI collaborated to create artwork (Figure 8.3).

As Mr. Anadol put it: "*AI will not create art unto itself, but it can help human imaginations create things they can dream up, but never realize on their own. I see data as a pigment.*"

In this effort, the artist used visualizations of various datasets to create virtual spaces for exploration. This project was a collaboration with neuroscientists from the University of California at Berkeley, generating artwork based on large volumes of EEG data. In another, the team trained AI to digests 1.7 million historical artifacts, then build a visualization inspired by "The Library of Babel" by writer Jorge Luis Borges. Later, the artist used datasets from every recorded TED Talk over 30 years to generate 3D visual datascapes of every question & answer ever asked in 7,705 talks. Using these techniques, Anadol has created "meditative artwork, immersive space" instillations in Los Angeles, Istanbul, and Seoul.

While Anadol primarily used AI ingestion of datasets to generate beautiful and visually arresting installation art, you can easily imagine other uses. For example, this could all be turned into dialog from NPC characters in a game focused on learning. Imagine a game in which players explored a version of

FIGURE 8.4 Using Generative Adversarial Networks to create relational databases of current events news articles and Cloud computing power from Google, artists like Jason Decker are able to use AI and large datasets to create compelling new types of artwork. (*Image Credit:* Jason Decker.)

ancient Athens and encountered NPCs who conducted Socratic dialogs with them based on AI that had deeply ingested these classic works of philosophy.

When creators start combining the ability of AI to digest vast amounts of information, synthesize it, and then map it to a new interpretation of the data, we can generate unique, evolving, and fascinating new types of content. This is creation in a way that would have been virtually impossible to achieve even 20 years ago; we should expect large datasets to create worlds, visuals, and other types of content for games over the coming decades (Figure 8.4).

As digital artist Jason Decker describes it:

These tools are still a bit outside the mainstream - one has to cobble together some Python scripts, relational databases and have a pretty beefy graphics card. Fortunately, Google has a Virtual Machine server that let's you run code in the cloud using their hardware, opening up these tools to a wider audience.

The key to getting good results is having the correct recipe of "prompts" to guide the AI into creating a work of art. The fun really begins when trying to create a specific look.

In making this image, I went as far as to purposefully editorialize the fighting in Ukraine at the time.

My prompt was: "atomic explosion cloud filled with skulls in a field of sunflowers; Zdzisław Beksiński."

The first line sets the scene, then I picked a famous Polish artist, who is pretty well known for dark imagery.

It's as if someone invented a new type of camera and we are running around taking snapshots of everything.

Procedural Content Generation

Can AI ingest enough stories that we can use these datasets to generate new stories that derive their language, plots, characters, and themes from all they have read? Yes.

With some clever direction from human creators, we can teach AI about what qualifies as certain types of meta-data on a particular character ("villain") or plot twist ("third-act surprise") or type of overall narrative structure ("The hero's journey.") By then feeding the algorithm enough examples, using some types of adversarial learning techniques to correct errors in understanding, we can teach AI about how humans think about stories, and what kinds of elements work well. From there, teaching AI to generate procedural narratives, plot, dialog, and so on is not overly difficult.

Indeed there are a number of novels, plays, and game stories that have already been written by AI. While most of these still belong in the realm of curiosities rather than creations that can stand up against the works of human creators, the gap is closing rapidly. And AI is just getting started.

Procedural game design, both narrative focused and otherwise, has along history in the games business. A person could argue that even very early games in the mid-eighties, like the innovative *Seven Cities of Gold* by seminal game designer Dani Bunten, published by Electronic Arts.[5] The game relied on large-scale world creation using procedural techniques and emergent systems driven gameplay. From a design standpoint, this led the way to a large number of games which relied on algorithmic world generation and population techniques; this was early procedural content generation. The techniques and visual sophistication of landscape and special generation have advanced considerably, even in the last year. For example, Nvidia's recent GauGAN2 (named after the impressionist painter) allows users generate incredibly lifelike scenes based on nothing more than a text description. While this may not differ fundamentally in character from its eight-bit world generation predecessors, the fidelity of the content generated is breathtaking. What modern AI gives us is vastly more sophisticated rulesets, and the ability to adapt these rulesets and parameters over time based on machine learning derived from large datasets generated by players. While these technologies are not new, the level of craftsmanship the can begin to deliver against in the coming decades will be so much better able to engage players that it may feel new.

Procedural content generation has a few problems though right now. One of these is that using AI to create content quickly runs into a problem that large procedurally populated worlds have since the days of Bethesda's brilliant *Elder Scrolls Arena* (an ancestor of *Skyrim*). Procedurally generated words and content start to have a sense of sameness before long, which players get bored of quickly. People are also very good at pattern recognition, and many complain about the problem of procedural content lacking the nuance and surprising originality of hand-authored content. This is sometimes referred to as the "1,000 Bowls of Oatmeal Problem."

In one recent example, the technically brilliant game *No Man's Sky* by Hello Games procedurally generated tens of thousands of unique planets for the user to explore and interesting life forms to populate them. But as one reviewer put it,

> The sheer number of possible variations of worlds and wild species is too large to fully comprehend, but because the variety is defined by a computer pulling from a restricted pool of options, animals appear more like slapdash creations than thoughtful constructions.

Researcher Kate Compton[6] describes the problem in this way:

> Using procedural generation, I can easily generate 10,000 bowls of plain oatmeal, with each oat being in a different position and different orientation, and mathematically speaking they will all be completely unique, but the user will likely just see a lot of oatmeal.

This is where just using large datasets to generate content or narratives is not enough. Instead we need a layer of directorial intent that pushes for memorable and unique outcomes and is coupled with sufficient Machine Learning to get better at crafting content that provokes the right kind of response from users. One approach to this problem that shows much promise is based upon procedural understanding of narrative archetypes like Joseph Campbell's *The Hero's Journey* or other common literary archetypes. Indie developer Scribbl has built an interesting example of this in a Procedural *Hero's Journey* generator.[7]

Using large datasets to generate procedural content is a good way of filling out game worlds and populating them, even creating basic narrative. And there are researchers doing amazing work assessing the different techniques that various types of Deep Learning are using to advance these efforts.[8] But this discipline will really come into its own in the coming decade as AI can be trained up on the kinds of narrative elements that players respond to and begin to act with more intentional authorial and directorial intent.

Using Data to Generate Music

Other types of content may be easier to effectively generate by ingesting large datasets. One example of this is music for games. By having AI digest massive libraries of music, which tends to follow well understood and predictable patterns, we can then have procedurally generated – even adaptive – scores which can easily capture a particular tone, mood, use temp changes to reflect changes in game state, and so on. In one interesting recent example, researchers in Salzburg even used AI to take fragments of an unfinished Beethoven symphony and create a full version.[9] For years, games have experimented with dynamic musical scores which would blend smoothly between different moods based on setting changes or other in game events. We should expect this to become easier for human composers to direct, relying to procedural generation informed by large datasets to create thousands of necessary bridges easily.

AI Helping Write and Find Bugs in Code

Beyond helping or generating interesting content for art installations or games, can AI help us program games more effectively? Definitely.

For years, we've been getting better at having machine learning finish up sentences for us in emails, or starting to suggest variables which might be appropriate for a particular piece of code. But in the last few years we've made strides in getting AI to help write the logic that makes programming effective.[10] On a basic level, hundreds of millions of lines of known efficient code can be used to train pattern recognition AI; then common tasks can be automated. Microsoft and Cambridge University have both collaborated on an early version of this kind of AI, called DeepCoder. An Oxford University team have built an AI assistant to help generate automated unit tests.[11]

In some game development companies like Ubisoft Montreal, new tools are being developed which help detect common types of bugs in code before it is committed to the shared source code repository.[12] By reviewing almost a decade worth of code written for Ubisoft games, the R&D division were able to train the AI on what common mistakes look like. As anyone who has ever worked in a codebase shared across hundreds of developers knows, the price of bad code or buggy data getting checked in can be very large, sometimes even forcing whole teams to grind to a halt until the error is discovered and the bugs fixed.

This is still a nascent field, but given the staggering amount of cost and human effort that goes into building modern entertainment software, particularly on large AAA titles, even small advances here are likely to pay huge dividends. And as our ability to train ML algorithms and more advanced Artificial Intelligence creators improves we should expect this to help offset the complexity of integrated systems required for the kinds of platform agnostic massively social online games we've been discussing.

All of this is fairly obvious so far though; AI can write prose, poetry, commercials, and music, of course they can write code! So what's actually next then? I suspect the first truly transformative advancement here will be when an AI agent can easily "ride shotgun" with a programmer in a modern interpretation of the traditional buddy system used when writing critical code. I also suspect that AI writing code in languages designed for humans is a little bit like trying to teach dolphins to play billiards. Sure, perhaps they can learn to do it, *but what games would they invent for themselves if they could?* The first computer programming language created by AI for humans to use will be interesting. The tenth will be amazing. And the tenth language created by AI for AI will likely be truly transformative.

Over the next ten years I suspect that the nature of "programming" may change dramatically, as we learn to use machines to act as our layer of interface to tell other machines how we want them to operate. For decades, abstraction layers have been used as a programming concept to simplify the ways humans needed to instruct machines. AI driven abstraction layers will likely be able to introduce new heights of software development, transforming not just game development, but most aspects of human society.

AI and ML to Aid Game Content Design

At Rovio we've been investing in machine learning for a number of years, with the key aims being to lighten the load on our game designers and be able to produce fun content at a faster cadence with less manual grind. In addition, we can also better predict aspects like level difficulty and likeliness of churn.

Ville Heijari, CMO, Rovio (Angry Birds)[13]

Big game teams engage hundreds, sometimes thousands of designers and content creators. For most of the last 20 years, the people who build levels for users to explore, zones in big MMOs, puzzles for puzzle games, and other types of game content, have had to do so manually. The tools that designers used to set up game content started very primitive, as anyone who ever entered data in a HexEditor remembers. Text files, spreadsheets, then.xml documents improved matters; eventually some levels of data validation based against schemas started to help further. Graphic editors and the use of sophisticated third party engine tools like Unreal or Unity further improved designers' ability to create game content. As we began to create tools for procedural generation of physical spaces, parameterized enemy statistic generation, and similar, things got better still. The advent of early Machine Learning simulation has allowed verifying the effectiveness of content, tuning level difficulty, and populating playscapes easier still. We should expect ML and AI assistant tools to continue to significantly improve this part of game creation over the coming years.

Helping Artists Make Art

Even more expensive and time consuming than a game's design content, the artwork that comprises modern games represents a monumental undertaking. Building out huge cities and explorable spaces takes a lot of brilliant artists a lot of time. As expectations for visual fidelity increase, driven by the relentless push of graphics hardware and competition, many game teams have ended up employing hundreds of artists for years in order to deliver modern AAA experiences. Despite huge improvements in 3D modeling, texturing, and animation software over the last few decades, this remains a very time consuming and technically complex process. A traditional animator can generate about four seconds of content per day. Deep Learning- and camera-driven motion capture technology can hugely speed this process. This is another area in which machine learning from big datasets has begun to change our approach.

By having AI ingest data describing the visual characteristics of landscapes, architecture, and even animals or humans we can train software how to replicate new versions of this kind of content in ways that would have taken human artists huge amounts of time just a few years ago. From an army of orcs massing at Helm's Deep, to digital destruction of urban populations in the newest Hollywood disaster film, content is increasingly being digitally created using tools that are guided by artists rather than being painstakingly sculpted and lit by them. Indeed, the skills of software at creating photorealistic visual content that is rapidly becoming hard to distinguish from photographs or film footage will change society in the coming years.

According to a recent report by VentureBeat: "Some experts project synthetic visual content will be nearly 95% of the content we view by 2027."[14] This is made possible only by huge improvements in the way AI and machine learning can speed the generation of such content. For games, this means that we will be able to build increasingly high-fidelity playscapes for players, populated with lifelike characters and objects for them to engage with, without needing to continue to grow teams in the way they've grown over the last two decades.

In only the last year, our capabilities using new techniques in machine learning are allowing AI to create many different kinds of content[15] at levels of fidelity which are very close to indiscernible from real life, or from work created by human artisans. As we will see in future chapters, this is about to open whole new vistas for creators, and start to blur some lines which humans have lived within for thousands of years.

Using Games to Train AI

We've covered the basics of how Deep Learning works to train AI, and even touched on some of the more advanced techniques, like Generative Adversarial Networks which can use multiple opposing Deep Learning networks to improve one another. But is there a way games and gaming can help train AI faster and create a virtuous feedback loop? It turns out there may be.

Some particularly nuanced and complicated tasks, particularly those involving highly complex systems with large numbers of fuzzy inputs or components which behave in ways that are hard to predict pose particular challenges for Deep Learning AI networks. As a highly practical example, let's take building AI which can effectively drive cars and trucks fully autonomously in real-world conditions. According to analysis done by the RAND Corporation, an American defense industry think-tank head-quartered in Santa Monica, California, "a fleet of 100 self-driving cars would have to operate 24 hours a day, 365 days a year, and cover 14 billion kilometers" to generate a sufficient real-world dataset to achieve a mean-ingful level of improvement over human drivers. They estimate this could take approximately 400 years to achieve if adhering to speed-limits.[16]

So car manufacturers, including Porche, have created simulators of which thousands can be run simultaneously. Could driving games played by millions of people be used to further accelerate this training? While the data from simulations and player drivers is not the same quality as data generated in real-world road tests, there are some reasons to be hopeful that this approach could yield fruit.

In another example of games providing data back to think-tanks, let's consider the so called "Corrupted Blood Incident" from Activision Blizzard's *World of Warcraft*. In September of 2005 the designers of this venerable computer MMORPG introduced a game element which infected players when they battled an enemy boss known as Hakkar the Soulflayer. In the course of this fight, some players would become infected. Thee infec-tion, called "Corrupted Blood" was highly contagious and could be spread to other nearby players and NonPlayer Characters. It could also be trans-ferred by contact with player-controlled pets in the game. This infection killed off low-level players immediately but could eventually be survived by some higher-level players. Due to a bug, the resulting plague extended across the entire game world, leaving cities piled with dead players. Many players responded by attempting to quarantine – running out to sparsely populated wilderness and so on, or not logging into the game – so as not to infect their guildmates. But quite a few did not, either ignoring the contagion, or actively spreading it. The United States Center for Disease Control – charged with studying and preventing the spread of infectious diseases – ended up studying the incident. In fact, a few years later, Dr. Ran D. Balicer, an Israeli epidemiologist published an article[17] in Epidemiology, a scientific-medical journal, suggesting that games could serve as models for infectious diseases.

WOW Event with a Contagion "Corrupted Blood Incident"

CDC inspired built models for training, useful in 2020 Covid-19 outbreak research.

This incident is particularly interesting because it shines light on one of the ways social games can be particularly useful for modeling. Many models can be far more easily build without the need for any human agency as an input. But because players did not behave as expected; rather than self-isolate and rest they continued to do things which were destructive to themselves and the goals of their guilds. As the world learned in the 2020 COVID-19 pandemic, this kind of human behavior turns out to be common. Because modeling complex human social behavior with all the wiles and peculiar counter-intuitive behaviors, which run counter to individual or group self-interests can be well simulated by large social systems, some games may be a perfect medium for it.

From these two examples, we can see ways in which games can assuredly be used to provide valuable data and in some cases the introduction of human players can create exactly the kind of counter-intuitive behaviors which AI Deep Learning models need to study in order to understand events in human populations. Can we imagine other types of games which could help provide valuable datasets which could train AI?

Could a tactical squad-based game like *America's Army, Ghost Recon*, or *Call of Duty* be used to generate behavioral metrics that could help AI generate squad-based tactics predictive learning?

Could sports games like Maddin be used to train AI "coaches" for the real-life NFL to pick plays more likely to succeed? Could similar games inform AI to improve draft picks in a sort of "Moneyball for AI"? Could player behavior at the pre-college level be used to help identify potential star players for college coaches to consider for recruitment as prophesied in science fiction like *Ender's Game* or *The Last Starfighter*?

Are there other types of gaming which would be well suited toward having players perform pattern recognition or matching mechanics which could have implications for complex mathematical problems? Imagine a Match3 puzzle style game that asked players to match and combine elements which were analogs to the kind of complex structures of molecular chemistry used to identify potential enzymes or similar.

The value of games for simulating large complex models may be precisely because there are things humans do which are unique, hard to predict, and which interact in very chaotic ways in large social systems. Games might be a perfect medium for such models.

Data and Analytics Wrap Up

By gathering metrics from users who play games, we can learn a lot about what these players prefer, what works to engage and retain them, what they are willing to pay for, and so on. Then by making subtle (or profound) changes to software tuning and data values, we can make the software even more effective. Machine learning across millions of users and automating some of this tuning gives us the ability to improve further still. And while some game companies have used these techniques for the last five years or so, this is an area that is still in its infancy. Making use of AI routines with access to vast amounts of user data and the assignment to optimize for particular types of user behavior will profoundly increase how sticky games are. This is a largely untapped area of game development which will change the industry over the next decade. Let's look at a few specific areas of opportunity.

First, for any free-to-play games (which is already and will become increasingly the vast majority of games played across the world), significant amounts of revenue are made from in-game offers made to players. They can choose to transact or not, and knowing what kind of offer to present to a particular player and when can make an enormous difference in conversion rates and purchase prices. Targeted offers could easily include information about a player's likely income level, overall wealth based on their postal code, probability of a particular day being payday, current levels of that player's family finance, credit scores. Slightly less sensitive data could easily allow a game to offer a player a birthday present offer, or the ability to send a friend who also plays a gift in game on their friend's birthday. Targeted offers for particular holidays are already common in free-to-play mobile gaming, and can get more sophisticated.

Are players more likely to make a purchase directly before or after lunchtime? (Theory: Before, because after they probably just spent some money on lunch and are sleepy!) I do not know, but machine learning could easily figure out the answer and then bias offers for the right time based on success rates across millions of players.

Machine learning algorithms can easily perform constant experiments with which in-game NPC is making offers to a particular player type, what types of words and language they are using in the offer, what scenario or challenge is being presented at that moment, and so on. Further, this can be tied to partnership offers to derive revenue like serving up targeted advertising coupons to a player's favorite local restaurant an hour before lunch time, etc.

Beyond monetization, even for games which are not free-to-play, there are lots of opportunities to use ML to increase retention and engagement. For example, players stick with a particular game a lot longer when they are playing with friends. Suggesting the right friends to players (based on awareness of their social graph, or just suggesting users in similar time zones, with similar shared language, playstyles, spend levels, etc.) can have a hugely beneficial impact on a player's enjoyment of a game. Detecting and adapting social groupings based on data analysis can be very useful here too. If 15 of 30 members of an Alliance have stopped playing (or massively changed their play patterns and left an Alliance) in the last three days, this might be a great time for the game to suggest that Alliance merge with another Alliance, before the predictable thing occurs and the rest of those players quit playing too. This kind of "churn prediction" is a particularly useful area of focus for training ML systems in games.

Games which are very good at tapping into large amounts of available data on users and building their software systems to make good choices based on this data, then learn from the outcome of these choices and reinforce good choice making in the future will have a huge advantage over the coming years. In the next two decades, the role of game tuning after a game is live will be far more important than the initial tuning values and systems behavior; this is the value of operating software-as-a-service in an age of machine learning and access to large and diverse datasets, with sophisticated abilities to draw connections between them.

The Coming Impact of Big Data

Whole books are written, entire advanced degree programs are now designed around the topic of data and analytics. Around the globe, great programs like the Rutger's Master's Degree (MS) in Data Science in California, or the IIM Kolkata in India are training new cohorts of students and professionals to think about and interact with data in new ways. To suggest that the advent of "big data" and increasingly advanced ways to process and teach AI to draw conclusions from it is changing every facet of human society is not hyperbolic. This is the century of big data.

For gaming, this represents a significant shift in how game architecture is designed and how teams are comprised and structured. We can already make meaningful incremental improvements to game engagement, retention, monetization through the application of data science thinking on the large datasets online social games generate. And modern mechanisms for growth marketing and user acquisition are heavily reliant on this technology. What's more, our abilities here are improving quite rapidly. But we are lagging far behind in knowing how to assess, visualize, and convey appropriate rights, controls, and permissions to various data streams or sources.

On some level, these techniques are not currently significantly changing the core of game design, or defining differently the things players do in games. Yet. But games which make use of this field of study will be able to attract more users more efficiently, keep them longer, help them enjoy the games more, and derive more direct and indirect revenue. But going forward, the techniques and ideas for AI companions, for connected ecosystems, and most of the other notions presented in these pages will only be possible because of the underlying data techniques described in this chapter. This makes the chase for big data techniques and the data scientists and product managers who can apply it a bit of an arms race; game companies that can effectively harvest and use data effectively will be much more successful over time than those that do not. Over the next 20 years, the winners in the game industry will be those who master data science to make their games better.

Large datasets will increasingly drive the ways in which we create the games themselves, by improving or altering the way we program game systems that define how playspaces work. Our ability to collect and have machines learn from large datasets will allow us to massive speed the mechanics of implementing game design content, and the artistic content that provides meaning and beauty to the environments players enjoy.

NOTES

1 https://theconversation.com/the-worlds-data-explained-how-much-were-producing-and-where-its-all-stored-159964.
2 https://time.com/5814276/google-data-centers-water/.
3 https://www.edwardtufte.com/tufte/books_vdqi.
4 https://www.youtube.com/watch?v=UxQDG6WQT5s.
5 https://en.wikipedia.org/wiki/The_Seven_Cities_of_Gold_(video_game).
6 https://www.gdcvault.com/play/1024213/Practical-Procedural-Generation-for.
7 https://scribbl.itch.io/procedural-heros-journey.
8 https://link.springer.com/article/10.1007%2Fs00521-020-05383-8.
9 http://espresso.economist.com/12f7312b4d9643975b72b9c5c032e2be.
10 https://www.wired.com/story/ai-latest-trick-writing-computer-code/.
11 https://www.stxnext.com/blog/will-artificial-intelligence-replace-developers/.
12 https://www.wired.co.uk/article/ubisoft-commit-assist-ai.
13 https://www.ign.com/articles/the-games-industry-on-what-gaming-might-be-like-in-2030.
14 https://venturebeat.com/2021/11/15/deep-tech-no-code-tools-will-help-future-artists-make-better-visual-content/.
15 https://unchartedterritories.tomaspueyo.com/p/ai-does-it-best.

16 https://www.economist.com/science-and-technology/the-hard-job-of-teaching-autonomous-cars-to-drive/21805753.

17 Balicer, Ran (2005-10-05). "Modeling Infectious Diseases Dissemination through Online Role-Playing Games". *Epidemiology.* **18**(2): 260–261. doi:10.1097/01.ede.0000254692.80550.60. PMID 17301707.

CHAPTER 9

Artificially Intelligent Characters

VIRTUAL CHARACTERS TAKE OVER THE WORLD. SOON

Humans have always imagined the role of clever familiars, wicked djinns, and wise oracles who could offer us comradeship and guidance. We learned the tales of the Golem, Pygmalion, Victor Frankenstein, and Wintermute. We understand that many gods have been made in the idea and image of men, at least by some creators and some believers. Humans create characters. And we dress and retool them like actors or archetypes over time to fit with what the populace responds to in a given place and age. Marketing campaigns create *persona*; they test what statements will be popular and with whom. Boy band composition and identities are relentlessly focus-tested; new hairstyles are tried on, new virtues or scandals or tattoos carefully honed over time in a commercial Darwinian process of selection. And some in the population have always wanted others they could birth, shape, change, or control. Technology is about to enable humans to create and command and interact with our own creations in ways which are expressions of these same human desires, but at a level of realism and immersion we have not seen before.

With Artificially Intelligent (AI) companions, all of these kinds of interactions with manufactured human-likenesses are about to become more commonplace, easier, and much stranger than we've seen before. Creating characters who are nearly indistinguishable from humans has now become a real possibility. And each can be unique, tailored to every

DOI: 10.1201/9781003291800-10

individual – for a specific role in that person's life even – and they can learn. They will not forget, and they can access every Library of Alexandria ever written. AI companions, far more advanced than Siri, are now a reality. They can evolve with incredible speed and rapid predictive accuracy based on the study of vast amounts of preference data. They will be omnipresent within a few years. They already mostly are, they are just quiet. Soon they can look like anyone you love, anything you trust, anything you want to see. And they will be a major force in the ways players interact with games starting within a few years.

Let's unpack all of this.

Speech recognition software can capture whatever you say with greater than 99% accuracy today. Speech recognition software like Dragon works beautifully in devices Google Home to the newest Tesla cars. Natural Language Processing can interpret the words you use to deduce what you may mean, and many of us use these technologies daily to help make our emails faster to write and more accurate. These systems can check the probability or common intent behind the phrases you stitch together. Deep learning algorithms, which are built on very sophisticated logic, mimicking networks of neurons in the human brain can train themselves to become ever more accurate at such interpretation. When it misinterprets, it can learn from that and not make the same mistake next time. Most of the technology behind each of these incredible statements – technological feats – is well established at this point. This is not new tech.

"Deepfake" technology for synthesizing and stitching together video and video quality 3D avatars that look like anyone, freshly invented or historical, making it easy to have a person or creature which is custom chosen by (or for) you. This avatar can easily be tied into conversational AI systems so it can respond to any person (or other AI avatars) who speak or input language. These AI characters will be able to answer phone calls, respond to messages, converse with you over Zoom. This means that every person can easily have AI companions at any and all times, on any device attached to the cloud. And they will be able to appear in games, play alongside human players just as they do now in many games, but with far greater verisimilitude.

Characters from some video games have been doing this for a long time. But their abilities and ubiquity will be getting significantly more advanced over the next few decades. And the characters no longer need to exist just within the context of the game; they can be in any and every player's pocket, or earphones or sunglasses. Think of Han Solo quipping, Confucius offering guidance, Nathan Drake chattering, Sponge Bob making fart sounds in the player's ear when their teacher speaks. Imagine *Mass Effect* crewmates which chimed in over the phone or headphones to remind the player that their ship had come into orbit around the destination planet – a perfect appointment mechanic reminder. Imagine your grandfather came in on a video call asking you to play Go with him again for your weekly game, even if he passed away ten years ago. Game companions can become as omnipresent as players want them to be or pay for them to be. As the technologies described above get more sophisticated, easier to incorporate into games, we will see the boundaries between games and life further lose focus and dissolve. Soon, many of the figures humans interact with will not be people, and mostly, the humans won't be able to tell.

ON AI CHARACTERS

Let's look at a few steps along the way that will get us from here to there.

AI-driven companions exist in many games right now, from Claptrap in the Borderlands series to friendly Non-Player Characters (NPCs) who journey with you for brief periods of time in almost every role-playing game, to personalities which drive the first-time user experience (FTUE) or tutorial experience. Indeed, we've come a long way from a game like Tetris, in which the player just interacts with a puzzle to modern incarnations of the puzzle genre, like *Matchington Mansion,* in which characters like Carol Renee and her cat help teach the player what to do and motivate them to move through the game. Let's think of these kinds of characters as the most basic form of NPC AI – really little more than a piece of 2D art attached to pre-determined messages from the game creators.

In more complex games like *Red Dead Redemption, Pathfinder: Wrath of the Righteous,* or *Mass Effect,* NPCs with complex branching story arcs follow or lead the player around, sometimes delivering thousands of lines of high-quality dialog in response to various player actions or the actions of other NPCs. These are usually driven by fairly straightforward branching dialog and stimulus-response trees. These sorts of characters have been a part of games for almost three decades.

But far more sophisticated versions of these kinds of conversational trees exist, mostly in products which are not games. While this basic technology has existed at a university and R&D level for a long time, these have just started to come into their own over the last ten years. Two great examples of these are Woebot and Replika, but there are many more (Figure 9.1).[1]

FIGURE 9.1   Replika is an AI Friend chatbot powered by Artificial Intelligence, created by Luka, Inc. (*Image Credit:* Luka.)

One of the more advanced consumer facing conversational AI in play over the last year or two, Replika is a purely recreational AI bot friend which allows users to engage in dialog about their lives. Replika allows users to choose a visual avatar for their Replika companion, then chat over the web or through a mobile application. Replika is the brainchild of Luka, Inc. a San Francisco-based conversational AI company, who have been training the bot through interactions with users since 2017. In Replika, you get to select an avatar for your friend, personalizing them by deciding on their gender, skin tone, hairstyle, name, and a few other details. Then your friend chats with you using a conversation tree and Natural Language Processing to interpret your responses. Replica has added a lot of features over the last few years, including a number of gamification elements that encourage daily logins, etc. Using in-game currency, users can buy other outfits, personalities, or domains of knowledge for their friend. They have also recently added a voice chat or call feature, which allows you to have spoken dialog with your friend. The overall effect is charming, though fairly shallow given the Replika's limited view into the user's world – restricted solely to what the user types or says, plus a basic and general-ized understanding of time. At the moment, Replika is only available in English (North American, Western US, Silicon Valley variant), which is indicative of one of the challenges with conversational AI. To build AI that can truly chat with any user in their own language, dialect, and slang is a complex undertaking, though fundamentally just a matter of exposing the system to sufficient content in those different languages. We should think of Replika as one of the first of a coming wave of AI companions that have been predicted in science fiction for decades. Within a few years, these AI companions will be good enough at conversation that they will truly be indistinguishable from other humans for the vast majority of humanity (Figure 9.2).

Another North American company is currently using similar technol-ogy for a different goal: Woebot Health is a behavioral health platform and products company based out of San Francisco whose primary product,

FIGURE 9.2 Woebot is an AI powered chatbot focused on mental health and based on therapeutic techniques including Cognitive Behavioral Therapy (CBT). It is the brainchild of Woebot Health. (*Image Credit:* Woebot Health.)

Woebot, is a conversational AI agent who engages with the user using the framework of clinically-validated therapeutic techniques, including Cognitive Behavioral Therapy (CBT). By asking the user questions and engaging in dialog, Woebot tries to help address stress, anxiety, relationship issues, substance use problems, and other common types of mental health issues that are more typically raised in counseling sessions with a human counselor. The brainchild of Alison Darcy, a clinical research psychologist who ran Andrew Ng's Health Innovation Lab in Computer Science at Stanford, Woebot uses automated conversational AI, which learns from every encounter with a user to get better target its responses. According to the *New York Times*,[2] there are more than 10,000 different apps focusing on mental health as of the time of this writing. But very few of them currently use AI and Natural Language Processing to attempt to converse with users in a way that builds relationship and trust over time. And while there are a number of valid concerns expressed about the ethics, security, and effectiveness of using AI bots to perform functions so essential to some humans' happiness, this genie is out of the bottle, and will not be stopped. Interestingly, many people report preferring AI counselors to human ones, because they don't feel judged in the same way.[3] Expect this to be one of the first of many consumer facing domain specific conversational chat driven agents which will begin to engage with people at increasingly intimate levels.

By looking at Replika and Woebot and thinking about the role of AI characters in open-world games like Rockstar's *Red Dead Redemption*, we can quite easily start to imagine AI-fueled companions for games in the future. The increasing sophistication of voice input into games and the ability for conversational tree bots to learn and improve over time will soon take us to a point where in-game NPCs will be able to have dialog that is as advanced as many human companions could.

BUILDING AI COMPANIONS

What steps would be required to build AI companions that could respond in a compelling manner in a basic conversation in a game?

The Character Visuals

- First you'd need a high-resolution 3D model, textured, "boned," with an animation set that allowed for a variety of hand and arm expressions that allowed the actor to emphasize elements of their articulations with gestures.

- You'd want to focus particularly on details and resolution in the character's face, especially the eyes, cheeks, and lips; humans are extremely attuned to facial movement nuances, and you're going to want the mouth to be able to move in a way that convincingly aligns with what the character is saying. This is usually done through morph targets which are interpreted from a text version of the character's dialog.

- A little additional work to ensure that the character fits into a scene with shaders, lighting, potentially cloth simulation for their attire, anisotropic shaders to simulate the visual qualities of hair, and similar rendering techniques aren't essential, but they can add to the illusion.

The Dialog

- Natural Language Processing techniques can interpret the conversational input from a player (or other NPCs), determine their likely meaning, and check it against situational context and other potential meanings for the most probable intent.

- Then the agent needs to generate a response they should say in return. Ideally this response can be checked against a database of the millions of times a similar response has been used to generate the desired effect to confirm that a potential response is the most likely.

- Once intent and basic word choice are selected, an additional layer to map these word choices to the character's particular slang, dialect, education level, or similar would be useful. (An erudite Victorian era Sherlock Holmes character would use different words than a Grand Theft Auto gangster character, for example.)

- Ideally the intent of the speech would be annotated with markup indicating emotional state of the speaker (e.g. angry, sad, emphatic) This adds an additional layer of considerable sophistication to the model and can also be used to drive expression and gestures which helps to sell the dialog performance.

- Now you'd have a line of text dialog with words that had a good chance of being convincing.

TEXT TO SPEECH

- The AI actor would need to translate the text and markup into audible dialog in that character's voice. Deepfake technology has advanced this kind of "voice skinning" a lot in the last few years.

- The markup can be mapped to lip-synch, eye movements, and gestures to further sell the illusion.

These steps gloss over a mountain of nuance in each step, but these are the basic technologies that need to be stitched together to create compelling AI actor companions who can engage in arbitrary dialog with players. Of course, this requires both very sophisticated Machine Learning models trained on very large amounts of data, and the input of human artists to create and refine the assets involved.

Next, imagine feeding additional inputs into the AI: visuals from AR-style glasses, audio or other conversations going on around the player, social graph information from the player's social networks to determine who their friends are, and how they might be playing the game, and so on. It's quite easy, then, to imagine truly sophisticated companions from games which might be "with" the player often, begging them to come back to play, warning or threatening them, making references to real-world events that might have bearing on the game. Moreover, by understanding other elements about a player's life, an AI companion might be tailored by an AI game "director" to act a certain way.

First popularized by Valve corporation's seminal cooperative zombie shooter, *Left4Dead*, the concept of an AI director will continue to evolve in prominence over the coming decades. In *Left4Dead*, the game dynamically adds events, enemies, and so on to the game session in response to how players are doing. More than just the kind of "dynamic difficulty" that has been around since early Nintendo games, the *Left4Dead* director sought to ensure that certain events that contributed to emotional intensity, hero moments where one player could save the day, and so on would occur. By paying attention to in-game events (a player's health, where players are in relation to one another, etc.), the game AI director would spawn new enemies of different types or create other in-game events to heighten the drama. The result was a game that felt different every session and kept players talking about their game sessions for years.

Now imagine this type of a system being fed inputs from real-world events surrounding the player. A game that set as its goal to uplift the mood of a player could discern that the weather was cold and gloomy where the player lived and engineer a change in the weather in game such that it was sunny and welcoming in the game world. An AI-driven fitness coach or workout partner in games which encouraged mobility or were built around exercise – as Nintendo's Wii and other console games have done – could easily receive input from a player's smart-watch, which allowed them to make recommendations about sleep, exercise, blood-sugar levels, or other biometric data. In a more sophisticated example, imagine that the game director heard the player being taunted or downtrodden by bullies on the schoolyard, then set up an option for the player to feel powerful and heroic by doing a good deed (like rescuing a kid from bullies) later and rewarding them for it in game. Perhaps the game could even subtly teach lessons that provided long-term emotional and behavioral benefits to players who engaged with the game (Figure 9.3).

For narrative-based games, like the superb *Choices* by Pixelberry, one of the great challenges has always been how to generate sufficient content. (Users typically retain very well in a narrative game they enjoy right up until they consume all of the content the game makers have created; then they are gone.) Imagine that AI game master or narrator was able to spin out an unlimited amount of bespoke content custom tailored to what an individual player responds to in characters, plots, or settings. This type of AI director could easily create fresh content scenarios based on recent news the player cared about, adopt local weather, details from last night's football game, scenarios based on battles from the frontline with adaptive NPCs based on humans who were present, and so on. Based on the amount of data the AI director had on a player, these games could present a narrative that was beautifully tailored and highly compelling to each individual.

The implications of truly aware AI agents who could exercise directorial intent when crafting scenes in games could be used to create genuinely powerful and influential bespoke in-game experiences for millions of players.

Two of these examples are straightforward and easy to do today with the right levels of integration between data streams; the third requires slightly more sophisticated interpretation and craftmanship than we could easily accomplish today, but within a few years, we should expect this level of social awareness from AI bots. Indeed, ultimately recognizing the

FIGURE 9.3 *Choices* by Pixelberry is a popular choose-your-own-adventure style of game which is a genre ripe for enhancement by AI directors and chatbots. (*Image Credit*: Pixelberry.)

emotional nuance in spoken language is just a few layers deeper version of Natural Language Processing reinforced by machine learning to confirm accurate interpretations of word choice, tone, and phrasing. Adding in social graph awareness of the individuals involved can further add context which can allow AI game agents to understand interactions between humans inside the framework of the game or outside. We still have a long way to go to train AI agents on softer human concepts, such as empathy, but while the ability to learn from millions of conversations between humans may not teach AI what an emotion feels like, it can certainly teach them how a real person is likely to act when faced with one.

INDISTINGUISHABLE FROM REAL HUMANS

In many ways, these examples of the ways AI characters in games don't properly communicate the impact the application of these technologies will have on people. We are not necessarily talking about pixelated or rendered 3D characters: we've developed the ability to generate genuinely life-like characters now, which are extremely difficult to distinguish from real people visually. Consider the examples provided by graphics chip-maker Nvidia in their experiment "thispersondoesnotexist" (Figure 9.4).

Using a collection of sophisticated open-source technologies, this website generates extremely lifelike human characters, which are indistinguishable from photos of real humans. By pitting two different Deep Learning algorithms against one another – one which improves the fake image, the other of which tries to detect parts of the image that look fake – in a process called Generative Adversarial Networks, the simulated humans can quickly become extremely difficult for humans or machines to discern from the real thing. From here to fully articulated, animated, vocalizing AI-driven avatars is a very short walk, measured in just a few years. By 2028, we should expect AI-driven characters at this level of visual fidelity to be regularly interacting with us in many contexts, inside and outside of games.

FIGURE 9.4   We can now easily create convincingly lifelike people who have not ever existed, like this computer generated character. This is not a photograph; this is not a real human. (*Image Credit:* StyleGAN technology, used by https://thispersondoesnotexist.com/.)

The tools for game makers to create and direct characters at this level are also being made powerful and either cheap or free, rapidly. MetaHuman, an Unreal Engine tool suite for generating lifelike 3D characters, ready to use in games, is available for free today in early access. With a collection of 50 fully created MetaHumans to use as examples, creators can learn how to generate their own 3D characters ready for real-time game usage, and ready to be paired with conversational AI using the techniques described above. Not to be outdone, Unity has recently acquired Ziva Dynamics,[4] a company that focuses on applying ML techniques to creating, and dynamically altering the fidelity of 3D human characters for deployment on different hardware, from mobile phones to high-end consoles with the goal of "democratizing real-time character creation."

But it is more than the unique new fictional or originally invented characters we need to start thinking about. New characters no one has ever met before pose one set of opportunities and challenges. But characters based on real humans pose a wholly different set of complexities, ethical concerns, and opportunities for game creators (Figure 9.5).

Consider the "deepfake" technologies, which have sprouted across the internet in recent years. Accessible mobile and PC applications now allow almost anyone to create decent deepfake videos but using more sophisticated software and hardware, various firms and individuals have created

FIGURE 9.5 This is not former president Obama speaking. This is a deepfake warning people not to believe what they see online. (*Image Credit:* ARS Electronica.)

hundreds of compelling, funny, or disturbing videos of dead celebrities or presidents singing, dancing, cursing, speaking in languages they never spoke, delivering speeches written by others, and the like.

Imagine now this deepfake technology being used in concert with social media uploads to create or allow users to create custom, bespoke in-game characters who look, sound, and move convincingly like a trusted authority figure, a beloved and long-gone relative, an ex-lover, or the bullies we mentioned moments ago. Can a trusted parent appear in a bespoke ad telling you who to vote for? Sure. Could an AI director in a game record footage of our hypothetical bullies messing with our hypothetical gamer kid via the kid's AR-enabled RayBan glasses? Absolutely. Could these bullies – looking and moving convincingly like the ones in real life then be dispatched with a sword in an adventure later that day in the game? Definitely. What if the kid's dead grandfather then showed up and delivered a lecture of forgiveness and an in-game reward? It is easy to imagine powerful scenarios, both superb and also terrible when combining these technologies for miming real people with an AI director setting up in-game scenarios.

One can imagine game like *Civilization* allowing players to interact with convincing historical celebrities, terrible revenge-snuff-games, celebrity-endorsed sing-along games which are far more tailored and realistic than *The Beatles: Rock Band* which was popular a decade ago. Imagine celebrity songsmith giving a personal invitation to a skilled player to come onstage and "perform" with the celebrity in front of millions of other players. What rights the dead (or living) have to their likenesses remains a hot open question, addressed in both courts and a recent episode of the science fiction television show *Black Mirror*. Already deceased celebrities like Tupac Shakur and Michael Jackson have performed "live" in concerts appearing visually using holographic technology. Other actors and stars, like beloved funnyman Robin Williams, have already written stipulations into their will prohibiting any Computer Graphics driven simulacra of their likeness to be used in any context until decades after their death. Regardless of the legality or ethical implications of the topic, it is clear that games (and other media) can and will make use of extremely lifelike AI-driven characters who carry with them all the emotional weight of real humans. This can and will be used for good and for ill.

Consider now, too, the criticality of security once these use cases start being combined and widespread. Imagine how powerful that virtual friend of empathetic therapist could be when Woebot meets a photorealistic virtual person with strong conversational NLP. Then consider the risk when hackers "abduct" your virtual best friend with sophisticated versions of the ransomware used today to lock up a person's PC. Contemplate blackmail extortion schemes when these same hackers threaten to expose secrets users and players have divulged to virtual therapists. What happens when they send convincing – horrifying – deepfakes threatening to torture an NPC friend a player has had for years (or worse, a virtual version of a real-life child or sibling?) What about when they threaten to release a compromising deepfake video of an avatar a top player has cultivated for years. Consider ransomware with deep emotional impact. These are the sorts of threats that will emerge from the shadows of these wonderful technologies.

As game makers, we have just recently gained access to a powerful new suite of tools – arguably more compelling than any that any writer or artist has ever had – because our ability to create lifelike characters and have them behave as actors who exert a level of informed autonomy tailored around a desired effect on a player is simply unprecedented in human history.

AVATARS

Other than real humans, there's another kind of simulacra, which are already in popular use in gaming and media. These are CG avatars, which allow real humans – players and otherwise – the option to appear as unreal characters in games. As opposed to the AI agents who look like real people, these are instead human-controlled agents who look like... something else. This is nothing new; one could argue that the original *Pac-Man* allowed players to appear as a hungry mouthy circle character being chased by ghosts. But the evolution of technology which allows people to map their speech or actions onto 3D characters – who can be as lifelike or fantastic as artists can imagine – is another aspect of character in games that we should consider.

With advanced movement tracking, cameras, and other affordable consumer technology that is now nearly standard in mobile phones, PCs, and many consoles, players will be able to appear as they wish in games but express themselves with all the kinetic and verbal nuance (or more!) that they can in real life. "Vtubers", like the incredibly popular Gwar Gura, with her millions of fans, allow real humans to disguise themselves as anime-style characters while streaming online video sessions. These characters act as puppets for Twitch streamers, whose real appearance and identities are hidden behind animated digital characters who act as masks. While this is fundamentally no different than the way in-game avatars in *World of Warcraft* or other games have worked for decades, the technology now exists to make these characters reflect a player's dialog, movements, and even emotional reactions.

We should expect games in coming years to allow players to take their created avatar characters in-game into out-of-game spaces to create performances in character on streaming services like Twitch. This technology now exists and is becoming increasingly popular.

Software created characters, like the popular Hatsune Miku, an animated character who is considered one of the first "virtual idols" uses vocal synthesis technology to allow "her" to deliver performances in animated series, sing songs, and even appear in ads for winter festivals.[5] For years, user-generated characters, like the "Mii" users are asked to create on Nintendo platforms have begun to appear as part of a gamer's profile; they will become much more ubiquitous. And imagine when these avatars start appearing to recommend what show you should watch on Netflix or what product you might like on Amazon.

THE FUTURE OF AVATARS

As we gain greater ability for everyone to create and customize both photo-realistic character avatars and heavily stylized characters like the VTubers discussed above, and as persistent virtual presence in various games, concerts, applications, and assorted incarnations of a Metaverse become more popular, we should expect gamers to care increasingly about their avatar. (Even more than many already do!)

Specifically, there are a few things which should become commonplace, and which will pay great dividends to those who make them easy.

First, a user needs to be able to create one or more avatar characters very easily and customize them heavily. Ideally, the tools for creating anything from hyper-lifelike humans to anime dragons, mechs, anthropomorphized pandas, and everything else under the sun. Creating unique, diverse, high-quality 3D models that can be deeply customized is not easy... But compared to many of the things we've discussed in this book, it is a well-understood problem with thousands of examples in games from the last 30 years. Making such a character creator highly accessible and work on almost any PC, tablet, mobile device, or console is a mild UI challenge, but also a fairly straightforward mission. A generalized universal avatar character creator, aided by a strong AI content-generation engine seems almost inevitable within the next few years.

The more challenging part is determining how to let users bring a version of their avatar into as many games and applications as possible. "Interoperability" is the phrase that has become shorthand for this set of challenges.

There are technical constraints to be sure: Different applications have different file formats, different rendering systems, different animation requirements, budgets for polygon counts and many other differences. The amount of detail that can be stored and displayed fast in a scene with a hundred players all running and jumping on mobile phones is typically much lower than the quality at which a single character can be shown while standing alone on a menu on PlayStation 5, for example. And yet, converting 3D models, materials, animation sets, between different 3D engines is also a common and well-understood problem set. And so are techniques for progressively degrading the fidelity of assets to suit the needs of a scene budget. With a little work adhering to file standards and the like, and some common and easy to use APIs to allow for importing characters, almost any asset could be brought into almost any game or application.

The bigger challenges deal with how to allow users to bring in any character avatar in a way that fits within the thematic or social context of the shared experience. For example, while having a moe anime shark-girl character as an avatar might work well for some shooters, even that would likely be out of place in a historical shooter game, like *Call of Duty: Vanguard*. Some games, like *Fortnite* allow for a huge variety of characters (though all in line with a particular art style) while this might well wreck the sense of immersion in others. Licensed content based on a particular IP (a Star Wars game, for example) might want to only allow characters true to canon in a shared space. Then too, there are concerns about which content is allowed for reasons of propriety; the kinds of highly adult costuming which might be appropriate in a *Saint's Row* game would not have been in *Disney's Toon Town*. Some games may simply never want to allow for avatar imports for these reasons.

To solve this issue, I expect that we will want to allow users to create multiple avatars to use in different contexts. A tagging system which allows the creation system, the user, and other users to attach metadata tags to a particular avatar would help identify an avatar's characteristics. Then a system of trust for particular users would need to be established (similar to the function served by user-authentication systems now.) And, of course, each different game or shared-space application would need to do the work of allowing avatar imports. This last will require some level of critical mass of adoption for a particular avatar creation system sufficient to create a financial incentive for game developers to believe they can attract more users by allowing avatar imports. To my mind, this is one of the more challenging problems with any real "Metaverse" that spans and connects lots of games.

To be clear, many players will not want to bring an avatar into many games. For many, playing a particular character, from Mario to Larry Bird is the fantasy that a particular game provides. And yet... it seems very likely to me that just as players typically go by a particular "handle" or gamertag – just as people go by a particular name in real life – users want to be able to decide how they look and convey their sense of unique identity and style in games and other shared 3D spaces. Would I want to dance around in a WaveXR concert for the Weeknd while looking like my favorite *World of Warcraft* character? Well... Yes, I suppose I might. And millions of other will want to, as well. Shared social spaces in games and in other applications will increasingly drive demand for customizing a player's appearance, and player's don't want to have to do this anew using a different system every time they want to explore a new game or space. For this reason, I believe it likely that the notion of common shared avatars which can be transferred from game to online event to VR meetup and so on will become commonplace by 2030.

ARTIFICIAL AND INTELLIGENT CHARACTERS WRAP UP

Soon we will be unable to distinguish artifice from reality when it comes to human-looking characters. Players will be able to interact in compelling, natural ways with digital characters in many different games. Players will also be able to choose how they want to present themselves in different online experiences and games and will expect their appearance and sense of identity to transfer between different interactive experiences.

NOTES

1 https://www.makeuseof.com/tag/unique-android-chatbots/.
2 https://www.nytimes.com/2021/06/01/health/artificial-intelligence-ther-apy-woebot.html.
3 https://www.forbes.com/sites/gilpress/2019/10/02/ai-stats-news-86-of-con-sumers-prefer-to-interact-with-a-human-agent-rather-than-a-chatbot.
4 https://www.gamedeveloper.com/business/unity-acquires-ziva-dynamics-to-democratize-real-time-character-creation.
5 https://en.wikipedia.org/wiki/Hatsune_Miku.

CHAPTER 10

The Future of Game Development

On my business card, I am a corporate president. In my mind, I am a game developer. But in my heart, I am a gamer.

– Satoru Iwata, Nintendo

THE ACT OF CREATION

We have visited now at length about the way the world is changing, the new power-connected device ecosystems will give us, and what kind of games we might make. But what should we expect to change about the way we make them?

What will the daily practice of making games be like in coming decades? How will teams work? What sizes and mechanisms for organizing our efforts will be most successful? What new tools will facilitate creation of even better games than we can today? How will financing game development work? Will there be any role for small, indie development teams or even solo creations? What is the future of game development, publishing, and distribution? What should I learn to be prepared for this future?

How will the ways we create the games of the future be different from the ways we've created the games for the last 30 years? This is still a very young industry compared to film, book publishing, or even television. The possibility for revolutionary change exists in the ways we build entertainment software; but I suspect we will see only one or two major changes. As

DOI: 10.1201/9781003291800-11

269

with previous sections, I believe we can draw good inference by extrapolating from some of the advances we've seen to date, some of them have just begun to show us the way.

One of the things we can count on to continue to drive advances in game development tools, techniques, and processes is the incredible passion of game makers around the globe. While the games industry has become a juggernaut of revenue and earnings, the majority of game makers with whom I have ever interacted began creating games because they loved the medium. Game makers mostly start as players; and as we've seen, the world is adding players at an incredible rate. Combine this with the incredible amount of capital that has poured into the industry – particularly during the COVID-19 pandemic of the early 2020s – and there are suddenly a lot of game makers! Gone are the days of a California-based Game Developer's Conference playing host to 200 people and calling itself a success. Beyond passion and money, a third force has massively increased the number of people trying to be professional game developers: Many universities and colleges around the world now offer degree programs at every level in game development. The best of these are led by brilliant game makers and provide legitimate broad-spectrum liberal arts or computer science based programs of study at an undergraduate or even doctoral level. Still others are technical or vocational programs of just a few course hours long, which teach eager students the specific mechanics of how to use a particular tool to create in-game assets. More gamers, more accessible and better tools, more money flowing in, and more university programs are creating new generations of game makers, most incredibly passionate about making their mark upon the industry and inspiring other gamers with their creations the way they were once inspired.

And, because gamers love to create games, many games themselves embed tools for building new worlds or adventures within their software. People have tried building game-making games for a long time, from early efforts like *Adventure Creator* by Spinnaker Software in 1984 to more recent hits like *Minecraft*, which, after being acquired by Microsoft Games, quickly spread to most every platform imaginable, allowing players to fashion their own custom worlds. *Fortnite* followed suite, and game platforms like *Roblox* added the ability for players to add in their own behavioral logic such that they could create whole games, not just content for an existing set of mechanics. This introduced game development concepts to hundreds of millions of players, but it also created a world of nearly infinite entertainment, mostly for free.

The relative ease of creating new applications and releasing them on the web, iOS, or Android stores meant that by 2020 the number of games released each month was far greater than any human could ever play all of in a lifetime. Literally millions of new games have flooded the market between 2015 and 2020. As a result of all of these factors, the games market is more competitive than ever before. And because none of the trends we just discussed will slow in the slightest, the competition for player's attention will becoming increasingly fierce. Game making for profit is now a bloody Darwinian fight for survival; the vast majority of games ever made will not generate a positive Operating Income.

For the majority of creators, this may be okay. People have and will continue to create things that interest them regardless of the profitability of the enterprise. From cave paintings to fan-fiction to art school, people create things because some members of the species are driven to do so. One of the wonderful things we can look forward to over the next 20 years is a world in which everyone is a game maker if they want to be (Figure 10.1).

And millions of games which are only barely built for profit cultivate active fan-bases. Many games can delight the world even if they don't

FIGURE 10.1 Games like *Wonderbox: The Adventure Maker* are continuing to make the tools that let players create their own games more accessible to anyone with a smartphone. (*Image Credit:* Aquiris Game Studio.)

generate much revenue, and this is laudable unto itself. Better still, almost every year has a few sleeper hits that end up creating surprise windfalls and making their creators wealthy and famous; *Minecraft* and Among Us both come to mind as recent examples.

But most games at any real scale take a team to build, usually wielding expensive software, decent hardware, a lot of discipline, and some level of funding. When capital or an established company with the war chest to bankroll development teams is available there are several well-traveled paths to investment, funding, determining the distribution of profits. For many creators though, their games are a labor of love, and they want to make their dream work by other more immediate means of testing out an idea for a game by generating funding from potential players.

Let's look at two specific mechanics of bankrolling the development of a game which have risen in prominence over the last few years:

CROWDSOURCING AND NFT SALES

First, starting around 2009 game makers started using websites like Kickstarter or GoFundMe to solicit donations for their creations. This proved to be very popular with players because it allowed passionate community members to gain insight into the game development process (often through video updates or blog entries accompanying fund-raising efforts), and it frequently allowed players to exert influence into the design and direction of the game; players could give money to demand the kind of game they thought they wanted to play. Despite a few large public implosions, instances of fraud, or cases where the end product simply never materialized, this resulted in the creation of a several beloved – if niche – games over the last two decades. Tens of thousands of gaming projects are still funded and run this way, and we should expect this will continue, in echoes of the Renaissance model of wealthy patrons funding artists.

More recently, game makers have begun selling off NFT assets – ownership registry entries for elements of games that do not yet exist – as a way of crowdfunding the development of the games themselves. Fueled by the explosion of value in crypto-currencies in 2021, fans are now buying up virtual items for games that have not yet been created. The developers take some or all of these proceeds and use them to develop a game that will make use of the characters or items that have so attracted the attention of fans. The fans hope for the excitement of a game that has captured their interest, just as with Crowdsourcing funding models, but now the model can also appeal to the greed motive; those NFTs that a player bought cheap before the game ever existed could well be worth many times what they originally cost if the game is a hit. This could be thought of as an unregulated way of buying shares in a promising game concept.

Will these models of selling a stake in a game before it has been created continue? Yes. They most definitely will. Particularly as blockchain driven smart-contracts become more advanced and more widely understood, many of the risks of fraud or vaporware that too often characterized early video game crowdfunding efforts can be reduced. And these models are perfect for indie studios, comprised of a few friends, who are eager to make their mark by creating something wonderful. We should expect increasingly complex forms of pre-order and digital asset sales to fund the creation of small (and maybe not-so-small) games for the coming decades.

INTERVIEW WITH MAURICO LONGONI: THE FUTURE OF USER-GENERATED CONTENT

Mauricio Longoni is the CEO and Co-Founder of Aquiris Game Studio in Porto Alegre, Brazil

TF: To start with, can you tell us who you are and what you do in the games business?

Mauricio: Yes, I'm Mauricio. I'm one of the founders and CEO of Aquiris, a video game development studio based in the south of Brazil. Aquiris was my first job ever. So, my first job in my life was founding a game development company in a country that didn't have a lot of track record in this industry. We built the business from nothing 15 years ago. So, that's what I do in the game industry.

I started with 3D modeling, animation, texturing, and later I moved to programming, where I spent a good few years leading the game development at Aquiris. After a while I moved to production where the knowledge of multiple areas was quite useful. As the company grew I got more and more involved on the business and operations side, to enable our teams to deliver great games. So, I touched a little bit on every area. I'm not the best on any of them, but I can talk about almost all development areas. And that's really helpful for someone who is building a business on games.

TF: I love to see how many new game makers there are around the world. And one of the games you've built and released recently, called Wonderbox, tries to expand the toolbox of game makers so that almost anyone can make a wonderful game. Tell me about how you built this product and why?

Mauricio: One philosophy we have in our company is that, it is a bit cliché but it's truer than ever I believe, is that "Content is king and people want good content." And I think our industry went for some time with too many copycats or believing too much that by copying mechanic here or there, you could make good entertainment. We don't think you can consistently mimic good, original, authentic content. We believe that we must understand what users want to play, make content that is authentic and genuinely fun for players to enjoy. Games that help them tell or live a story, or even be someone else. Live in a world that they couldn't have access to.

When we started conceptualizing Wonderbox, what we wanted to create was a place where people could play a fun adventure game, and make it their favorite. A game where they could feel like they're a hero or they're living in a different world. And then, when they finish that, they didn't have to wait another 3–4 years for the sequel for the game to come out. They could just go out and play something that someone else created for them, or even create something for themselves to play or share with other people. All within the same platform with the same familiar rules.

And with Wonderbox, we also wanted to close the gap between creators and players. We wanted players to feel like they were in power to create cool things just like the creators that made the games for them. If you play a Zelda game or any other cool adventure game you like, you kind of feel like you want to build that as well, right? You want to be able to build that world. And in order to do that, before Wonderbox I would say, you'd have to have a lot of resources at your disposal, a whole huge team of game devs to build your own world. Not very practical for the average player. And we wanted to enable people to do that with a very simple toolbox. Something that was easy to pick up and build those adventures without too much technical knowledge.

I believe there is a movement that started some years ago when the game engines democratized development a little bit. Where the ordinary developer could make a game because now there was an engine that took care of the sound, animation, all that stuff, right?

And now games like *Roblox* and Dreams, and Wonderbox, they are enabling the ordinary player to become a creator too and share their creation with the world. And with Wonderbox, we wanted to take a step ahead and make it very simple, very beautiful, very organic and we didn't want to create a game maker or an "anything maker." We wanted people to have a very good understanding of what they could create with Wonderbox. It's an adventure maker. They can play adventures. They can create adventures. They can let players to play their adventures and it's simple, they don't have to create complicated logic, everything is in the toolbox. It would be perhaps too complicated if we tried to make the possibility of making an FPS or a racing game all within the same tools. Then, we would have to start adding some kind of programming into that and that was not our goal.

TF: One of the things that seemed unique to me about the Wonderbox system you built is that it allows people to make these games, these adventure games, using just their phone. You don't have to switch to a PC. What made you decide to do that? And, how do you think about the types of tools that creators of the future will be using?

Mauricio: That's a very good question. The phone is the device you use the most nowadays, right? So, if you want to create your world in the adventure game you like, want to create your own adventures, tell your own story. And if you can't do that from your phone, if you can't do that from the device you're playing on it wouldn't make a lot of sense. And it wouldn't be as simple and accessible, right? So that's the reason why we wanted people to be able to create with their phones first. They'll be able to create on their PCs as well, at some point when the game is there. But first and foremost, the mobile device is the device that we most use. And it had to be simple to create on that device.

For the future, that's an interesting exercise. I think that the phone will continue to be very strong. As I mentioned, a PC will be a possibility as well very soon for Wonderbox. And people will continue to create on their workstations, right? People are very agile on a PC with the mouse. And I don't know, in 20 years from now, maybe they will be doing that through some kind of AR device or virtual reality device.

We see some of that already happening. Through the glasses and the controls that we have, and all this is in the market right now. You already have something called the VR artist, right? You can see videos on YouTube about people painting things in VR. Maybe that is a way people will be creating games in the future as well?

TF: Tell us a little bit about what the game development community across different cities in Brazil looks like.

Mauricio: Brazil is a country with a lot of talented people in tech and art, which are the ingredients you need for making games. And it's also a very large country with a good number of very large cities. So the scene is very different in Porto Alegre, where we are, in the South, than in São Paulo or Rio or Manaus. You have different realities in different cities. But, the community and the development environment is growing a lot lately. And it makes me proud, not very happy I must say, but proud that a lot of people that worked at Aquiris were poked by game studios around the worked and are now spread, working in top global companies, and that's great. It's great because these are people who grew and learned from a local company and developed their talent here. And now they are working at other global companies, at some point they will give it back to the local market, right? They will train someone else. They maybe come back and open their own companies. And then you feed the environment, right? And you create the conditions to grow.

Of course, we have the biggest companies in San Paulo. It's the largest city and it's the most obvious one. But in the South, you have a very thriving community as well, in Porto Alegre, Florianopolis. You have a good number of companies and a lot of the talent that goes abroad come from these places.

TF: Right now, I think the top grossing games in Brazil and across most of South America are probably *Free Fire* and a few other games that are built in South Asia. Do you believe that local content creators, local game makers have an advantage in building games for their particular region, or do you think that any developer anywhere can end up building a hit game for any region?

Mauricio: In my opinion, it's the latter. With some twists I believe that... for Brazil specifically, Brazil is a market that is very global. And if you're in Brazil, I don't think you're in a competitive advantage to develop content for the local market because you're here or because of some specific cultural thing. As long as you can create high-quality content, high-quality entertainment, you can be successful here just like you would be in the US or Europe or Canada, or North America in general. For other regions, maybe regions with very specific cultural differences, like building games for the Asian market, I think it's a little different maybe because they consume content in a different way, in my humble opinion. And with the very few visits I made to some of those countries and how I saw people consuming content there. I believe that in the current market, especially post Covid, you can't think that you need to be in a particular place to build content for a particular audience.

Of course, going to these places and living life there a little bit, understanding how people think helps a lot. But I don't think Brazilians like something in particular and because I'm here, I can produce specific content. If I can produce good quality entertainment I think it will be successful in Brazil, in Canada, in Europe, in the US, maybe in Asia with some adaptations.

TF: We've got about three billion gamers in the world today. By 2040, we will have four and a half billion gamers. What are the things that get you the most excited about the coming world as a creator?

Mauricio: I think it's the fact that games are becoming less niche. As the market matures gaming is becoming just general culture. When I was a gamer as a young person my parents didn't play. But now,

I will play with my kids, and they will probably play with their kids, and we all, three generations, will be part of a growing base of gamers worldwide.

So it's becoming part of our everyday lives. Part of the social tissue in a way, because it will become one of the main, it is already actually one of the main entertainment mediums as we know well. And moving forward it will be more and more. But also, I think that technology will allow us to close even more the gaps between creators and players. With Wonderbox we're trying to close that gap.

The technology to power that is still a little unstable and I don't know exactly how the future will unfold for the digital ownership of assets that we are seeing. How the NFTs will play out, blockchain, obviously. I don't know if that is the right technology. I don't know too much about that yet. But I think that we will be closing the gaps between players and creators.

There will be more ways where I will be able to create content and put it out for players to play and maybe monetize on top of that. Not in a weird way where the developer of the game gets 90% of the revenue of what I would make as a creator. But in a stable way or just like today with other mediums, I can make a video and put out on YouTube and monetize on that the quality of my content. Maybe with the right technology we will be able to build platforms within games where players can create an adventure, put it out, and they can get paid by players who play their game, right?

If people pay for a full Zelda game, why wouldn't they pay for my 15 hours long supercool adventures made in this other platform called Wonderbox? Why not? Of course, these games will have to hit critical mass and have the right technology to make that interaction between creators and players smooth enough. But I think that gap will be much smaller and I think that's very exciting.

HITS

Hits vs. Games

Still though, when most people think of games they think of large budget products with significant professional development teams, large marketing budgets, and global distribution. This is the segment of the market that attracts huge capital investments and most of the media attention.

Let's talk for a moment about the cost, timeline, effort to create and market a hit. For big tentpole AAA console games in 2021, a major publisher would likely expect to spend between $75 million and $250 million in development costs, carrying a team of 100–300 people, plus outsourcers and vendors and consultants for two to six years from initial concept to worldwide release. One should then expect a similar amount to be spent on marketing before any of this outlay can start to be recouped. These costs have increased year over year, excepting that the jump in graphics technology from PlayStation 2 to PlayStation 3 caused a step-function increase in the cost to develop so much high resolution content. At the same time, concerns about working hours, staff burnout, and "work-life-balance" further bloated development costs. Then the Covid-19 pandemic of 2020 and subsequent years reduced almost all teams around the world to being 100% distributed and "work from home" at least for a while. This shift has further increased costs, at least in the short term. Game development teams for AAA products are now large and require a huge array of highly specialized talent; and so do the organizations required to support them. G&A functions and HR teams have also scaled up hugely in order to deal with the complexities of larger teams, big budgets, and the accounting implications of global distribution and sales. Civil unrest, concerns about "Diversity, Equity, Inclusion" and other social concerns in the West have further increased the amount of game makers and support staff required to ensure employees feel comfortable working on a team. Big games are getting bigger and more expensive to make.

As an example, the original *Halo: Combat Evolved*, released in 2001 on the first Xbox cost an estimated $10 million to create in 2001. *Halo* 4 cost an estimated $40 million to create in 2012. *Halo Infinite* is estimated to have cost over $500 million to create by 2021.[1] We should expect these costs for AAA games built in North America and Western Europe to continue to increase, at least for a while.

Mobile products are also not immune to a similar curve, though one that started smaller and more recently. In 2013 building a top-quality mobile game from concept to world-wide-release could be accomplished for $2–5 million dollars. In 2020 a top game will regularly spend more than $15 million to come to market, and truly grand games, like 2020's *Genshin Impact* by MiHo Yo was estimated to have cost more than $100 million to create, and carries an ongoing yearly development and live operations cost of more than $200 million each year. (Fortunately, the game also grossed more than $1 billion in revenue in 2021, so the costs continue to prove worth it to those who can land hits.)

And we should not expect costs to increase in a purely linear fashion, just as they have not over the last two decades. Because, as discussed, the hardware and levels of immersion afforded games is not increasing at a linear fashion. And proper integration to high quality of almost any of the types of new interfaces and output devices we've discussed in previous chapters will serve as step function increases in cost, just as we saw between 2005 and 2015. Building hit games for consoles and PCs is already very expensive, and this only continue. Add global distribution, 30 languages of fully localized speech and NLP dialog trees, 8k VR headsets, smart clothing integration, top-of-the-line AI customizing in-game behavior, and you can easily imagine the first billion dollar yearly-dev budget by 2025, and perhaps a ten billion dollar development budget by 2042. It takes a lot of smart people, well coordinated and using the best tools and services to stitch all of these complex solutions together. Top end games' production costs are going to continue to rise.

The size of the bets required to compete in the top grossing charts for PC, console, and mobile games is increasing rapidly. This leads to a lot of characteristics in the business which influence how games like these are made. At a corporate level, this leads to large amounts of consolidation in the gaming space; indeed, in the first six months of 2021 we saw more M&A activity by volume and by total dollar value than in all of 2020,[2] which was a record setting year. Beyond the huge war chests and risk appetite for longer-term paybacks required to fund software development projects at this scale, recent changes to the way games can be advertised (Apple's changes to the IDFA model, among others) have further encouraged consolidation; game companies with a bigger portfolio of products (more games!) are more effectively able to use targeted advertising to acquire new players. As has always been the case, larger companies who are able to offer a bigger book-of-business to agencies and distributors are able to negotiate more favorable deal terms. Finally, the advent of machine learning means that game companies with more users are better able to algorithmically tailor in-game offers, events, anti-churn techniques, and other data-science driven techniques simply work more effectively with larger data-sets to learn from. For all of these reasons, the game industry is consolidating rapidly. Multi-billion dollar acquisitions have been commonplace over the last year, and this will continue. Indeed, follow the chain of ownership up from any successful game released within the last three years and you're likely to bump into Embracer Group, Tencent, Microsoft, or one of a few other massive companies.

The commercially successful portion of the games industry will continue to consolidate over the next few years. And given the need for distribution, complex hardware/software ecosystem integrations, and increasingly large budgets and data-sets to accomplish much of what we've discussed in this book, we should expect the big tech companies to fund increasing numbers of the hit games of the future. Indeed, when you contemplate many of the more complex types of features and systems we have discussed here – AI directors taking input from player biometrics, for example – it's easy to envision teams for some of these games needing to be quite large. As a result it is also quite easy to imagine all "big" games to be released by three to five total companies by 2042, similar to the way five major phone manufacturers dominate the market today in 2021. (Apple, Samsung, Huawei, Oppo, Jio.) Indeed, it is highly possible that these companies could end up being the publishers for 90% of commercially successful tentpole games by 2042. And this even ignores the possibility of the majority of games moving into some sort of shared "Metaverse" type ecosystem adjudicated by one super-sized conglomerate, government, or DAO. While these kinds of megacorps might seem the province of science fiction right now, we are inching closer to this reality daily. The oligarchy of the gaming industry seems a distinct likelihood.

INTERVIEW WITH THEA CHOW: BUILDING THE BEST IN THE WORLD

Thea Chow is a Game Lead at Supercell in Helsinki, Finland.

TF: Hi, Thea. Tell us about yourself and your role in the games business.

Thea: Hi, Tim. Right now, I'm a game lead at Supercell. I've been working in the games industry for the last ten years, my background is in production, with a focus on project management and team leadership. I have had the privilege to work with many different types of teams, team sizes, and products – from the early startup mobile gaming days, to console games, to the most recent evolution of entertainment on handheld devices.

I've seen the industry evolve over the last decade. And it's super exciting, right now, to be a part of that.

TF: I'm curious... Today, there are about three billion gamers in the world give or take. By the year 2040, there will be four and a half billion people who play games. How do you imagine the way we make games needs to change in order to get ready for that world?

Thea: I think it's important to broaden our perspectives when we make games. Gaming is such a young industry. For a long time, it's been defined by small groups of people for their own interests, and for those like-minded to enjoy. And I think it started out as "entertainment that I want." It is about creating what I want to play, or what we want to create together, and sharing that out to others. Because it is made for ourselves, it is fun, and that's part of the reason we have seen waves of creativity and innovation.

But when we start thinking about scale... when we want to entertain millions and billions of people in the future, it's no longer just about you, or me. It has to be about a variety of perspectives, from many different people. From the technical point of view, this means building infrastructures to support all the different ways people have access to their devices, from the low end to high-end devices, and also connecting between different types of platforms.

The other aspect is creative: what kind of content we put out, the writing that goes into it, etc. The type of things that motivate people to continuously engage with a game, is as varied as the breadth of audience we reach. Gaming already reaches such a broad market, and that will continue to grow. And so, I think that having as many groups of people who are finding new ways and broad ways to serve the audience will be important.

TF: When you think about building games for lots of different cultures on lots of different devices, one of the challenges is that this tends to lead to bigger and bigger teams. What are ways that you think we should be imagining the structure and organization of game teams in the future, in order to avoid bloating ourselves to two or 300-person teams?

Thea: I think it's a decision we make around why we are making a game, who it's for, and the business goals. There are certain games for which it would make sense to have 2–300 people during its life-cycle, for example – if the game is content heavy, requires frequent updates, and tied to licensing processes. That ties to the goals of audience and business. But in any case, I think one of the best ways to start a game, is making sure that the people that you get on board first are those who can tangibly contribute to the product. So, starting from the core of the unit, and then making sure that the people that are in that unit can create and innovate. After that, it can scale.

If you have five to ten people with broad enough imaginations, they will figure out what they need to build at the core, that can eventually scale to serve millions. And if what is built looks promising, maybe they eventually need the team to grow a bit bigger. But, you start off with a strong, shared vision among a small group. Scale should depend on the lifecycle the game is in, and what the players need.

Nowadays, when I think about some of the different games out there... let's say: *Clash Royale* or *Clash of Clans*. The dev teams are not that big, certainly much less than 100 people. And it still reaches billions of players across the world. There are other games from Supercell that operate with teams under 30 people, so it is possible. But just consider that the games we make are not tied to IP we license from, so there is less process and time involved. And I think in the future, there are many opportunities to create games of all types, involving different operating strategies. But it has to be a choice to say: let's try and create something completely from scratch on our own, we're going to do it with a small group. And we'll avoid any overhead that's attached to that. But also understanding that, depending on what your success criteria are, the return on your time, the dev timeline, and scale reached may be different. You can have big teams that fail, but equally you can have small teams that fail. That is why it is important, in either case, to have both a strong vision, a plan on how to get there, and the ability to adapt.

And if the idea is to be quick, small, and agile – there should be decisions made around the type of art style that you choose, the type of audience that you're reaching, and basically designing the entire vision around the constraints you have of team size. On the other hand, there are big dev teams that support games like *Genshin Impact*, which is now hundreds and hundreds of people. It can be equally successful, but require a much higher startup cost.

I think that rather than say, in the future, it has to be one way or the other, what I see is both ways have their own vision and they have a very clear idea of what market they're going for. And successful games, regardless of size, will have a group of people in there that is driving the growth forward. So, I think it's very important to have, also in the team, a division of labor around what you're trying to do.

So, if a team is to grow, start with a strong core, and then grow it thoughtfully. Always make sure that within even a bigger team, you have different tracks and different groups that are serving specific purposes. So, one group could be about experimentation, and really trying to innovate on something that works. And that group will not be trying to ship updates every month. They are focused on being a lab and being innovative.

And then, you have a group that is just purely focused on execution and content. And then, you have a group in the middle, that's working on reaching a broader market and looking at features that serve them. So, I think you can build teams within a big team as well, if that makes sense for the product. Those teams can still feel organic, and they can still have full ownership over the areas that are responsible for.

And you would also pick the right people for those groups. I think designing the team and designing the growth is just as important as the actual team size itself, and where that number actually lands.

TF: That makes a lot of sense to me. I'm curious... One of the reasons that teams have gotten a lot bigger over the last 20 years, is because of the complexity of the content and the software that we build. Do you believe that there are new types of tools that will help people build more with smaller teams in the future?

Thea: I think so. I think a lot of them are either on their way, or they are already here. I can see that in what Unity have developed, and they will continue to grow their tools. *Roblox* is another example of providing a platform for anyone to make games. I think there are many aspects of games that can be almost commoditized. So, nowadays, you can make your own RPG really easily, because you have libraries of images and graphics, and if you want to do something... If you simply want to tell a story, you can actually do it with one or two people.

And the tools available now can help in any case. From doing something indie, all the way to bigger teams where engines are now looking at supporting groups by providing code chunks that you can use, or certain features and functionality that you can just take. It should be getting easier and easier to prototype things.

A lot of the guesswork in known game mechanics have been removed. So, it's easy to recreate it, and quickly put it together and see if it works. Of course, there is room for innovation, but it helps when you can easily grab the parts that you don't want to reinvent the wheel on, and free up time and mental space for tackling the hard problems.

In the future, I can see a world where anyone interested, can make games themselves. I think the world is getting more and more technologically advanced, and people are savvier. And I can see games being another way in which people choose to express themselves.

People are happy making YouTube videos, now. Twenty years ago, you can't even imagine singing a song on your laptop and then getting famous out of that. You also cannot imagine being an artist and posting your work on DeviantArt, and making a living from online commissions - that's something new. So, I think games will also go through that as well. In 20 years, people may be making games and sharing them with each other, in the same way they make videos and share them with each other on

TikTok and Instagram. I think it's going to go through that type of really cool Renaissance.

TF: I love the idea of a whole world of game makers. Do you believe AI will play a significant role in how we create games going forward?

Thea: I think AI is helpful for being a tool that's used within either making decisions for game design, or being a part of a system within games. I think AI can help us simulate human behavior, and learn more about them. It can help us run the simulations a lot faster than we can just playtest by ourselves. And also, learning behaviors and developing profiles based on replay data from thousands and millions of users, and then helping us make objective decisions.

We can also design the AI within the game, and AI itself will become probably more capable of emulating human behavior. And so, as AI gets better, the types of experiences we can provide that evoke authentic feelings, will also grow.

TF: What advice do you have for someone who is a teenager today and really wants to be one of the game makers of the future?

Thea: I would say, start acting on that creative energy and begin making things. There are lots of tools now, especially online, that you can use to make games for yourself and your friends. Learn as much as possible – read books, consume information about the world, and learn as much as you can about technology, tools, coding, where the future is headed, etc. I truly believe we're going through a few decades, maybe even a century of rapid, unprecedented technological innovation. The types of games you make, and how it is presented, will evolve alongside this.

I'm quite envious of you teenagers, because you're at this time in your life where you are just getting started. And if you can just learn as much as you can, about all the really cool things that are going on... You will have a head start. Get knowledge, express the creativity, and just make games! You don't need to join a studio, in order to start. If you are unable to, then don't even bother going out to a studio and interning. Just go online, watch videos, go on *Roblox*, and make something. There are so many platforms now to promote your own work. Always push yourself to learn, and never lose that creative spark. And I think the next 50 years, the next 100 years,

you're going to be in a really good position to just make anything you want.

TF: That is awesome.

TOOLS AND TECHNIQUES

But there is a countervailing force which can offset these increases as well.
Tools and technology available to game makers – already very good in
many cases, compared to the techniques of old – are getting even better
rapidly. Modern game engines, programming languages, 3D modeling
and animation tool suites, scripting editors, and the like promise to continue to allow skilled game makers to do more faster. Let's take a look at
some of the ways they help us now, and how they might improve.

Better Engineering Tools

Programmers write code that makes the features and systems of a game
work together. The technologies they create or stitch together bring a game
to life on client devices and in the cloud. The programming languages
and interfaces that modern software engineers ("programmers") use have
evolved a lot in the last 50 ears. The original *Pac-Man* was written in C, a
language created in 1972. Unreal 5, currently the most advanced publicly
available game development engine and tool suite in the world is written
primarily in C++, a popular, portable language. More modern languages
like Java, Python, Ruby, Elm, and even Lua are common as well, and a
typical game project will incorporate several different languages into its
tech stack. Most of these languages continue to evolve every year or two,
adding new features, standards, and adapting to new popular software
development patterns. This evolution of language – almost all of them –
should not be taken lightly, it results in significant increases in efficiency
and capabilities every year across the industry.

Here are a few of the specific improvements which have enhanced the
programming ecosystem for creating games in the last few years:

- Machine Learning for testing and tuning

- Headless command line testing for fast local iteration

- Large-scale cloud testing simulation abilities

- Automated continuous integration of changes to a codebase to vet
  changes and measure impact

- Better structure to modularization techniques

- Better documentation

- Integrated Development Environments that allow programmers to code, compile, run unit tests, and test our client simulations all from within the editor

- Improved scene optimization tools

- Enhancements to device profiling tools to combat the explosion of target client devices

- Distributed build systems to make compiling code and data fast

- Easy to use methods for distributing builds to teams to make collaboration easy

We've visited already about ways the combination of powerful CPU and dedicated powerful GPU have rapidly advanced display capabilities and the visual presentation of games. But it's worth looking a layer deeper into how profound this impact has been in order to extrapolate what further evolution here might mean.

As Zaitrarrio Collier, a pioneer of 3D graphics technology and member of the original 3D Studio team at Autodesk, writes:

> GPU's reinvigorated the adoption of vector processing for a specialized use case, highly parallelized vector and trigonometric operations which are key requirements for high-performance rendering and graphics pipelines. The high levels of parallelism that became possible through the evolution of GPU's essentially drove other advancements that required new software development methodologies. Further, the development of specialized programming tools made these features generally accessible to the average software developer. This ultimately led to new ways of developing key graphics systems.

The result of this combination of dedicated programmable hardware, easy to access languages and tools for authoring shaders (frequently no longer even the purview of programmers) has made it possible for almost any team to create games of incredibly high visual quality. Sharable libraries of customizable visual effects have further reduced the need for dedicated graphics programming teams on many games (though those seeking to push the edge of visual fidelity or stand out still tend to employ a few geniuses who specialize in this arena).

Beyond this domain-specific movement from dedicated code to libraries and tools in graphics, much the same thing has happened in other disciplines of game programming. Rather than writing custom behavior code for how in-game opponents behave, many teams can use off-the-shelf libraries of AI behavioral scripts. Audio middleware solutions allow for very advanced real-time mixing of sound effects, music, and spoken dialog. Physics, cloth, and other complex physical property engines allow for realistic object behavior which once had to be coded by individual game teams. And off-the-shelf engines handle much of the heavy lifting of scene optimization, from automating Level Of Detail (LOD) solutions to handling real-time synchronous network traffic.

This speaks to a generalized force that will continue to help the industry: A great solution need not be reinvented for each new game. And as the industry moves into its fortieth year of maturation the number of battle-tested existing libraries, routines, and tools that have been honed over many versions continues to increase. This will continue.

More evolved languages, better integrated workflows, and moving many of the tasks which used to consume engineers' time to other disciplines will all help both reduce the number of engineers required to make great games, or allow large teams to do even more.

Content Creation Tools

And professional tools for creating content are becoming vastly more powerful as well. From the early days of 3D Studio (which itself was an amazing breakthrough at the time!) to modern incarnations of Autodesk's Maya, 3D asset creation tool suites are nothing short of incredible today; and every year they are getting better. Other tools, like Houdini are beginning to innovate on procedural workflow with powerful history tools make working with animations much easier than it used to be (Figure 10.2).

Procedural animation suites, character generation tools, and wonderful new tools for generating and populating natural or fantastic terrain make content creation that once took a small army of WETA level artists accessible to a team of one or two creators. Adobe Substance Designer has transformed the way creators approach building surface materials, textures, ad visual effects. Simplygon massively speeds asset optimization.

New types of haptic and tactile interfaces for creators allow the creation, sculpting, surface painting, and other types of art creation using advanced

FIGURE 10.2 Houdini software empowers artists with procedural game development workflows for modeling, world building, character FX, rigging and animation, VFX, tool building and more for Unreal and Unity. (*Credit:* SideFX Software.)

input and displays which were impossible a few years ago. For VR design and modeling, tools like Shapelab allow creators to sculpt in 3D using VR headsets, much as a traditional sculptor might (Figure 10.3).

And, of course, the Unreal Engine deserves a special paragraph unto itself. The industry leader for the last two decades, Unreal allows almost anyone to create 3D scenes, assets, and populate them with relative ease. More recently, Epic's new Unreal 5 tech demo, *The Matrix Awakens* set the whole industry abuzz, demonstrating a procedurally created city and photoreal characters from the popular Matrix franchise along with special effects which would have been impossible for Lucasfilm's Industrial Light and Magic studios two decades ago... All in real time, running on a PlayStation 5.

Collectively, these tools are now making the creation of very high-quality assets accessible to millions of users around the world. As AI assistance further facilitates creation of these scenes, we can truly start to understand the possibility of collectively created spaces which might start to approach something like a real "Metaverse."

As Zay Collier puts it: *"This democratization of creation of 3D scenes, animations, and all the rest broadly led us to the point where talking about building metaverses to which millions of authors can contribute content is a realistic possibility."*

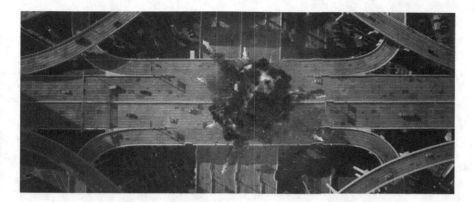

FIGURE 10.3   Unreal 5 released *The Matrix Awakens* technical demo in late 2021, demonstrating the future of real-time 3D graphics tools. (*Image Credit:* Unreal.)

Increasing Competition for Talent

We've talked a little about the way the sheer number of games released across all platforms each month has increased the competition for players. But let's look at a few other ways competition will continue to heat up in the games business.

First, despite all of the university programs and game makers self-taught on *Roblox* or Javascript, the competition for first class talent in the games business has never been hotter. At least in late 2021 the amount of capital flowing into the sector, the allure of get-rich-quick crypto schemes, the dissolution of geography brought about by a pandemic that accelerated the commonality of work-from-home arrangements, and the collective walk-out of the "Great Resignation" in 2021 have led every game company and team I can name starved for talent. Competition for experienced game developers – programmers, artists, designers, producers, project managers, and all the rest – is hot. Wages here are likely to continue to increase, at least at the mid-level, because these projects take complex skills that take decades to train. Competition for talent will increase.

In the last decade, we've seen game development companies build out lavish offices filled with perks like onsite barbers or massages, complimentary catered meals, baristas, and the rest. Aided and abetted by Zoom and other video-conferencing tools, more recently we've seen flexible work hours give way to the promise of "work from anywhere forever" for top talent. This has led to a class of game developers who are able to relocate to low-cost desirable locations, Fiji beach resorts, and the like while drawing six-figure Silicon Valley wages and other lucrative forms of compensation like stock options or retirement fund matching accounts. For top talent with proven abilities to act as force multipliers for teams and deliver top grossing games, this will continue. However, at the lower entry levels of the business, we should expect to see wages remain fairly modest: There are no guild restrictions, few serious efforts at unionization, millions of people can learn the basics in online courses or at community colleges, the tools are getting much easier to use faster, and I suspect as many kids want to grow up to make video games as would want to grow up to be soccer or basketball stars. As technical skills and the population increases, entry-level jobs will likely not increase in compensation.

Increasing Competition for Licenses

Increasing costs lead to another type of competition within the industry: The competition for coveted licenses which attract users. As development costs soar companies need ways of reducing risk for big projects. One of the biggest risks for any game (or entertainment) is the difficulty of accurately predicting how many people will care about it enough to try it out. In the increasingly shrinking retail sector, digital download numbers on closed platforms like PSN, or in the wide open world of app-downloads, volume is everything. Since the cost to create a software product can be quite high, but the incremental cost to acquire another customer can be quite low, almost all digital entertainment ends up being a volume business. To attract million or hundreds of millions of users requires a lot of marketing and community effort to make them aware of the product in a crowded market. One way to make this heavy lifting a little easier has been to make things with characters, in worlds that people already love. Marvel, Star Wars, James Bond, Harry Potter, *FIFA*, and other mass-market consumer brands are not a guaranteed way to delight the multitudes, but they are a much surer bet than creating something brand new. This is the reason that so few blockbuster films each year are "original IP" – the cost to raise awareness and the difficulty of effective predictive modeling of customers and revenues lead the risk-adverse to bet on understood franchises. In the gaming space, license holders know this and are able to demand significant concessions for the licensing rights to top franchises. Since entertainment is inherently zeitgeist driven, consumer fatigue with some brands which oversaturate the market is a very real risk. Licensors know this too, and so wise license holders attempt to curate only top-quality products with a particular brand and carefully manage release timing. All of this creates great competition among game developers for the most beloved characters and brands. As industry consolidation and development costs both increase, game publishers and entertainment companies of all kinds will continue to seek ways to leverage marketing efforts from one medium (a movie, for example) across other mediums (like games). As a result, competition for top brands will increase. What will be the top grossing piece of linear content (like a movie) in 2042? I do not know, but there are two bets which seem safe: It's probably a brand you have already heard of, and there will assuredly be a major video game released using the same characters and world that year.

Distributed Teams

There is a high level of joy and efficiency that can come from in-person creative collaboration. However, not every team can always be together physically. Indeed, models for distributed game development have been common for more than a decade as a way of leveraging the best possible talent, smoothing out the economics, and engaging local expertise for publishing games. These practices were rapidly accelerated by the Covid-19 pandemic starting in 2020, which drove thousands of game development teams into forced distributed collaboration. Zoom, Slack, and other tools for remote collaboration enjoyed widespread adoption and also improved remote collaboration. People learned to work remotely, and many of them decided they preferred it to in-office collaboration.

Does this mean that we can expect creative collaboration on game projects to be increasingly conducted using distributed models in which team members are not all in the same location physically? Yes. I believe so. The tools are good enough to allow for many types of sharing to work effectively. And many people have decided they prefer this, if only because it saves them a commute and gives them more time to spend with their families.

However, remote distributed collaboration is likely not as effective as in person collaboration. According to many (hotly debated!) studies, remote teams suffer from a roughly 20% decrease in productivity[3] compared to in-person standards from pre-Covid. These studies are backed up by observations from almost every games industry leader I know. Teams can build games without being physically co-located, but they probably cannot do it nearly as well or efficiently.

Certain phases of game operation (once a game is live, for example) and some types of tasks (e.g. deep engineering code optimization), which rely more on focus than creative collaboration, may be as or even more effective. But early concept work, pre-production design efforts, and reaching alignment and consensus across multi-discipline teams definitely seem to be much less effective when a team is fully distributed. The core issue here seems to come down to communication. First, despite superb video-conferencing and shared digital whiteboard software, many people report that building consensus and eliciting the best ideas from team members is more challenging without the subtle visual behavior cues that humans have evolved over tens of thousands of years in tribal structures. Second, telepresence through a window on a screen rarely commands as much of a person's attention as an in-person engagement; sometimes it can be hard to block out other events happening in real life in order to devote focus to a group of thumbnail sized portraits talking. Finally, the loss of serendipitous "ah-ha!" moments that arise from chance meetings around a coffee machine, or by walking by and glancing at something on a colleague's monitor are hard to replace. It is possible that as distributed work models become more established, and people get more accustomed to them, some of these detriments will be reduced, but at the moment, truly distributed teams seem to be at a disadvantage.

In an effort to have their cake and eat it too, many companies are allowing workers to work remotely some of the time, but mandating or encouraging in-person events for collaboration a few days of the week. This model, often called "hybrid," is a partial solution, but really only works if a team are still largely located near the same city. As teams become more distributed, as employees decide to decamp from the major game development hub cities, and as employers learn that they can hire hard-to-find talent from afar, the games industry will be forced to come up with more effective solutions to make hybrid or fully distributed collaboration more effective.

Independent Contractor and Unionized Models of Talent

Disenchanted with the primary model of game development and publishing employment for the last three decades, many game makers in North America and Europe have pushed for a change in organizational structure. Traditionally corporations have funded game development by paying salaries, bonuses, profit sharing, providing health-care and dental benefits, etc. and then treating game makers and their supporting staff as employees. Complaints about long hours have been common, as have concerns about uncertain employment when projects go bust or fail to reach expected returns on their investment.

In response to these concerns by labor, many developers, testers, and the like have proposed either an independent contractor model, similar to that followed by the North American film and television industry, along with the unionization that is common within some disciplines there. Such efforts at unionization of the North American games business have been particularly vocal within the United States, where concerns about a lack of government provided health-care and other social safety nets have driven many developers to seek ways to better secure their futures.

Could an independent contractor and or a unionized model for certain types of labor work within the games business? Absolutely. The net result would likely be increased costs to develop, more even distribution of benefits and wages, reduced hours, and a change in profit margins for publishers. I would expect such discussions to continue in the coming years, though I remain broadly skeptical that the nature of the business – where roles are highly differentiated, processes and tools are in a constant state of innovation, and the workforce is still relatively small – is as well suited for labor unions as more traditional industrial-era industries.

Still, great games cannot be made without skilled and dedicated craftspeople, and if the equivalent of a Screen Actors Guild were formed for artists, producers, and even programmers, we could see large changes in work practices at big publishers. Alternately, since, unlike coal-plants, game development hubs can move to wherever there is talent who desire to make games and can be trained, this might simply lead to publishers moving more development capacity to jurisdictions without strong legal support for unions. Indeed, the rapid distribution of the workforce brought about in 2020 and 2021 as a result of the Covid-19 pandemic has likely weakened the likelihood of unionization taking hold. As the saying goes, "If you can do your job from anywhere, then someone anywhere can do your job." And with the sheer number of fans who would love the chance to make games professionally, while the industry always has a shortage of top talent, it rarely lacks for fresh blood who want to learn.

DAO

Decentralized Autonomous Organizations (DAOs) are a relatively new type of organizational structure made possible by smart-contracts of the type that are possible on some blockchain technologies, like Ethereum. In a broad and basic sense, DAOs allow members of the organization to vote, share resources, or similar based on predefined rules which are written into the nature of the chain ledger that defines the DAO. Using these kinds of organizational structures, for example, every owner of asserts stored in a treasury could automatically receive a vote based on the percentage of the treasure they had verifiable claim to. From 2016 to 2022, DAOs have been used to accumulate funds to attempt to purchase the original version of the US Constitution, direct investments like a mutual fund, free an individual from prison, and build an assortment of technologies. Theoretically, this type of organizational structure could form the backbone of a game development team, allowing verifiable ownership, decision-making rights, and ultimately distribution of revenue generated by the game.

With a clear goal or charter ("Let's make the best science fiction RPG ever made!"), a mechanism for community discussions ("Here's a link to our Discord server and our GitHub repository!"), a treasury ("Donate to the cause in BOO coin using your Metamask wallet!") to pay for labor, a Governance framework and set of rules ("Code checkins must be reviewed by at least 3 Alpha members before submission"), and an ownership model ("Every 100 BOO gets you 1 vote!"), a DAO could be set up to coordinate and organize almost any sort of project.

Those who are bullish on the concept of Decentralized Autonomous Organizations see them as a sort of utopian approach to the future of human organizations, offering more egalitarian opportunities than traditional capital driven corporate or private partnerships. Almost any endeavor could be described and organized as a DAO, and since the mechanisms for compensating members of the organization for their contributions to a shared goal (like making or operating a game!) can deliver value through cryptocurrency exchanges largely without supervision, taxation, or easily enforced regulation. This makes this a very interesting future organizational structure for distributed teams who are interested in building a particular game together without incurring the overhead costs of offices, payroll, and the other traditional hallmarks of forming a business. And since ownership or membership in a DAO can be as exclusive or large as desired, there are opportunities to revolutionize crowd-sourced funding for games. DAOs may well blur the distinction between game makers and communities of fans, leading to widespread and accessible ways of collaborating to create games.

Is it possible to imagine the Metaverse as a service owned and run by a DAO comprised of creators? Perhaps. Is this a utopian fantasy or real possibility with Defi? That's hard to say.

INTERVIEW WITH ALEXANDRIA SEPULVEDA: THE FUTURE OF REGULATION

Alexandra Sepulveda is an entertainment and tech attorney in California. She has represented Uber Eats, Cameo, Udemy, Kabam, and others.

TF: Hello! Can you introduce yourself and tell us about your role in the tech business?

Alexandra: I've been an attorney since 2004. In that time, my career has taken me to a number of high-growth companies, from Kabam, where I was second-in-command to the General Counsel and oversaw the day-to-day legal operations, to Udemy, an online education marketplace that went public this year. I helped those companies navigate periods of explosive expansion. I was also responsible for large enterprise deals on the Uber Eats legal team when the pandemic first hit in 2020.

TF: Speaking of growth, one of the things that is really exciting to me is that we're in a world where there are almost three billion gamers today and by 2040, we're going to have about 4.5 billion gamers on the earth. I'm interested in how the wild west of online social spaces changes over the next 20 years as more people get online and as it consumes an ever bigger part of people's lives. What are your thoughts on this?

Alexandra: One of the things that has been incredibly exciting to see is the fracturing of the online entertainment market in general. There are so many places for consumers to play and gaming companies to service. Let's say that you want to play online social games with people who are generally in your same age group. There's a space for you for that. If you want to play MMO games exclusively, there's a space for that. Same thing with games like *Roblox* where you are actively participating in the creation of the gaming experience and the environment itself. If there's something that you're into, there's a place for it. I just think that when we look back on this period of time, we're going to see it as the dawn of an important new era. From a commercial perspective we're in the earliest stages of understanding how we can unlock value within it.

TF: When we think about the amount of data that everybody generates by being online – whether data they create in *Roblox* as a user or consumer data that they generate through their online behaviors – we've just started to see regulations on this emerge throughout the world. What are your expectations for changes in the regulatory environment for user-generated data over the coming decade?

Alexandra: I think there are some potentially dangerous outcomes. Many of us in the legal space have taken a wait-and-see approach. You don't see too many companies directly engaging with regulators to try to get ahead of things. More often, regulators hear a consumer complaint about some online service, then slap a law into place to address that particular issue. Then it ends up encompassing a ton of other business behavior. And in many of these cases, the game industry didn't anticipate their behavior getting wrapped into the regulation.

I hope that we're going to see more companies engage with regulators upfront and have an open conversation. That would be better than what's currently happening too often – companies reacting to laws by filing a lawsuit. Only then are they engaging with the government to say, "We'll listen, I know what you're trying to get at, but this isn't the right way to go about it." I don't see that happening enough right now. My hope is that does happen in the future.

TF: One of the challenges that we've seen in the online social gaming space is that services can be run out of anywhere, built by people anywhere, and played by people almost anywhere. Regulations tend to adhere to the borders of countries or trade blocks like the EU. Over the next 20 years, can you imagine larger regulatory bodies beginning to attempt to regulate online commerce and behavior?

Alexandra: The keyword in your statement is *attempt*. We're absolutely going to see people try. What we've seen from our experience in gaming is that gamers are not interested in being regulated. They are going to seek out spaces that specifically give them the operational freedom that they're looking for. When we look at things like the blockchain systems, like Ethereum, like other places at the intersection of unregulated structures and monetization, we're going to see a lot more action for gamers in that space because it's going to provide more freedom from regulation.

TF: I read recently about the sheer number of conversational AI chatbots that are performing therapy functions in apps users can download on their phone. I read about a bunch of data breaches where people's private confessions to their therapists had been hacked. Do you believe that over the next 20 years we will start to see a need to license AI serving a professional function just the way we require licenses now for therapists or for attorneys?

Alexandra: The challenge that we're having on this particular topic is that there are people who grew up in the internet age and there are people who did not. People who grew up in the internet age are very used to the intersectionality of technology in their lives. What I mean by that is that when that person does something – for example, go to a website then click "I agree" to the terms of service and privacy policy – they understand that in doing so they have effectively agreed to the rules that are there.

The challenge we're having is that there are people who are used to a world in which these kinds of interactions happen in person; they don't run most of their life online. In time, for more and more people, interacting with nonhuman elements online will become the norm. Scenarios in which people say, "Oh, I'm suing because I didn't understand that I was interacting with a virtual therapist. I didn't know my data could be hacked!" will become increasingly rare.

My guess is that we're going to get the technology to a point where actually the virtual therapist will be nearly as effective as the in-person therapist. We're going to see a flip. Disclosures will say, "By connecting to this website, I agree that I'm going to be chatting with a human being and that human being is capable of errors, omissions, etc." There's a whole laundry list of human mistakes that we human beings make. That's where I think the world's going to go.

TF: When you think about the world of labor laws, when it comes to the video game industry, we've seen some move toward unionization in some countries and we've also seen a move toward greater distribution with DAO style groups and similar. What are your predictions for the way that the employment and labor conditions for game makers will change over the next 20 years?

Alexandra: The regulatory environment is in a state of tremendous upheaval when it comes to the freelance economy – and a lot of gaming companies rely on freelancers to create value. You're seeing a push and pull between advocates for gig workers' rights and companies whose business models are predicated on more flexible working relationships with talent. This is one of this century's great labor law debates. We'll see how it shakes out as legal and legislative institutions try to catch up with the reality on the ground, but my prediction is that we will see more structured relationships between game makers and freelance talent.

TF: What area of the law do you believe is the ripest for disruption as the gaming market expands massively over the next 20 years?

Alexandra: I think it's going to be privacy. Today, the cycles it takes for an issue to move from "Consumers don't like you doing this with their data" to an actual law being put on the books are so long. By the time the law is passed, gaming has already made another quantum leap. We're going to learn that people, gamers in particular, are willing to provide more information about themselves in exchange for a more personalized experience. The law will eventually catch up to that.

What's more, the actions of companies in gaming-adjacent verticals will influence consumer perceptions about privacy. If one big tech company makes a big, unfortunate splash, the operating context for lots of gaming companies and online service providers will change in a heartbeat.

INCREASED COMPLEXITY

Increasing Complexity of Publishing and Distribution

The market for distributing and publishing games is diverse, complex, and will likely get moreso in the coming decades.

Let's take a look again at a 2021 year end snapshot of where games are distributed and the revenue they generate (Figure 10.4).

We can immediately observe a few things about where we are today, and where we are going.

As more of the world gets in on the fun of gaming, we can see that the mobile market comprises a little more than half of the total revenue from the business (and the overwhelming share of the players.) And mobile gaming is on the rise. Console gaming comes in next, but is in decline. PC

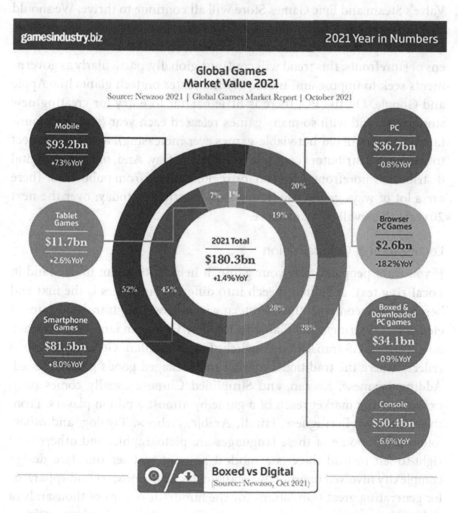

FIGURE 10.4 At the end of 2021, the games industry globally drove $180 billion in revenue broken up between mobile, console, and PC. (*Image Credit:* Gamesindustry.biz.)

games come in third place, holding relatively flat. We should expect these trends to continue.

As a result of widespread broadband with high bandwidth capacity, we should expect the move to digital download distribution models (and away from retail) to continue, particularly outside of North America. Retail distribution of games, by 2030, will likely be exclusively in specialty shops and comprise an insignificant part of the business.

Digital distribution through App Stores, the web, dedicated platform storefronts on consoles, and PC side digital distribution storefronts like Valve's Steam and Epic Games Store will all continue to thrive. We should also expect to see a much more fractured distribution ecosystem develop. On mobile platforms in some counties (like China) there are already dozens of storefronts; this trend will continue globally, particularly as governments seek to impose anti-monopoly mandates on tech giants like Apple and Google. On the PC, there is little barrier to entry for creating new storefronts, and with so many games released each year (and the mountainous library of old-but-viable-games ever increasing), we should expect to see more distributors continue to enter the fray. And, of course, digital distribution storefronts are ideal for regional focus from publishers. There are a lot of ways games can be digitally distributed today; over the next 20 years there will be many more.

Localization & Culturalization

If you want people to play your game, it helps if they can understand it. Localizing text, and often speech into different languages is the first and best way to accomplish this. Western games have long translated tutorial elements, UI strings, and dialog in to a few European languages to start. So-called EFIGS translation (English, French, Italian, German, Spanish) reflects where the traditional market for packaged goods games existed. Adding Japanese, Korean, and Simplified Chinese usually comes next, expanding the market reach of a game by almost a billion players. From there, Russian, Portuguese, Hindi, Arabic, Hebrew, Tagalog, and others follow. Since some of these languages are pictographic, and others read right-to-left instead there is a modest amount of User Interface design complexity involved in properly localizing. And the process and apparatus for generating great translations for the hundreds or tens of thousands of strings that exist in a game can be quite time consuming and expensive.

Add in recorded audible dialog and the complexity increases considerably: First, the game team needs actors to perform the spoken lines in each language supported. Second, for high fidelity games, having characters lips moving as if they were speaking in one language while the dialog is heard in another can be deeply distracting, as anyone who tries to watch foreign-language films with dubbed-over dialog knows. It is possible to have 3D animated characters lip-synch effectively to whichever language the user is hearing, but this further adds complexity.

In short, just localizing game content is a big undertaking and expensive. This will inevitably increase in coming years as more users expect to play games in their primary language.

But increasingly, game publishers have learned that simply translating a language is rarely enough to create a massive hit. "Culturalization" is a practice that refers to changing other game elements to make it more appealing for a particular market. This often involves altering art elements (to make characters more appealing to a particular region, or to remove culturally sensitive elements like skulls or religious symbols). It can also regularly involve changing a game's economy progression systems in order to adhere to regional play preferences. For example, average hours played per day can different quite greatly by region (Figure 10.5).

This means that the rate at which gamers consume content can vary hugely. Often designers choose to slow down progress in response.

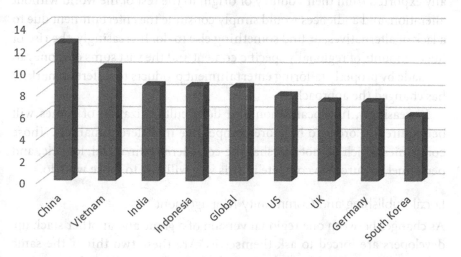

FIGURE 10.5 Average time spent gaming varies considerably by region, making some publishers conclude that tailoring game progression economies by region can result in more engaged customers. (*Source:* Tim Fields, Data Statista, 2021.)

Alternately, there are some features which are more popular in some countries (autoplay, for example) which might be seen as likely to make a game more appealing. Every feature or content tuning change may seem small, but taken in aggregate, they can result in a great deal of work, even requiring different teams.

Adherence to Local Custom & Regulations

As discussed elsewhere in this book, the role of governmental regulation in the games industry has been fairly modest for most of the last 20 years. This will not remain the case. Even today, from California to Belgium to Beijing, there are local laws that game makers and publishers need to take into account. GPDR dealing with data privacy, COPPA laws which seek to protect children, Toubon laws which force equality of translation, lese majeste laws which provide penalties for speaking ill of a sovereign, and a thousand other varied local ordinances can trip up game makers who are caught unaware. This will increase.

Finally, there are cultural sensitives that need to be taken into account when publishing, marketing, or operating games in particular regions. Scantily clad female characters on a game's loading screen are likely to be met with frowns in the Middle East, while games in China need to censor huge amounts of potentially politically sensitive conversation from players. In the twentieth century consumer goods and entertainment were generally exported from their country of origin to the rest of the world without alteration, and audiences would simply consume the entertainment due to a lack of alternatives, or find something else to do. Increasingly, the rise of huge amounts of regionally specific content and the vast sums of money to be made by properly tailoring entertainment products to different markets has changed the approach.

Increasingly, full localization and deep culturalization of games will be required in order to be more competitive in different markets. Those companies which do not marshal the considerable financial, logistic, and personnel resources to compete in this way will lose to those who do.

Local Publishing and Community Management

As changes between one regional version of a game and another stack up, developers are forced to ask themselves: Are these two things the same game anymore? Should people playing two fundamentally different games be allowed to play together? What if one group can advance much faster than another? This hardly works in competitive games.

This forces developers and publishers to debate if games can be built and operated for the whole world simultaneously or if players should be segregated by territory. There are significant technical, regulatory, design, and economic implications to each choice. Increasingly, we are seeing massive rewards for those games which engage in regionally astute publishing and custom tailored versions for those territories with sufficient population to warrant it. This is likely to continue as increasing global demographics create massive markets out of emerging countries.

Forecasting

As the costs to create great games continue to mount for all the reasons we've discussed, it becomes ever more important for the entities funding these games to reduce the risk to their investment. The approach by which companies forecast what it will cost to make a particular game, how much it will cost to operate it, and what return their might expect on their investment is usually almost unique to that company. Indeed, those who are great at it are able to increase their ratio of hits to misses and generate tremendous value for their shareholders. While the results of these kinds of efforts are often decried as harmful to innovation, they are also essential to being able to fund the creation of massive projects.

The rise of vast amounts of data and increasingly sophisticated techniques for forecasting product success will continue to drive the importance of predictive modeling in the games industry. As game development budgets for AAA products move toward billion dollar development and global marketing budgets it will become essential for game developers to understand – at least at a rudimentary level – how these techniques work.

Advanced data analysis from past products and sophisticated forecasting models will increase in importance over the coming decade.

On Bots and ID

Video games have engaged in-game agents referred to as "AI" since the ghosts in *Pac-Man*. We've talked a lot about them throughout this book. As we've seen now, these characters bear little resemblance to the true early Artificial Intelligences we are creating now and nothing like what is coming. They don't typically exercise any form of machine learning, don't usually build up data on anything; instead these simple agents behave according to a set of rules often referred to as a finite-state-machine to determine what to do when faced with circumstances in the game world. (An example of this from the ghosts in *Pac-Man* might be: "What do I do when I reach the end of my current path?" And the two choices might be "Go right:" or "Go left." The bot profile would have some criteria for deciding, like "Go right 50% of the time" or "Always go right.")

Players and game makers often refer to these in-game machine driven agents as "bots." And the way bots are used by players and developers alike, and some of the problems they create have implications that are worthy of discussion.

There are a number of uses basic bots provide in games:

First, they are great for providing simple NPC opponents to be defeated. (Imagine the hordes of enemies a player is expected to shoot in a game like Contra.) They also regularly provide for in-game NPC companions for players to play, fight, and adventure alongside.

Second, bots can provide game development teams a very useful way of simulating thousands of game sessions for testing purposes. Since having human QA teams test every combination of characters, playspaces, equipment loadouts, skills, hardware configurations, and the like would be prohibitively expensive, (and might take hundreds of years!) game development teams often build up bot matches which can be run automatically, tracking various information about framerate, crash rates, load times, win or loss rates, and so on. This kind of test automation making use of even simple bots which mime player behavior is essential to effectively testing multiplayer games.

In 2020 almost all online real-time multiplayer games make some use of bots of one kind or another. This is done to train players before throwing them into higher stakes competition. It can also be an effective way of ensuring quick matchmaking times for players who wish to jump in and complete quickly.

In most real-time multiplayer games (*Call of Duty*, *League of Legends*, and so on), establishing teams of players is essential to ensuring a high-quality match. Depending on the number of players concurrent in the system at any given time, this can be a daunting challenge. The game matchmaking system needs to consider a number of factors. Player skill ranking using variations on the venerable ELO system developed by Hungarian physicist and chess master Arpad Elo) are usually considered. But factors like geographic location and its impact on communications latency can be equally important. What language does the player communicate in? Are they a spender or a non-spender? Do they have social affiliations to a particular clan or guild? What type of play patterns do they exhibit? Are their communications profane or family friendly? The specifics of a given game design will determine what factors matter most to ensuing a great experience for the greatest number of users possible, but the more factors that need to be considered the smaller the pool of available users to be matchmade against at any given moment. Since players don't want to wait for an hour (or even five minutes!) before being given the chance to jump into a match, and since poor matchmaking quality can ruin a player's experience, delivering fast and high-quality matches is essential. Invariably except for games with very high numbers of concurrent users at all times, this leads developers to thinking about how to employ bots to sub in for players.

Then too a player may choose to quit a game or be dropped due to a bad network connection. For team based games this can result in a very poor experience for other players. Various solutions have been tried to solve this problem, but one common approach is to simply have a bot take over for the player who has dropped.

Finally, over the last few years, lots of mobile RPGs have begun to allow players to engage with content using "Autoplay" features in which their characters move and fight their way through parts of the game autonomously. Usually this kind of feature can be unlocked after a player has demonstrated mastery over a particular piece of content such that they can then "farm" resources granted by completing that content over and over. This type of game mode often allows players (particularly on mobile or PC games) to play the game in a more casual or "idle" way, devoting a small amount of attention to the game while otherwise occupied. Creating bots are a simple way to allow for this kind of lower-friction engagement for many players.

So bots have a variety of valuable uses for game developers and players alike. However, hackers can also create bots which can be very destructive to games. First, players can engage hacker bots to automatically play the game for them, which can break the game economy or give some players an unfair advantage over others either by playing nonstop and performing repetitive game actions while players are away, or by reacting at machine speeds that make them impossible for honest players to compete against.

This may not seem like a huge issue, but in games where fairness is considered a critical component of play the rampant use of bots can make players abandon the game quickly. Imagine if every chess match you tried to play was actually against a Deep Blue level chess-AI who could crush you rapidly without fail; chess would quickly cease to be much fun to play. (You are unlikely to try to run a foot-race against a

Ferrari; the metaphor is fairly analogous.) The presence of hacker created bots which present as real players can make other players feel the same way. Bots ruin games.

And so developers devote design, programming, and data-science resources to detecting bots. Win rates outside of the standard deviation, analysis of metrics for speed of decision making that no human could replicate, memory or application variations which imply the presence of hacking, and a variety of other techniques allow game devs to try to catch cheaters using bots. And hackers know about these kinds of checks and build ever more sophisticated bots to evade detection in a game of escalating cat and mouse as old as the story of crime and criminals.

And this is true even before we consider games with prizes or payouts in real money, crypto-currencies, or NFT assets which have real value to players. As we expect both RMG (Real Money Gaming) and crypto/NFT games to become an increasingly big part of the gaming ecosystem in the coming decades, the problem of bots who can make these games unfair will grow. Imagine a game with a million dollar prize for the winner in which the victor is accused of cheating by employing a bot. All of the complexities of steroid doping, testing, lawsuits, etc. that occur in sports will be likely to occur here. Bots will become an increasing problem for games as the stakes get higher.

One avenue of approach we could imagine beginning to gain steam to combat botting and other types of hacking is increasing demand for more secure methods of player identity verification. Rather than allowing anonymous players to jump into any game and start to play, games can require digital verification of a player's identity. When a player logs into a game, the game can verify a digital identity (often by requiring login to some other trusted service, from Facebook to Google to Apple, or some proprietary account system). This account verification is often cross-checked against the player's geographic location (reported by IP address or similar) to ensure that it checks out. In some countries, like China, these methods are being coupled with a third layer of biometric verification using facial recognition technology to ensure that the person playing the game ties into a government issued ID. As of 2020, game publishers are required to verify player ID in China to ensure compliance with restrictions on the amount of time players under 18 are allowed to spend playing online games. In India, the Aadhaar card digital identity system seeks to ties into iris scans from every citizen.

While this is initially intended to be used to ensure government services are being properly administrated, game companies should expect (and may value) the enhanced ability to ensure fairness, combat bot usage, purchaser fraud, other types of shady behavior.

Of course, there are numerous consumer privacy concerns with widespread tracking and biometric identification. Ensuring the fairness of games may seem small compared to the "Minority Report" implications of potential misuse by state, corporate, or non-state actors. However, as game makers and gamers we should expect that increasing reliance upon identity verification will become standard in games over the coming decades. By 2040, I would be surprised if a player is allowed to play any game on any device without submitting to biometric identity verification.

Wrap up on the Future of Game Development

It isn't unreasonable to say that gaming is humanity's top hobby at this point. And unlike painting, or writing fiction, or making their own movies, millions of people seem to want to engage as creators, not just consumers of games. Incredible advances in the accessibility of hardware and availability of low-cost or free software used to create content for games have made this form of expression possible for the masses. Programming languages and the general environment for providing instructions to machines and working together with teams large or small are getting so great so fast that what once took dedicated experts is now in reach of many more creators. The tools and engines for creating games have become democratized such that we can all create games for one another.

But the business of making and marketing hits continues to grow in cost and complexity. There is fierce competition for talent and for the kinds of powerful licenses that can help drive widespread awareness and financial success for the best games.

A few forces which have yet to really influence the industry – most notably the impact of machine learning and AI creators – will begin to change the way teams approach building software and content in the coming years, resulting in a richer and stranger canvas of personal expression. The ways teams are organized and the business structures which facilitate creation are potentially on the cusp of some radical shifts as well.

The next 20 years are likely to be an even more profitable (for some), thrilling, and stranger ride than the last 20 have been for game developers. And there will be a lot more of us.

NOTES

1 https://segmentnext.com/halo-infinite-development-cost/.
2 https://www.appsflyer.com/blog/trends-insights/gaming-mergers-acquisitions/.
3 https://nypost.com/2021/06/12/remote-workers-put-in-longer-hours-but-were-less-efficient-study.

Conclusions

> So we beat on, boats against the current, borne back ceaselessly into the past.

So reads the final line of F. Scott Fitzgerald's *The Great Gatsby*, a tale of the world – or at least the United States – 100 years ago. Jay Gatsby made his fortune by bootlegging liquor, a recreational drug. Today's empires are built selling recreation as well, though consumed in a very different form.

And as we conclude our investigation into extrapolating what the last 20 or 40 years of game development have taught us, I cannot help but reflect on the ways the world has changed, is changing, will change.

And I cannot help but consider how different our world is now that from the Roaring Twenties of the yesteryear, from one century ago now. The past may not be dead and buried, it may not even be past, but its voices feel increasingly drowned out by the cacophonous roar of voices of the future, all speaking, Tweeting, proclaiming at once in a hundred different languages. Ten times more people enjoyed my last game than were alive on Earth in Gatsby's time. Tens of millions of people study computer languages today, almost none study Latin, a near pre-requisite to be considered educated a hundred years ago. Because of the sheer staggering power of the Malthusian growth curve humanity is on, the past is all but an irrelevant footnote to the future now, and every year that will become more true. I propose that the next decades will be defined less by the past and more by a future whose gravitational pull and momentum is so strong that its arrival feels like an inevitability.

Are we making a better world by making better games? By dragging more gleeful, curious players onto the worlds we create? Is adding one and a half billion new habituated gamers over the next two decades a net positive for humanity? In a world increasingly designed for addiction by

DOI: 10.1201/9781003291800-12

unfeeling algorithms whose sole purpose is to increase the amount of time humans spend starting at their screens and the amount of money they spend on digital products… Is this the world we want to build?

Throughout the writing of this book, and hopefully as you have read it, we cannot help but wrestle with questions of privacy, addiction, and many other complicated concerns. The techniques and predictions described in these pages are about building "better" games, which retain users longer, engage them more deeply, and monetize them more effectively. If you make games for a living, this is your job. And the Age of Intelligent Machines is upon us, such that optimization and even the act of creation will increasingly be shaped by these relentless forces of optimization, cold intelligences who perceive players as highly fungible.

And so, on the one hand, some may think of this as a bleak or cynical pursuit. But I propose we could – must! – look at it in a different way.

Well-built games make the lives of billions of people better every day. We help the weak feel powerful, letting them swoop in and save the day by helping their alliance mates. We encourage the lonely to find friends, sometimes fulfilling lifelong romance, by introducing them to others with shared hobbies. Games can bring color into lives that are too often gray. The entertainment we create and perfect can take the minds of millions off the hardships of their day-to-day. By giving the people of planet earth these wonderful games that they can play on the devices in their pockets, with their friends, completely for free if they wish … By doing this we spread happiness and delight even in dark days of pandemic or war. By entertaining the world, we can bring people together even when they are forced to be apart. Our games really do make people's lives better. Because they can carry our games in their pockets, into their bedrooms, to school with them, sometimes into the final chambers of their lives. They give us their time, and they voluntarily give us their money, because we make them happy.

As game makers, we must believe in this low-grade, common nobility of the entertainer.

Go forth and use what you can from these pages to build wonderful toys that make the world a better, more fun place.

The world of the past is gone. The world of the future is ours to create. Let's try to make it a good one with what paltry magics we have at our command.

So we beat on, boats pulled by the current, borne ceaselessly into the future.

–TF
BOLD POINT, 2022

Index

Printed in the United States
by Baker & Taylor Publisher Services